This book is due for return on or before the last date shown below.

24|·01·+

JAN 2014
Catalogued

cost: £19.99

792. 23 FAV.

THE COMIC MASK
IN THE COMMEDIA DELL'ARTE

ANTONIO FAVA | Foreword *by* Simon Callow

Actor Training, Improvisation, *and the* Poetics of Survival

NORTHWESTERN UNIVERSITY PRESS

EVANSTON, ILLINOIS

Northwestern University Press
www.nupress.northwestern.edu

Printed in Canada

10   9   8   7   6   5   4   3   2   1

ISBN-13: 978-0-8101-2368-7
ISBN-10: 0-8101-2368-1

Library of Congress Cataloging-in-Publication Data

Fava, Antonio, 1949–
    [Maschera comica nella commedia dell'arte. English]
    The comic mask in the commedia dell'arte : actor training,
    improvisation, and the poetics of survival / Antonio Fava ;
    foreword by Simon Callow.
        p. cm.
    Includes bibliographical references.
    ISBN 0-8101-2368-1 (pbk. : alk. paper)
    1. Commedia dell'arte—Technique. 2. Improvisation
    (Acting) 3. Comic, The, in literature. 4. Masks in literature.
    I. Title.
    PQ4155.F3813 2007
    792.230945—dc22

                                        2006026839

Printed on acid-free paper.

Edited by Francesco Zimei
English translation by Thomas Simpson
Photographs by Ermanno Bono and Franco Pilati
Masks worn by Matteo Bartoli, Donata Bori, Dina Buccino,
Luca Cairati, Antonio Fava, Ferruccio Fava, Marcella Fava,
Luisa Galfano, Marino Galvão Jr., Fabrizio Paladin

☞ Contents

"Commedia dell'Arte" is a phrase rather recklessly bandied about in the English-speaking theater. When I directed Milan Kundera's play *Jacques and His Master* in Los Angeles, I was astonished to see the actors who were auditioning for me appear in knee pads and track suits. On inquiring of them why, they said that they had been told that I was doing the play Commedia dell'Arte style. Assuring them that this was not the case—nothing could have been less appropriate—I asked them what they thought it meant anyway. "Physical," they replied. "Lots of pratfalls. And masks." And that, it must be admitted, is what most productions in England and America which claim to honor the Commedia tradition amount to: masks and a lot of jumping around. Even Italian productions which purport to be done in Commedia style are simply somewhat stylized: there was an enchanting *Venetian Twins* given by the Stabile Theatre of Genoa in London some thirty years ago, in which the great Alberto Lionello played the title role(s), but despite an occasional archaic gesture, it was essentially a high-spirited farce, wonderfully funny but completely in the mainstream of modern theater practice; masks may have been donned but very briefly and for purposes of concealment, not, as in Commedia, for purposes of revelation.

We are, all of us in the theater, haunted by the idea of Commedia, partly because the prints and engravings of it that have come down to us so clearly embody an essence of theater but also because the whole corpus of dramatic literature until the nineteenth century is haunted by it: Shakespeare, Ben Jonson, Molière, Marivaux, Beaumarchais, Goldoni (it goes without saying), Nestroy, Holberg. Wherever there are witty servants and domineering masters, young wives and old husbands, pompous pedants, thwarted lovers, or bragging soldiers, the Commedia is there in spirit and also very often in form. What we respond to in it is the energy that leaps out of the old illustrations, a fundamentally theatrical vitality which takes hold of and possesses its characters, fabulously exotic but somehow instantly recognizable. All over England and America at this moment there are people trying to bring back to life that energy—popular, earthy, and rude—and to inhabit those characters. The books on Commedia fill shelves, beautifully crafted masks can readily be purchased off the peg, the repertory of physical gestures it was the outcome of weeks of rehearsal, while in fact it had just been put together ten minutes before. There was a startling kind of corporate life to it which was very impressive. After each improvisation, Fava himself would stand up and give a simple report on what we had just seen. If it worked, he would say how it worked and how it might work better; if it didn't, there were precise reasons why. These comments were factual, practical, without personal judgment. He was analyzing what he had seen from the perspective of certain very clear rules.

Now, this is uncommon in most theater work, where everyone is very shy of rules. The individual method, the personal contribution, are carefully respected, even tiptoed around. In music, of course, it is very different: music is either in tune or it's not; the rhythm is correct or it's out of time; the note is the right length or not. There is room for variation, for subtleties, but the essential rules are concrete and easily articulated. In the theater, an enormous amount of time is spent trying to find a common language to describe the desired result. Fava's directness was curiously refreshing, and I was keen to know more, both about these rules of his and about the secrets of transformation, since transformation is the actor's art par excellence, though increasingly rare in our theater. It has acquired a rather bad name in recent times, thought to be external, a putting on of something rather than a releasing of something. Well, these young men and women in Reggio Emilia had put something on—a mask—but for the rest, their physical lives seemed to well up spontaneously from within them; indeed, the most striking thing about their work was how connected to a center their bodily impulses were.

My curiosity about this was satisfied last year when Fava came to London to give a Commedia workshop as preparation for work that a group of us were doing on a version of *Punch and Judy* under Daniel Kramer's direction. "Punch," of course, is a derivative of "Pulcinella," and his and Judy's show has some points of comparison with Commedia scenarios, but what we were really interested in was the ability to create large archetypes that were also filled with life and truthful impulse. Fava duly gave us a crash course in Commedia. In one week we each played all of the characters, attempted some of the classic *lazzi*, and worked on scenarios of our own invention. My fellow actors were mostly from what is called the Physical Theater tradition—Marcello Magni, Toby Sedgwick, and Linda Dobell—one of us was a comedian (Phil Nichol), and another (Lizzie Hopley) had a great deal of improvisational experience in addition to an acting background; Daniel, who directed, had a wealth of experience in movement, modern and classical, in Decroux's Corporeal Mime, in the Viewpoints technique, and in Laban; he had also studied with Fava. I was the odd one out, the only one from what is called the "straight theater," though I rather fancied myself as a more physical actor than most: the word made flesh was my gospel as a performer. However much I might love words, I believed passionately that the actor's whole instrument had to be engaged at all times.

I quickly learned my limitations and self-delusions. I can't speak for the others, but it was one of the hardest weeks I have ever spent in the theater. Partly this was because Fava, one of the greatest teachers I have ever encountered, works by demonstration. To watch this shortish (slightly shorter than me), stocky, fuzzy-bearded man transform instantly and absolutely from one of the fearful, hungry, cunning Zanni (Pulcinella, Arlecchino) into the swaggering, flamboyant Capitano, into the pompous, blinkered Dottore, into an idealistic young Lover (female), or the fussy, outrageous, and frankly camp Pedrolino, and then to be told to get on with it oneself, was profoundly daunting. Apart from anything else, it is physically draining. The focus and concentration required—even for a sleeping Zanni or a swooning lover—are a shock to the system, a system, that is, like mine, accustomed to relying on voice and subtly nuanced words to convey so much. For me, too, the loss of one's face and all its expressive possibilities leaves one feeling bereft. All the expressive energy has to be relocated to the spine, into the muscles, into the feet, the arms, and the hands—to the very tips of the fingers. Even more demanding is suspending the familiar process of creating character by accumulating detail. In this work one has to completely surrender to the needs, the instincts, and the self-image of a creature dominated by very simple drives. Psychology as such is by no means absent—in fact the psychology of each of the types is absolutely watertight and organically consistent—it is simply that the emphasis is on what it is to be human rather than what it is to be this particular human. There is a Zanni in all of us, a Dottore, a Brighella, waiting to be released, and that is what the Commedia is concerned with, rather than Zanni X, Dottore Y, Brighella Z. The collective creative act that brought the Commedia to life puts onto the stage a representative and abundant selection of humankind going about its daily business, making love, looking for food, impressing the neighbors, earning money: a ship of fools, perhaps, or a human Noah's ark, and this is what we as actors have to strive to realize. I felt at the end of the week that I needed to reconsider everything I knew about acting.

It has long been my personal belief that the purpose of the theater, as opposed to that of any other medium, is the enactment of the collective psyche, and the Commedia is the most direct route to this of which I know, with the significant exception of Greek tragedy, not so much its antithesis as its complement. In his book, Antonio, my friend and teacher, expounds the profound roots and enumerates the liberating rules of the Commedia, both as a complete system of performance and as a worldview. His remarkable book is deep, sharp, challenging, and authoritative, but its purpose is not to sit on the shelf or rest on the student's lap: it is to create actors who will allow the Commedia's ancient blood to flow through their veins, who will give themselves over to the vital energies and deep-seated impulses of the characters, and to make us recognize ourselves while roaring with laughter, appalled and yet somehow enchanted by the human arrangement in all its mad glory.

This book is about the Commedia dell'Arte and about the comic mask.

We won't deal with improvisation from a historical standpoint, although we embrace with respect and love our sense of belonging to the tradition and history of the Commedia dell'Arte. In these pages, we put forth the terms of a method for the understanding and practice of a living form of theater, active and moving, that has been stupidly given up for dead by a book-bound vision of theater. Nobody says Shakespeare is dead, but Commedia, they say, is dead. Why? Obviously, Shakespeare is alive because we have his texts, but improvisation cannot be regarded in the same way, notwithstanding much documentation. Given the impossibility of conserving records of actors' improvisations, there can be no word-for-word analysis. Words in this *arte* are strictly connected to deeds, to *actio,* to the live situation that is at once both the comic play unfolding and the unique performance under way. The mind of a *zannante* doesn't think of writing down a line beforehand or even afterward, except as a record of something finished and done (the case of the Commedia dell'Arte texts that have been handed down to us).

From the position of someone working onstage, the impossibility of recovering texts of a particular genre is immaterial to the goal of knowing that genre and making something of it in performance. People who make theater do it neither in homage to the past nor for future beatification; they do it (at least they should) for the audience present at that moment that wants to have a good time. Whatever it's about and however it's done, theater takes place in the now, in movement, wherever speech and silence, action and stillness, reveal a present moment under way.

More than any other, the Commedia dell'Arte is the genre of theater that expresses the *present* as it moves. This spirit animates our intention to synthesize our two-decade experience in improvisation. We won't narrate a story or compile a historical summary; rather we shall propose a method and explain a project.

To begin with, Commedia dell'Arte is a powerful training method, not to be neglected by any stage artist, that provides the ability to expand what we normally call the *psychological* into the *multiexpressive* play of mask performance.

Commedia dell'Arte is not mime, dance, pantomime, masqueing, circus art, street theater. Commedia dell'Arte is full, complete, total theater, which includes—in ways we shall see—all the techniques and disciplines of the varied forms of theater. But it remains an absolutely autonomous and independent genre. In Commedia, psychology is present everywhere and subject to two fundamental principles: total physicality and collective meaning.

First, psychological intention is expressed through the actor's total physicality. For example, when a typical actor, trained in the familiar psychological methods of twentieth-century theater, must include the entire audience in his gaze, he will carry out this action in an immobile way with a single, unchanging facial expression (in this case, usually an "intense" one). Only the eyes will move. If, on the other hand, a Commedia actor playing a Zanni character wants to achieve the same effect, he or she will do the following:

- ☞ Before taking action, consider the audience as a gathering of individuals rather than as a mass
- ☞ Move his or her gaze from one spectator to the next, indicating with head and eyes precisely which individual spectator is singled out, then move to the next, then the next, and so on
- ☞ Without obviously stopping at each and every spectator, make a "selection" from each part of the hall, to suggest a sampling of the entire crowd

In singling out those representative spectators (just a few), the actor will engage a distinct rhythm, from one viewer to the next, not like a metronome, but syncopated, jazzlike, as though to personalize each contact, for example, passing rapidly away from a gentleman to pause more insistently upon a lady, and scanning the group in the rear with a distinct *glissando.*

The actor's body will adjust directionally and provide parallel actions suited to what he sees, such as waving and showing admiration or contrapuntal, independent actions, such as scratching, adjusting oneself, and so on.

Why all this? Because, in putting human behavior *into a mask,* gazing at the audience becomes no longer an action of that individual character but rather a representation of the human behavior that goes with the genre: Zanni (the human being named Zanni) looks at the audience (being in the situation of one who looks at an audience). *Doing the thing* turns into *the spectacle of doing the thing.*

As for the nonmasked characters, in Commedia dell'Arte the commitment, the requirements, the technique, and the rhythm are all the same.

Whether the character wears an actual mask or not is a factor derived from the evolution of the types, which we'll discuss in chapter 5, a factor with aesthetic and behavioral consequences for each of the different characters but not an abridgment of the principles imposed by the original, primordial mask.

The second fundamental principle is that psychological intention always assumes a collective meaning. The actor studies collective behavior: Zanni starts in fear at a sudden loud noise because everyone starts in fear in such a moment. He reacts quite plainly because fear induces everyone to react plainly. The actor attributes this behavior to Zanni (the character) and elaborates it through technique, style, and all the conditions that undergird the presentation of that character and his fear in that moment.

Building the "psychology of a character" in the Commedia dell'Arte calls for the actor to combine these elements: study of collective psychology; *putting into mask* the collective behavior by applying it to the character, its gestures, traits, and poetry; and making that behavior *unique* through the necessarily unique style of the performer. The result will be true to the tradition and, at the same time, the immediate moment of performance when the artist communicates with the real, living, present audience, with whom that artist shares the culture and rhythms of expression, mutual understanding, and complicity.

Anyone who practices Commedia dell'Arte as we do, with passion and conviction, knows that the two principal interpretive models that have driven twentieth-century performance—that is, losing oneself in the character and its opposite, the so-called alienation effect—have no application to Commedia.

The continuity of Commedia dell'Arte means the perpetuation of a great artistic and cultural heritage with universal value. Since its very beginning, the themes of Commedia are fundamentally human: love, the stages of life, money, sex, possession, hunger, war, sickness, fear, and death (both that ever-present, hovering, unspeakable bogeyman and also the familiar stage character of Death, now costumed as an irresistible woman, now as an important man, but always repugnant). Above all, for every single character, always and everywhere, is the theme of all themes: the permanent emergency of survival itself, here and now, this minute, this moment, this second. As for its "Italian-ness," the Commedia represents a powerful counterbalance to the hegemony of the great European authors and stands in equal dignity with Shakespeare, Lope de Vega, and Molière (with the greatness of Ruzante at the dawn and Goldoni at the sunset of "historical" Commedia).

The thoroughly Italian origin and development of Commedia should never be confused with trite folklore about the "Italian masks," which has nothing whatever to do with the first principle of the Arte, which is to say a trade, a craft, a business, and a specialization; in effect, the modern concept of acting as a skilled profession. Folklore relegates Commedia to clown shows, passing off the characters as homegrown representations of the various cities throughout the peninsula, each of which, the story goes, has cooked up its own symbolic character, expressive of the native genius of all Italians. Instead, a proper analysis of this professional discipline of theater par excellence, which is universally and for good or bad denominated Commedia dell'Arte, must first clear away this and similar tenacious stereotypes. Commedia stands for theater, acting as a discipline, and Arte signifies trade and profession and implies commerce, business.

At its birth, Commedia is above all a practical idea: a theatrical spectacle fashioned to be sold to make a profit capable of sustaining the artist and financing further artistic projects. This invention, which forms the base of all modern theater, is an Italian one, but an invention conceived for application across a much wider area than merely the Italian peninsula (at that time, of course, still not a unified state). The area encompassing Spain, France, Austria, Germany, and England crossed national boundaries but was perceived nevertheless as a culturally "coherent" continent, throughout which inhabitants recognized one another as sharing common traditions and perceptions.

The historian Roberto Tessari, with strong symbolic connotations, suggests January 18, 1801, as the date of the death of the Commedia dell'Arte. On that day, the Cisalpine republic prohibited masked performances. In our opinion, however, the historical death of Commedia is, as they say, greatly exaggerated. Commedia certainly comes to an end as an industry, but the culture of the mask and its public use survive. They continue in puppet and marionette plays and among street mimes who carry on a repertory of bad routines which still provide a distorted glimpse of how the original actors must have performed. We see the traces of this mask culture in circus performers, such as the Calabrian Bajazzu and the Commedia Infarinato, who will later be called Pagliaccio and will lend his smock and name to the figure we now call Clown. The Italian masks achieve an often-triumphant destiny through transformation into a number of European variants, especially in French and English pantomime. They have lived on in popular festivals with great dignity, in particular in the south of Italy where Pulcinella has maintained an uninterrupted historical continuity, and not only in Naples.

I am the son of a Calabrian Pulcinella of the people, Tommaso, who worked the villages in the countryside around Crotone in the mask and costume of Puricinedda, playing a guitar he beat for rhythm, enlivening local festivals with *lazzi*, songs, serenades, comic sketches, and outrageous comic-epic tales with cynical-tragic undertones. These tales live on, modernized, in my own shows. It feels indeed strange, therefore, to be told that Commedia belongs to a distant and irretrievable past. Unless, that is, we choose to think of the Commedia dell'Arte exclusively in terms of its dominant icon, the inevitable Arlecchino as portrayed by Carlo Goldoni.

Giorgio Strehler's famous production of Carlo Goldoni's *Servant of Two Masters* (staged first in 1947 by the Piccolo Teatro di Milano with Marcello Moretti as Arlecchino) did not launch the rebirth of the Commedia, for which it is often given credit. Rather, that production presented a very particular interpretation of a very particular text and was a terrific artistic achievement, but to call it a new beginning for Commedia is misguided. Certain misunderstandings derived from that production have yet to be clarified. For example, the fact that Goldoni's servant character named Truffaldino becomes Arlecchino in the Piccolo Teatro's version suggests the archetypal superiority of Arlecchino over Truffaldino (otherwise, why make the change?). But in truth, whether the character is called one or the other name is less important than the fact that both are names for the character role of a Second Zanni. You can object, "If the names are interchangeable, what does it matter what we call him?" But then why change the name from Goldoni's Truffaldino to Strehler's Arlecchino? Is Arlecchino a symbol of something, while Truffaldino isn't? Ahi!

Arlecchino, Truffaldino, Tabacchino, Traccagnino, and the other "ino" characters in the Commedia are the same in that they all correspond to the structural element we call the Second Zanni. Placing Arlecchino over all the others creates a superstar Zanni and thus a protagonist, a lead, a matador of the Commedia. This is entirely mistaken because Commedia develops according to the structure of the acting companies, which depends upon the synergy of equally important specialists. Featuring Arlecchino over the others pays homage to a "frenchification" of the Commedia, of which Goldoni himself sadly became a victim in the last years of his career. There is no question that Strehler's staging of Goldoni's *Servant of Two Masters* is a masterpiece of directing. The piece is not, however, Commedia dell'Arte or Commedia all'Improvviso or *zannesca*. Nor is it a rebirth of Commedia dell'Arte. Nor should it be considered an absolute model for actors now creating Commedia.

Commedia does not need to be reborn. Whoever does Commedia today is carrying on a continuing tradition. I consider myself to be carrying on that tradition, and as such I proceed along the double track of fidelity and renovation.

Commedia dell'Arte, or Commedia all'Improvviso, is obviously alive and well. It exists, and not as a revival, or a fad, a charming toy, or an outlet for underemployed actors. It can be these things in certain cases, but the phenomenon of Commedia remains obstinately alive. Only in Italy, where it was born, do we grumble about Commedia; we tolerate it as a tiresome leftover that we should free ourselves of. But the rest of the world sees it more clearly: Commedia is the expressive and artistic patrimony of everybody. It has meaning and universal value as an extraordinary stage discipline of training in physical control and the best possible rapport with an audience. (Shall we say it? Yes: the world envies us for this!)

The activities that resulted in the conclusions and convictions expressed in this book began in 1980 in Reggio Emilia (performances, courses, workshops), and continued until 1985, with the inauguration of the Stage Internazionale di Commedia dell'Arte, which remains today the most important and prestigious training institute on mask comedy for young actors throughout the world. This resource has been further enriched by the opening in 1989 of the Scuola Internazionale dell'Attore Comico. Our goal is the continuity of the Commedia dell'Arte in theater today on an international level.

To render this project as stimulating and clear as possible, we have enclosed in these pages our "science," which, like our shows, has not been formulated beforehand at a desk; rather it has grown day by day.

This point of arrival aims to be a contribution to the proud unfolding of the *Improvvisa* as a scenic art: refined, popular, and open to all languages and all cultures.

It is also a point of departure.

☞ The Comic Mask in the Commedia dell'Arte

1 | The Mask

WHAT IS THE *MASCHERA*?

The *maschera* is first of all a physiognomorphic object. The actor puts on the object by placing it over his face and therefore acquires the face modeled by the mask itself, along with the characteristics that the mask is intended to express. The actor takes on all the expressive consequences imposed by the mask, including both physical behavior and qualities of character. Each mask's form is a combination of signifiers imposing distinct characteristics.

As soon as it is put on, the mask is *put into action, made alive* in the context of a ritualistic, staged, festive fiction. He or she who puts on the mask makes the *actio*, becomes an actor, *actualizes.*

Everything changes in the stage artist once the mask is on. Body, voice, language. Everything must change: by putting on a mask, an actor can no longer act or speak as he does in daily life.

A modern actor of Western culture who has not passed through a strong experience with masks, once the semblance is put on, tends to delegate. He slips into the mask and waits—or believes—that the mask itself will put into action all its aesthetic dynamic signifiers, simply by virtue of the presence and visibility of the mask itself. Beneath or beyond the mask, our actor "performs the text"; with proper pitch and pronunciation he loads each word with nuance and seeks out its subtext, no longer concerned with what the character says but rather with what the author wants to say (which, our actor naturally presumes, is totally different from what the character says). In all this, no attention whatever is given to what the character *does,* or should or could do or not do (after all, *not-doing* is an extremely dynamic action if motivated by the situation and played by an actor capable of action). Once again, the modern Western actor merely reproduces and is therefore not truly an *actor,* one who makes, who carries out the *actio,* who actualizes. This is the kind of nonmask actor we have inherited from a century and a half of obsession with psychology in theater. We must explain to this actor that the mask is not the explosive but the detonator. The explosive is always the actor.

Certain necessary qualities must be acquired by the stage artist. Others already exist in the mask, and still others must be achieved by the mask maker, to confer a complete result that perfectly coincides with the expectations of the actor and the audience. The audience always understands "miraculously"; that is, it perceives what is being communicated to it through the theatrical performance. It always either enjoys or is bored by the show. The audience is never wrong (except in cases—regretfully frequent nowadays—when overly difficult stage language induces it to feel guilty for not being "up to its level," when, on the contrary, it is actually the artists who have been unable or unwilling to make themselves understood).

While the actor must acquire the complex, difficult, and exquisite science of knowing how to delight, the audience naturally possesses the ability to be delighted: it "knows" when to laugh, when to applaud, when to be bored or moved, without ever having studied.

Necessary Conditions Within the Actor

With or without wearing a mask, the actor is a mask and gathers within himself a series of projects.

The actor appears on the stage of human culture as a necessary project; the cathartic or, on a still more basic level, the apotropaic representation of life and death constitutes a primary human necessity. If fear is an instrument for survival because it allows us to recognize danger and to react for the survival of the individual and the group, it is nevertheless a source of anguish, which itself undermines survival and imposes a search for solutions.

The problem of fear is felt by the entire community as a totality of the single fears felt by each individual. The community must resolve the anguish caused by fear. The common interest in a solution guarantees that it be applied and carried out collectively.

The representation of fear leads to the momentary resolution of the collective and individual anguish provoked by the fear itself.

The repetition and structuring of the representation of fear generate a state of equilibrium between the unavoidable, continuous return of fear and the means of handling, withstanding, or bearing the fear. Thus is theater born. It instantly organizes itself in means, ways, and genres, all of which are aimed at catharsis, at purification, at overcoming anguish. Serious, tragic, dramatic theater offers thoughtful, moving, and intimate relief. Magic theater reassures without openly explaining *why* but effectively spreads the sensation of having escaped from something terrible. Epic-heroic theater allows us to participate in unforgettable triumphs. Mystical theater saves us through spiritual elevation or the superiority of thought. But above all, comic theater discharges anguish with an efficacy and rapidity unknown to the other genres.

It's curious, this condition of superiority of the inferiority of the comic. The aim is high: complete catharsis, purification, relief from anguish, but the means of attaining this catharsis are low. In fact, they are the very meanest. That's the natural state of the comic character. Critics have always seen in the comic only the lowest level. They have always distinguished—not necessarily with a negative attitude—between the superiority of the serious forms and the inferiority of the comic forms.

This matter doesn't disturb us, because we believe it to be the necessary effect of an opposition which critics have been mere instruments of. To elevate the comic means to neutralize it, to deprive it of its power to make us laugh. This arrangement is therefore as it should be.

Comedy literally shatters fear, releasing collective joy expressed in raucous, liberating, communal laughter. The comic actor neither arouses emotions nor raises questions. Rather, by exposing them to destruction, he resolves them. The laughing spectator is relieved. He is saved.

The sacred origin of *risus* (laughter) gives the spectator something more than safety from danger, relief from anguish. The sacredness of laughter renders the laugher immortal. He who laughs is immortal. Certainly, it is only a brief immortality, lasting the duration of the laugh itself, but with the certainty that the laugh, and with it, immortality, will be repeated. To the long and tormented catharsis of tragedy, comedy opposes an irresistible, brief, intense series of catharses, loudly expressed by the whole assembly.

The actor therefore defines himself as an anthropological project. The community manages its fears through a dynamic representation of the fear itself. The actor creates codes and symbols, organizes and structures these representations, and joins a category of specialists, whose original authority is surely religious and comes before the creation, invention, shaping, and putting-into-action of these saving representations.

Notwithstanding the social status in which actors have found themselves in different phases of history (almost always infamous and low), the actor immediately takes on and occupies an important presence in the community, which learns to recognize and console itself through his symbols in movement.

The necessity of putting symbols into movement makes the actor into an *expressive project*. Representation does not exist without a form that contextualizes it, develops it, explains it, that clearly contains what would be otherwise inexpressible. Given therefore a certain expressive form destined to perform a precise collective function, the actor becomes a specialist. His specialization permits him to perfect, improve, amplify, and vary his expressive project.

The great consequence of this is the *artistic project,* when form finds its autonomy, its self-unfolding. Form blends into content, becomes content itself, the object, the goal, without having renounced its original aims, often unconscious of its own complex formal elaboration, which is exalted—particularly in its effects on the spectator's psyche—by the varied paths to beauty now opened by the forms. This is art.

The *signifying project* concludes the necessary conditions. In the moment of representation, meaninglessness no longer exists. Not-signifying is not possible. It is impossible for a representation not to signify, no matter what the circumstances (especially when the effort is to represent nothingness). Everything is sign; everything signifies. Because of this, the actor, the stage artist, by becoming an artist of the sign, must always calculate and control the expressive and narrative process. It is useless to overload a representation with meaning when meaning already exists autonomously and the artist is merely the vehicle, the reelaborator, the one who selects. The weight of individual signifiers risks growing to the point of suffocating the intended joy of the message. The artificer has the responsibility to construct a perfectly signifying artistic machine, by managing the equilibrium of the meanings among themselves and between the meaning and form.

Necessary Conditions for the Mask

The mask is a useful project. The use of a mask is often necessary for practical reasons. It is called for to characterize, to create a character who is obviously and unequivocally that certain thing. Makeup alone may not be enough or be poorly visible or faded. The facial mobility and mimicry of the actor, even when excellent, are subject to inconsistency and confusion. From a distance, all facial expression is attenuated and becomes vague and therefore ineffective on an expressive level.

A mask never fails. It is constructed beforehand; its expression is controlled; its fixity is determined beforehand, inalienable, guaranteed to be clear, with a clarity that connects the intentions expressed by the performer and the comprehension of the spectators.

A concatenation of intentions is, in the last analysis, what an actor does when he "performs" a mask. The audience perfectly reads the actor's play when all the intentions of the character are expressed with a clarity that is always active in the actor, even when the actor performs a character that is intended to be vague, such as one with confusing, ambiguous behavior. A shadowy quality, obscurity, and ambiguity are to be understood as poetic characteristics of a role that must be performed with "scientific" clarity. The clearer the expression, the more clearly will be rendered the "shadowy, obscure, ambiguous" qualities of the character.

In the play of the mask, the concatenation of intentions is emphasized, exaggerated, pronounced, and maniacally specified. A concatenation of intentions elaborated to achieve credibility in the character's behavior will produce an effect of formal exaggeration of the reality that the actor wishes to describe. Thus the mask will have achieved its function.

When the mask goes into action in a comic setting, it does not stop representing "true" things. To make things appear true, we must arrive at the level of creativity called for by the meaning we intend to express. We are not seeking the credibility of true truth, the real, or the truth of "realism" but rather that of formal exaggeration. We demonstrate a recognizable, known truth but in a different form than that found in reality. This truth is deformed, excessive, in order to confer on the represented fact the sense of an exemplary occurrence.

Exemplarity historically fixes the represented fact. To achieve as well as possible this historic fixity of the fact (banal, common, and private, if taken by itself), the actor proceeds by fixing all the audible and visible aspects of the character and the action, the factors we call *maschemi*. By fixing these elements, with or without an actual mask on his face, the actor enmasks.

Enmasking implies the continuous fixity of the expressive models. The fixity of the mask clarifies the character and constrains the actor to distribute onto other parts of his body the expressive variety of the character's intentions. Fixity here stands for the capacity of synthesis of a character and its poetic potential. Actor examples of poetic fixity are Charlie Chaplin, Laurel and Hardy, Totò and Peppino, Jacques Tati, and Roberto Benigni.

We are now at the expressive project. Having established the utility and necessity of clarity between actor and spectator, we need to specify the content of a single mask. The expressive project aims to define a character but cannot neglect consideration of the practical requirements involved in acquiring the mask desired.

The Form or Cut

The form or, more accurately, the cut of a mask of the Commedia dell'Arte constitutes a simplification and humanization of the masks already present in various manifestations of popular and elite culture, which developed and spread throughout Europe during the Middle Ages.

For the first Commedia dell'Arte actors (who originated in the 1530s and 1540s), it was a matter of being immediately recognizable as "familiar" figures that were simultaneously "surprising." In that era (beginning in the sixteenth century), masks were common both during celebrations and in daily life. The comics bring this costume to the stage but cut their phantasm specifically according to certain guidelines:

1. Anatomical proportions
2. Strongly caricatured but rigorously human facial features
3. The elimination of the lower lip, taking the form called *mezasola* (in Neapolitan), *menzagiabbatta* (in Crotonese), *crosta* (so-named by scholars Ferdinando Taviani and Mirella Schino),[1] or *mezzamaschera* (half-mask). This permits the mouth to be free to speak, sing, and emit sounds without obstacles but also gives an illusion of overall mobility of the face through the exaggerated mobility of the free part of it.

The Proportions

The proportions of the mask are anatomical, but the mask is not anatomical. The mask is a wholly different face than that of the person wearing it. The distinction must be clear. A mask that adhered totally to the face of the actor would be a virtual portrait of the actor and therefore superfluous. The overall volume of the mask is proportional to human anatomy, but the individual features of the mask, as we shall see, are grotesque and excessive.

The Features

The features of the mask, with their protuberances and hollows, are the mask's physiognomy. They have two functions, one expressive and the other structural: expressive, in that they embody and illustrate the character; structural in that they constitute the armature of the mask and confer resilience and strength.

The Character

Knowing the character in advance, the mask maker can give the fixed personage his own interpretation. At the same time, however, we must take account of established tradition. Long noses are inevitable for the primitive Zanni, huge, curved noses for the Magnifici (Pantalones), snub or little noses for the Zanni whose names end in "ino" (Truffaldino, Arlecchino, Trivellino). Actors today want perfectly anatomical masks that they can hardly feel, with big openings for the eyes. Such masks would be little more than makeup. The primitive Zanni characters must have little eyes and big noses, so as to suggest a vaguely proto–human being, something just above an animal. The fierce frown of a Capitano must not be diminished by wide-open eyes that reduce the impact of his continuously flashing, furrowed brow, essential to that character.

The Separate Parts

The separate parts are the forehead, the eyes, the nose, the cheekbones, the lip (always the upper one), and the overall shape. They are formal exaggerations of their human equivalents. The nose, in particular, is subject to disproportion and deformation. The cheekbones, the brows, the forehead, the lip, and the outlines are the parts where the mask maker may exercise his skill, always however with respect for the fundamental humanity of the type he seeks to create and the recognizability of its character.

The Bumps

The red-tipped bump on Commedia dell'Arte masks has been explained as the vestige of the ancient devil's horns of medieval masks from which Commedia masks are said to be derived. This theory, proposed by many scholars and certainly evocative, can be accepted as an addition to tradition but not as the definitive explanation. The original Zanni characters were based on an extremely common social type of the era: the bumpkin in the city. These types crowded into the rich, beautiful cities of the Paduan plain. Padua, Milan, Mantua, Ferrara, Bologna, and even Florence were invaded by natural Zanni in search of casual labor, willing to take on any heavy task that might temporarily guarantee their survival.

These impoverished yokels spoke a ridiculous language, their mountain dialect, which sounded "wild" to the ears of the citizens of the city. They moved awkwardly, they were simpleminded and laughable. The observation of these types led to the formation of the Zanni character and the invention of the *zannata* (Zanni sketch), the earliest form of the Commedia dell'Arte. The devil is added in later as a cultural referent little by little once the Zanni type is already successfully established and its professional practitioners begin to look for more prestigious "genealogies."

The development of the "ino" Zanni, with his snub nose and entirely black face, belongs to a later phase. The insolent "little devil," trickster and provocateur, results from a "culture" that the actors accumulated in the course of a century of practice and tradition.

Not only do the Zanni and other servant characters have their bumps, bumps are also worn by the aged characters and even by the masked Capitano. Are they all devil figures? No; rather, they all have skin problems. It is normal they should have such growths and sores in an era that little valued personal hygiene, when nutrition was lacking or entirely insufficient (especially for the Zanni, both the real and the stage ones, eternally struggling with hunger and starvation), and when medical remedies were mostly in the hands of "charlatans."[2]

The Head: The Mask in Relation to the Head (Hair, Beard, *Camauro*, and Jaw)

Hair always consists of the mustache, eyebrows, and the hair overhanging the forehead and extending as far as the sideburns, which often join the mustache. The hair is similar to the beard, almost always artificial, which the actor adds to the chin, if judged necessary, to complete the mask. When the beard is natural, the mask's hair should match the beard but not naturalistically.

In putting on the mask, Commedia tradition calls for the use of a *camauro*, a small black hood or bonnet that completely covers the head, including the hair and the ears, with a strap that passes under the chin, so as to frame the face mask.

The *camauro* has a complex function:

1. By covering the hair and ears, it conceals from audiences the real parts of the actor that would give away the fiction, the "falsity," creating conflicts of credibility and causing unconscious distraction for the spectator.

2. It guarantees the stability and security of the mask on the actor's head throughout the performance, preventing shifting and sliding.

3. It absorbs sweat, so that it won't drip into the actor's eyes, and it isn't visible to the audience, for whom the actor maintains the highest respect.

4. It adds a poetic quality, perpetuating the evocative, ancient tradition according to which the servant's head was always shaved (the servant characters were the first to wear the *camauro*, and its usage was then extended to all the other mask wearers) as a measure for preventing

lice. By association the shaved head came to stand for infamy, as well as signifying "hot-headed" (that is, insane) characters, for whom shaving the head was a means of cooling them off and thus reducing their insanity.

There remains the lower part of the face, that part not covered by a mask. This part should be treated with makeup and applied elements that continue and complete the effect of the mask.

The Hands

Having taken care of the head, the rest of the body is dressed in a costume. This leaves the hands, the only naked part of the masked actor. The hands must never touch the mask, because they could cause it to shift, because they could knock it, causing an "empty-box" sound with no spirit in it, but above all because the hand is naked, untreated, not theatricalized, not "masked," and therefore its contact with the mask might betray the theatrical falsity of the mask, thus risking its function and expressivity.

The Color

The maximum effectiveness of the mask as a visible object is guaranteed by the perfect legibility of its features. For this reason the mask must be monochromatic. Additional colors would certainly have a decorative effect, but they could reduce the recognizability of the character. What monochrome is called for? There is a great deal of insistence that the Commedia dell'Arte mask must be black. Why black, precisely? Black is the color of the devil and of hell. But it must be repeated once again that the devil and his habitat do not completely explain the fact of the mask's blackness. The infernal theory of color—as for that of the horns—presents itself as unequivocal; it imposes black as the only chromatic option for the mask. But as we shall see, this cannot be enough.

The first known images of the Commedia dell'Arte, known as the *Ludi Zanneschi*, published in Rome by Lorenzo Vaccaro between the 1560s and 1580s, show Zanni and Zagne (that is, female Zanni) without black coloring. The following two centuries of iconography (prints, drawings, watercolors, paintings, and other forms) of the Commedia show us masks that vary from white to black, passing through every possible shading from beige to sepia to brown. In some cases there is even the addition of flesh tones to add a realistic touch to the grotesqueness of the forms.

We believe that masks originally became black solely as a result of use. The masks that illustrate this volume (which we have made with leather), when they are freshly made, have the light color of natural leather, but in the course of two or three years of use in performances and schools, they become very dark. One day they will be black. This certainly makes for a good explanation.

Naturally, the sophisticated actors of advanced Commedia dell'Arte wished to provide a reason for that black color and, always seeking a prestigious cultural genealogy, they were pleased to trace their descent from the figure of the devil which, in the popular mind (a culture and mentality that include all the social classes), is a tempting and terrible source of trouble. The troubles created by the devil force their victims to invent solutions, to take dynamic countermeasures. The devil makes and unmakes, obligating others to make and unmake. By thus making and unmaking, we are all compelled to move forward and make progress. The devil imposes an evolutionary vision of life. This diffuse philosophy has spilled over into the practices of the *zannanti* since the very beginning, giving birth to the ingenious, intriguing servant, "diabolical" but without malignity, a devil who is no longer evil but who conserves the original quality of making and unmaking things in a continuous, incessant, apparently useless alternation, a pure vital energy that requires no further explanation than the fact of its own existence. This presence of the devil in the Commedia dell'Arte is extremely poetic and completes the double social and cultural origin of the Zanni, in part poor peasant and in part poor devil.

Moved by a pressing sense of duty that is not his own, and driven by a solemn wish to do good, the crypto-devil Zanni upsets the lives of all the characters, including his own. In the general confusion he comes upon a solution for everyone's troubles, a solution that was always present but which could come to flower only in consequence of the general confusion.

Aesthetic degeneration, which leads the original Zanni-devil to "evolve" into the playful little black-faced prankster, creates a trivial character too knowing to have sociocultural substance. We are now in the rococo era and our little "ino" has become a snobbish, pedantic, pushily "likable" servant dressed in elaborate, sumptuous livery, who no longer has anything in common with the original poor peasant/poor devil who dominated European stages up through the end of the seventeenth century.

At a certain point the black of the mask becomes a fixed element of the Commedia costume, preferred to other colors, and rather than waiting for it to darken naturally through use, it is blackened in the process of fabrication. But even in this case we must ask whether the symbolism of the color is the only reason for the practice. The blackening of the mask often has the significance of anticipating the aging of the leather. We jump over, in effect, the youth of the mask, thus overcoming the discomfort of the new object. We eliminate the discomfort we feel when we put on a new piece of clothing or new shoes for the first time, we free ourselves from that sense of separation between our bodies and an untrimmed, extraneous object.

If we look at the mask only as a symbol, we risk losing sight of all the physical, practical—we might say sensual—aspects that link an object to its user, which have so much importance in the conception and history of the mask itself.

If we wish to concentrate our attention on the symbolic meaning of the color black (although black is not unique in this sense), we must introduce a rather disquieting meaning that may lead us toward the ultimate meaning of the mask: the mask represents a *redivivo,* one who has returned from the dead, who has seen that which cannot and must not be witnessed. Now that he has returned, he no longer remembers, he has lost consciousness of what he experienced, he does not know that he knows what "the normal ones" do not know. Phantom, *redivivo,* demon, spirit, zombie, black as the abyss of the unknown, the mask emerges suddenly, humanized momentarily to carry out its task of initiating "the normal ones," the spectators, into that state of *low superiority* that is the condition of anyone who laughs.

Today we must be up-to-date: the advanced technologies of theatrical illumination available today, as well as the capabilities of video and photographic reproduction, are introducing new motives for altering the color of masks.

Black, good-bye. Dark, so long. Clear masks. The mask should be visible, subject to photography, video, and film. Excellent. Welcome to the clear mask.

But let it remain monochrome.

SYNTHESIS OF THE PROCESS OF FABRICATION OF THE LEATHER MASK

Idea and Project

The conception and project of making a mask presuppose a background that we will presume to be already acquired: knowledge of the subject matter, the era and its culture, which are necessary to justify abandoning the rigor of tradition in favor of a personal reelaboration.

By conception and project, we mean an appropriate clarity of conception before proceeding to the manual phase of building a mask. A mask to be worn onstage cannot be improvised or entrusted to a vague freedom of inspiration, which is too often invoked in artistic creation.

A theatrical mask subjects the mask-making artist to a series of creative renunciations that favor the functionality of the object in its use onstage, keeping faith in functionality as an essential aesthetic principle. The idea becomes a project when the compromise between creative impulse and functional requirements is achieved.

Design

The design constitutes the first concrete rendering of the idea and the project. Sketching in various ways the mask one is imagining allows one to consider its appearance and limitations, to correct it, and bring it closer to the desired result.

Optional Phase: Plaster Cast

We are aware of the phase known as "plaster cast of the human face," as a support to the development of the mask. We skip over this phase in the fabrication of our masks. In our practice the determination of measurements of the anatomy and the features is undertaken as follows:

1. The layout of a typical face is the reference for certain cuts and for the production of masks destined for general use, for use in our school, in gestural and thematic experiments with different actors, in requests for masks that come from all over the world.

2. Individual measurements for personalized masks are taken directly from the face of the person in question and used during the phase of sculpting the model. In many cases, standard masks are personalized in a final phase. Personal adjustments almost always concern opening up the eyes and fixing the lips to allow correct pronunciation by the actor. In case of problems, we alter the mask according to the wishes of the performing artist.

Matrix (Model)

The model is the wooden sculpture upon which the leather is embossed to take on its exact form. At times additional quantities of leather can be used to create additional effects.

Wood is the material most suited for the model. Responding elastically, it is perfect for sculpting, which facilitates the treatment of the leather over its surface. Wood absorbs part of the humidity in the leather (which is worked while wet), which prevents the formation of moist areas of separation between the wood and the leather, as could happen with materials such as metal, ceramics, or plastic. Using wood, we can fix the leather onto it at certain moments in the work process. We use primarily pine, fir, and cembra pine.

The model is a sculpture and should be considered a work of art. The leather mask embossed onto the model is also a work of art, above all in its final consequences, which is to say, its use onstage.

For these reasons, while the leather mask may be realized by assistants, the model must always be sculpted by the mask maker, who is its sole creator.

If the model is exquisitely artistic, the *crosta* is two things: a work of craft in its execution, of art in its final result.

Leather

An irreplaceable material. The leather to be preferred is that taken from the flank of the animal, soft, naturally cured if possible. In any case, only leather is acceptable. No other material is so well adapted to *shaping*, contact with the face of the actor, the continuity of skin to skin, and the creation of a beautiful, light, adaptable, and functional object, rich with evocative allusion and symbolism.

Recently, there have been actors in our schools who support animal rights, who have—with admirable courtesy, in truth—spoken about the cruelty contained in every mask, which is only obtained by killing an animal. We have offered them several alternatives:

1. Masks in paper. Even when made of recycled paper, these require the killing of trees. A paper mask also has a very short life, so a professional actor can expect to go through about twenty versions of the same mask in the course of a year's worth of rehearsal and performance.
2. Masks in plastic. Plastic pollutes and derives from polluting industrial processes. It is always stiff and uncomfortable against the skin, as well as unhealthy and, frankly, ugly.
3. Masks in metal. Besides the impracticality of a metal mask—at least in the setting of a prolonged, extremely active, exhausting activity like the Commedia dell'Arte—metal also can only be obtained by impoverishing nature.
4. Masks in wood. Wooden masks exist in many cultures, in particular, Japanese Noh masks offer a sublime example. As for Europe, the alpine regions of Switzerland, Austria, and Italy produce beautiful and important wooden masks.[3] It is a marvelous material and can easily be obtained in recycled form. Nevertheless, Commedia cannot make use of wooden masks because they would be heavy, stiff, bulky, and—due to the nature of the material and

the means of fabrication—they would be outsized and protrude too much beyond the face.

5. Masks in fabric. This solution also offers some interesting possibilities. It would certainly be possible to obtain an attractive surface; lightness and adaptability are guaranteed, and even the ability to absorb sweat. But here's the problem: no complex and strongly characterizing form can be obtained with fabric. The masks would turn out elementary to the point of inexpressivity. To obtain complex, expressive masks with fabric, it would have to be plasticized with chemicals, which would make the mask stiff and unhealthy.

6. Masks painted on the face. This would no longer be a mask. A mask is a mask only if it forces the actor to reimagine himself with a whole different face. No matter how elaborate, a painted mask maintains intact in the actor the perception of his own visage and, in the audience, the sense of the individuality of the performing artist.

We have singled out in the tradition of the Commedia the existence of a complex play of aesthetic-symbolic counterpoints among the various options for *masking,* as follows:

☞ A character mask worn by the actor
☞ Character makeup: l'Infarinato (a servant character with a heavily powdered white face)
☞ Combined treatments: the quarter-mask of the Dottore or, on rare occasions, of the maidservant
☞ Fractions of masks: only the nose, cheeks, or forehead
☞ Plastic deformation of the visage with deforming makeup elements
☞ Characters without masks or particular treatments—except for beautifying makeup—who are adopting the *social mask*
☞ Characters with exposed faces that are heavily made up with the double aim of expressing character and enhancing their attractiveness, such as the whole plethora of maidservant characters

All these options exist together in the Commedia. The addition of a mask painted on the face could cause the collapse of the delicate equilibrium built up over centuries. All the options listed here have made their appearance when called upon and have exchanged dynamics of use linked to their characters. For example: an Infarinato and a Second Zanni are both servants, but the Infarinato represents a certain concept of evolution of the Zanni, in that the Infarinato's powdered white face coincides with the achievement of a status in which the primary problem of survival has been resolved, while the Second Zanni is still floundering around desperately. That's the meaning of his huge nose, his ragged hair, his bumps, the leathery effect of his skin surface. They are all masks, but none are just any old mask.

Now, the addition of—or worse, the substitution of a leather mask with—a "virtual" mask painted onto the face would lead to confusion of the balanced play between the existing options. Our opinion is that the mask painted on the face—which we have seen onstage on numerous occasions, always with a certain irritation—manifests a phenomenon of masking that is totally alien to the principles we have brought forth here, when it is not, in fact, an expedient to justify an entirely lacking *sense of the mask* on the part of the performer.

7. Masks in latex. This is an interesting material, but decidedly inappropriate; it is totally impermeable, suffocates the skin, and is genuinely damaging to the health of the actor.

Since the mask is essential, it must be made with the most suitable materials. No slaughter is carried out in order to make a mask. We make use, I would say we make noble use, of an animal product that will be produced and employed whether we use it or not.

The Mask-Detonator

The mask is the detonator of an expressive explosion entrusted to the actor. This explosion is made up of signifiers and meaning:

At the moment of appearance, the mask immediately suggests who he is (what human and social type), what he will and will not be able to do, what he "promises" (what dramatic project he contains), and what his life is like (his permanent behavior).

This takes place for all audiences of any culture, even without knowing anything about the Commedia dell'Arte or mask theater in general, even without knowing the language spoken onstage. The evidence, the manifestation of the character in all his vitality and humanity, is the most meaningful artistic and communicative result of the mask.

Any functional object (any object for any function), when produced with full respect for the needs the object is intended to fulfill, is also a beautiful artistic object.

The mask has always been a functional object: a cultic object, a reliquary or symbol for a cult of the dead; an apotropaic fetish; a persona, a ghost, a sorcerer, who simulates other beings in the widest possible forms of representation; a protection for the face and eyes, for respiration in dangerous activities (work, sport, or daily life); a simple accessory for hiding one's actual identity (especially in the eighteenth century for harmless social uses, but the regrettable modern use for violent or criminal activity); an ideal object for play and celebration during the great traditional festivities (Carnevale, Halloween).

The mask is always useful. And it always unleashes something beautiful, strong, and mysterious but also ambiguous, elusive, attractive-repulsive.

Only in recent times has the mask become an object to hang on the wall, a souvenir of one place or another, a tourist-photo extravagance. In these "aesthetic" uses, the mask is running the risk of becoming meaningless and decadent. Devoid of dynamism, the mask becomes empty. The art of the mask is an art of movement in space and time, of movement as the sign of the spirit in anything, in everything, even in that which appears static.

The comic mask is rich and powerful in content:

1. It substitutes private psychological expression with expression that is dynamic, epic, and in which the meaning and the message are identical.
2. The head of the performer acts as though it were a single great eye, whose center focuses on its target. The audience sees what the mask eye sees; it has seen what the mask has seen. The mask sees only if and in the moment in which it performs the act of looking, otherwise it is blind, planted on a clueless head.
3. The mask causes the atomization of the visible. Body, space, things, other actors, the public: each is separate, acting and interacting with the mask.
4. The mask is always in search of confirmation, it always requires an explanation. Whatever takes place, takes place for real, but that's never enough; it must be verified, explained, narrated on the basis of what is already known or at least already seen. This certainty is determined by observing the fact, the details of the fact, and the audience, or rather a representation of the audience composed of certain spectators selected *rhythmically,* moment by moment. In order to do this, the mask is *launched* toward the audience. Technically, the entire mask looks by *pointing* wherever it looks.
5. The mask establishes the ambivalence of the character, which we schematize thus. The character

Knows who he is	Doesn't know who or what he symbolizes
Is aware of his prosaic mission	Is unaware of his symbolic mission
Is filled with limitations	Possesses extraordinary abilities
Is nonpoetic	Produces poetry
Is one among many, "Mr. Nobody"	Is an anthropological model, a concentration of human and social meaning

6. Each comic mask, alone or together with others, is loaded with universalized cultural precedents. It carries forward the popular epic that, on different levels and not always well known, is nevertheless recognized by the audience. The audience knows in advance what to expect from the mask. It will thus appreciate both the confirmation of the familiar and innovation, as long as the innovations do not contradict or subvert what is already known.

The actor-mask is distinct unto itself:

1. He neither mixes nor superimposes the action of masking onto the private, the intimate.
2. When he makes use of themes drawn from the realm of the private or intimate, he does so spectacularly, "maskingly." To apply this principle, he must return to a basic fact of the Commedia, the distinction between *commedia*, the exposition of the events, and *spectacle*, the "gratuitous" development of the *fabula* (play), which involves actors and audience throughout the time of the artists' performance, even when the time is consumed with digressions (problems and accidents that have nothing to do with the commedia), entertainment (the dynamic intermission), initial greetings, thank-yous at the end, apologies, and enjoyment of the success of the show.
3. The actor-mask is always in play. The prologue, the synthesis, and the epilogue are not literary facts but situations which emanate prologues, syntheses, and epilogues.
4. The skills required of the actor-mask are not sufficient unto themselves, but must be fit into the play. An example with juggling: Brighella pulls chestnuts from the fire. They are burning hot, he can't hold them in his hands but the rule prohibits him from letting them drop, so he juggles the chestnuts. An example with acrobatics: Pantalone is suddenly asked for a loan. His powerful emotional reaction to the prospect of giving up his money—internal on the psychological plane—translates itself externally as a backflip. Naturally, Pantalone himself is not an acrobat; even if he were in his youth, he is now too old for acrobatics, he can't even hop voluntarily and fails when he tries. But putting a strong internal emotion into mask-play a strong internal emotion necessarily translates it into something visible and spectacular. The backflip is therefore the *external* expression of an equivalent *internal* movement. This should demonstrate that the supposed superiority of the internal over the external is a useless exercise, given that the exteriority that comes from the mask is the *externalization* of an explosive internal dimension that must be externalized to be manifested, explained, said. It is an eruption. And

like all eruptions, it emerges from somewhere deep, deep down. Skills are not ends in themselves, but in service to great poetry. An example with vocal and instrumental music: a serenade can constitute an important moment in the unfolding events of the story, with relative comic disasters that take place during the musical execution, translating it into *gestural music*, strictly connected with the dramatic situation.

5. All the actor's play is subject to *enmasking*, to being rendered dynamic: body, gesture, voice, speech, language.

6. The actor-mask is spatial. He does not move around like a *biopuppet* in an alien setting, but performs actions in a space that is as free as possible, that becomes modified, shaped, given meaning, by his actions.

7. The actor-mask is nonpsychological. He does not create a single individual with a unique psyche but rather situates the human being in a given situation. He is profoundly aware of collective behavior.

8. The masked actor is humanizing. He does not create abstractions but rather formally exaggerates human reality, maintaining it always within the limits of the recognizable and the comprehensible.

9. The masked actor combines his unique and unrepeatable human and artistic peculiarities with the universal and archetypal qualities of the mask. He obtains his own personal version of the popular epic contained in the mask. He guarantees, by virtue of this combination of personal and collective qualities, the continuity of the tradition.

10. The masked actor of the Commedia dell'Arte is an *epicomic* artist.

Theatrical comedy bases its expressive particularity on universal laws that have still not been entirely decoded, but which we will attempt to summarize here as follows:

The *comic* is the conscious and intentional organization of the *ridiculous*, which is involuntary and disorganized.

The ridiculous is always a regrettable and shameful accident.

The comic is always intentional.

The ridiculous, though it always provokes laughter, also provokes—subsequent to laughter—feelings such as sadness, compassion, and pity, or sensations such as discomfort, intolerance, and disagreeable sharing of the shame of the victim. These feelings are provoked by the evidence of the tragic side of the occurrence that has plunged the victim into ridiculousness. The ridiculous is a problem for the witnesses as well as for the victim.

The comic intention presents itself as a momentary solution of the problem: the representation of the ridiculous relieves the spectator of the fear of the ridiculous. The comic character takes on himself all the misfortune that the spectator fears in the daily unfolding of his existence. When laughter is triggered, a catharsis has taken place. Catharsis is not an attribute only of tragedy. It is a purification that brings consolation. All consolatory relations are cathartic.

Spectacle in general dispenses catharsis, even though at times this occurs only to the tiniest degree.

The masked actor is comic when, through his character, he takes on the suffering and pain that the audience fears in its daily life. In order to obtain the laughter of the audience, the mask exaggerates, deforms, miniaturizes, and enlarges. He does this with words, his voice, his body, and gestures. The word is to the voice as the gesture is to the body. The comic mask is composed as an application of comic principles. The actor must apply these principles throughout his expressive being. The features, the form and color, the exaggeration of his character, his highlighting of physical defects—which ennoble themselves as defects of character and behavior—and despite all this exaggeration, the concreteness, the need for truth; all this clearly indicates the *comic intention* contained in the mask.

The comic mask imposes the formal exaggeration of reality. The comic actor never departs from reality but pushes it toward its most extreme expressive consequences.

THE MEANING OF THE MASK

What does the mask mean, what does it represent in general? Without wishing to offer here a "history of the mask," we need at least to attempt to define it in its universal meaning. In its very earliest (before becoming a character) and very last (once personification has taken place) analysis, the mask represents the following:

1. He who is wearing it, who performs actions in another life, whether preceding, subsequent, or parallel
2. He who witnesses and therefore sees the representation of himself in another life, whether preceding, subsequent, or parallel

It is difficult, if not erroneous, to claim that the mask represents death. Unless, that is, one wishes to give an entirely positive connotation to death by conceiving it as a part of a progression (different from the process of decomposition). This is difficult to reconcile within Western culture, which sees the physical death of the body as the end of the being itself. This vision of death is absolute in modern Western culture on a scientific level and as a brutal nightmare. Spiritual remedies from superstition to mysticism have not resolved the negative definition of death in the common imagination. If that's the way things stand, why believe that the mask represents death? The mask *tout court*? Certain masks? Perhaps, but not the comic mask, not the mask of the Commedia dell'Arte, which is at one and the same time a utilitarian object and an artistic principle, and which causes, at the moment of its appearance onstage, the immediate forging of an eminently social contract of complicity between actors and audience, a guarantee of civil and peaceful coexistence, of collective intelligence, and the capacity to overcome baser emotions in the name of progress, as happens whenever comedy is not gratuitous.

Gratuitous comedy, the gravest sin of the comic, involves the refusal of the superiority of inferiority, which is the most complex and most important poetic manifestation of the comic as a social, cultural, and artistic expression. The superiority of inferiority is a clause written into the contract of complicity between actor and audience. With a sort of reverse touch of Midas, the comic actor demolishes, destroys, puts everything he touches on the lowest level, down on his level. The audience is situated at an intermediate level between the actor's lowest of the low and the higher level of represented reality. The audience watches everything collapse around it and takes part in a sort of rebirth into a higher order by virtue of the systematic lowering of everything around it. The middle level, that of the spectator, is the dimension of reason, of civility, we might say of democracy that reconciles the high with the low. Extremes are resolved through comic representation. The audience is an accomplice in all this. When the audience is not an accomplice, it is decidedly contrary and refuses to play along. It won't laugh, it doesn't want to laugh, it makes itself into an *agelasta* or it exits, it abandons the game.

There is no doubt that the mask also contains the meaning of death, in the sense that the comic mask itself is a certain remedy to the sense of the absolute negativity of death. The comic mask makes death a mere obstacle, though unavoidable and insurmountable. Death becomes *recuperable*, like any other manifestation of life as rendered in the popular comic tradition, which makes the most terrifying scarecrow a mere obstacle by affirming the circularity of life, allowing time to continue, and denies irreversibility in favor of continuous return, besting in efficacy all curses, prayers, mysticism, and psychoanalytic couches.

The mask therefore is not death but rather *that other life,* the one we want to know more about. It has already taken place. It has not yet taken place. It is taking place virtually onstage, not the representation of some ideal life but life explained, understood, made acceptable. Life is affirmed; in fact, everything that happens in a comedy is always and only a crescendo of complications that could be resolved with a single gesture, a single word. Why doesn't that happen? Why does it take two or three hours (which often signify two or three days) to make sense of the mess? Why, besides the length of time, does it take an entire comedy, which is after all the entire lifetime given to these characters to manifest themselves? The sensation we have in a comedy of many things happening, perhaps too much of it useless (and that it would have been simple not to make that gesture or say those words and everything would have been avoided; or rather, it would be simple now to make that gesture or say those words and everything would be resolved), is very strong. But all that chaos is not useless. On the contrary. In the first place, there is no drama, or representation of drama, without conflicts, problems, defects, excess, and confusion. Absence of a dilemma is the perfect negation of drama, the absence of the need to represent, the absence of need for theater itself.

No less important, the apparently useless agitation of the characters in the Commedia dell'Arte signifies the epiphany of life in its biological sense, life that has no need of explanation except its own unfolding, its noisy manifestation. The vitalism, therefore, of the Commedia dell'Arte.

Death and life are the rebounding or mirror images of a movement, a rhythm, an action that makes use of historical linearity (fable, narration, the rational and chronological succession of facts) to affirm an eternal impulse, a *circular time* (the cyclical mystery of life). The mask is not merely the simple and obvious symbol of all this; it is the *action,* the *lazzo par excellence.*

"*Lazzo*" (the plural form is *lazzi*) is a sort of magic word in the practice of the Commedia dell'Arte. It is said to derive from the expression coined by the first comic actors, *fare l'actio,* to perform the act, the scenic action. Torresani suggests that it derives from an expression in the dialect of Lombardy, "quite probably from the Lombard 'acc'; still today in some of our towns, 'acc' means 'uncoordinated gestures mixed with witticisms.'"[4]

In comic slang, *lazzo* indicates any solution adopted onstage to provoke laughter in the audience. A minimal *lazzo* is a quick gag, a maximum *lazzo* is a brief, fully structured scene. *Lazzi* form part of the repertory of an actor, who uses them as a sort of supply of sure and effective comic solutions, adaptable to all comedies. A *lazzo* is always linked to a particular character. The Commedia is based on fixed types which we find, with slight variations, in all comedies and which develop a poetics common to all the actors who perform that type. Actors create their *lazzi* on the basis of general comic principles, but they are then adapted to particular characters; thus we have *lazzi* for the aged characters, for servants, for the Capitano. The Lovers usually get wrapped up in *lazzi* but rarely produce them. Their seriousness—which is itself comical, a product of expressive *excess*—prohibits them from participating in jokes that tend to be considered vile or base. But the Lovers can produce *lazzi* when their psychophysical condition has reduced them to such a desperate state that their behavior becomes base; a sufficient example is that of the state of insanity produced by unbearable amorous desperation.

Through his *lazzi,* every actor elaborates his own style, his own comic poetics. *Lazzi* are gestures and actions, both situational and verbal. A verbal *lazzo* is called a *bisguizzo;* this is a virtually forgotten historical term of unknown origin that we would like to try to reintroduce into common usage.

Lazzo and mask are inseparable. The *lazzo* is the putting into action of the mask. The mask is the image and visage of the *lazzo.* The *lazzo* is the enmasking of the character, who cannot abstain from making *lazzi,* because creating *lazzi* is a natural function of being a mask. The actor will always figure out a way to integrate *lazzi* into the action and unfolding events of a play.

DEFINITION

The term "Commedia dell'Arte" is a late invention, attributed to Carlo Goldoni and untraceable before his use of it. But the genre it names is implicit in the word *arte,* which refers to the professional character of improvised theater, which remains its distinctive characteristic throughout its history.

Commedia di Zanni, zannesca, Improvvisa, italiana, mercenaria, delle maschere (Zanie Comedy, zannesque, improvised, Italian, mercenary, of the masks, respectively); these are the most frequent terms used to define Commedia. But Commedia dell'Arte remains the most accurate expression, because it identifies perhaps the most historically significant aspect of the "invention": professionalism.

Professionalism in theater and in performance in general no longer constitutes a novelty. Nevertheless, our sense is that of a progressive distancing of the actor from his creative responsibility. This abandonment of responsibility grants the actor a relative personal tranquility about the results of his work, but it also produces an inevitable frustration and creates a general flattening of theatrical expression.

We hold that the Arte must be reaffirmed in this sense, that performing artists, with the strength of a discipline that makes it possible, must return to being the ones who determine the destiny of the performing arts.

The Commedia dell'Arte has known numerous historical phases. To classify and describe them is the work of a different book. We propose here to provide a basic orientation. Our attention is focused here on stylistic evolution resulting from certain key changes, which leads in a continuous development up to the work we are doing today.

STYLISTIC EVOLUTION

In its origin, Commedia is all *zannesca,* from its first appearance no later than 1538 until the arrival of the actress, the woman performer, an event that is traditionally fixed at 1560. This phase is characterized by a heavy-handed farcical form made up of brief sketches that are obscene and aggressive. Only men perform, playing also the female parts, the so-called Zagne. All are masked, and they represent a poor, ugly, filthy, often deformed humanity, aggressive but not evil, generally cowardly; all in all, *grotesque.*

In 1560 the actress makes her triumphal entrance. It must have been a shock for everyone, including her fellow actors, audiences, and authorities. Secular authorities were in favor, but the religious authorities were furious, and they never ceased to preach and launch anathemas against this new development, to the extent that they preferred—with some reservations—the castrati to real women during the triumph of bel canto, in the seventeenth and eighteenth centuries.

The idea of putting "real women" onstage in women's roles is undoubtedly a consequence of the professional mentality that drives continuous improvement of the product and its reinvention. Whoever first had the idea had a good one, because it was visually attractive, explosive, instantaneously imitated by all other companies, and carried a sense of the future. The most important consequences of the arrival of the actress onstage, other than the event itself, can be found in the structure of the comedies performed, which now required more complex situations and a larger cast to accommodate the growing number of characters. The new figure of the female Lover, for example, necessarily calls for the male Lover, a previously nonexistent character. The character of the Courtesan is introduced, drawn from the learned comedies written by the elite humanists, who had taken it from Latin comedy. Another new character is Fantesca, a young female servant played as a sort of screwball. There is a series or sequence of images in the *Recueil Fossard,* which still today constitutes the most antique iconographic document of the Commedia dell'Arte. Its precise date is uncertain, but the engravings are dated between 1560 and 1580, the period in which we locate the phase when Commedia established its definitive structure.

Among the images, called the *Ludi Zanneschi,* is one that shows us a Zagna (that is, a male actor playing a female role) assisting Zanni in the delicate operation of intestinally cleaning a Magnifico, physically strong and hunchbacked, who looks back at his "doctors" and their equipment with an alarmed, supplicant expression. In another image, Zanni plays a flute for the Magnifico, who dances with an *Innamorata* (Female Lover). The Zagna-actor and the Lover-actress, female characters but not both played by women, must have coexisted during this phase.

The great interest of the *Ludi Zanneschi* resides, beyond that of defining the passage from transvestite actor to female actress, in the suggestions that the images offer for a systematic reintroduction of the Zagna into our principle of Commedia's continuity. We may now entrust the role of Zagna to actresses, carrying out a sort of correction and nonrenunciation that did not take place in history but is today entirely justified. The first actresses rejected the male way of playing a woman, which invariably consisted in grotesque caricature, featuring hypertrophied feminine attributes and masks no different from those of the male Zanni. It appears that they did not, however, refuse to embrace obscenity, if we can trust an image from another series in the Fossard collection, in which we see Arlecchino maneuver his hand between Franceschina's thighs, and if it is true that a certain reincorporation of the ancient *nudatio mimarum* was not infrequent.

The actress who appears onstage refuses and rejects:

1. The mask covering her face
2. Physical deformations
3. Sexual unrecognizability, a refusal that will develop into the refusal of individual unrecognizability

She affirms the exhibition of herself as a recognizable individual, separate from her character. This determines the slow, progressive, and fatal decline of the use in theater of the mask-object.

INFLUENCE OF THE ACTRESS

The arrival of the actress imposes a rapid evolution on dramaturgy, which borrows the model of Plautus, that is, Latin comedy, which had been rediscovered and diffused during the preceding century and was by now well known to the professional companies.

We must give credit to erudite comedy, which chronologically precedes Commedia dell'Arte, for having stimulated the modern rebirth of comedy through the rediscovery, rewriting, translation, and emulation of Latin comedy. All the erudite plays have in common the modernization of the classic plot. The modernization manifests itself in the use of common speech rather than high literary language, costumes that reflect contemporary fashion, and settings in modern urban locales. It does not use masks.

The mask never appears in erudite comedy; apparently its use was not even under consideration. But perhaps the use of the uncovered visage falls within the general criteria of modernization, the reappropriation in a modern key of a timeless, ancient, eternal art.

When the Commedia dell'Arte companies find that they need to adapt their dramaturgy to the new influx of personnel, they do not turn directly to Plautus for help but rather to his intermediaries, the Renaissance humanists and their comedies, translations, adaptations, and certain of their scenic practices.

The masks then in use, by now unassailable, remained. But the newly arrived female components of the companies draw from erudite comedy the principles of the modern and the recognizable. No masks therefore. The face is fine. In fact, it's better. What kind of woman is this new woman actress if you can't see that she's a woman? Where would be the novelty in that? Keep the mask for those who are naturally ugly: the fools, the grotesques, the aged, and keep the natural face for those to whom nature has given beauty. That is, to the women, and to all those who love poetry.

SIXTEENTH-CENTURY DEVELOPMENT

By the late sixteenth century, Commedia, which is now termed "Perfect Comedy," counts on the presence of all the definitive types: male and female Servants, the Magnifico (Pantalone), the Dottore, male and female Lovers, and the Capitano.

Some important experiments of the time have no historical consequences, such as the ultra-chauvinist one-man shows of Giovanni Gabrielli (who died between 1603 and 1611), whose name in art (that is, stage name) is Sivello. In compensation, however, Gabrielli will invent the mask of Scapino, which fixes the role of First Zanni.

There is also an enlargement in repertory, which no longer includes only comedies but now also "serious" works.

From the hopelessly stupid Fantesca we pass to the intelligent female servant, who later comes to be called the Servetta.

The melodious and musical vocation of the Commedia dell'Arte is confirmed in this period, when it almost becomes a musical genre, creating the first serious effort at melodrama (which will soon be called opera). The experiment by Massimo Troiano and Orlando di Lasso in 1568 in Munich is a very early sign of what is to come, but between the end of the sixteenth and the beginning of the seventeenth century, in the *Comedia Harmonica* or

Madrigalesca (although apparently not theatrical in form), musical dignity is accorded to the *buffi* (fools) of the Commedia. Some examples of this development include *Pazzia Senile* (*Senile Insanity,* 1598) and *La Saviezza Giovenile* (*Sage Youth,* 1604) by Adriano Banchieri (1568–1634), and *Amphiparnaso* (1594) by Orazio Vecchi (1550–1605). *Amphiparnaso* is a true Commedia play put to music. The text was by Vecchi himself, under the supervision of Giulio Cesare Croce (1550–1609), the legendary comic poet, author of the *Tremende Bravure del Capitano Bellerofonte Scarabombardone da Rocca di Ferro* (1596) and the *Testamento del Zan alla Bergamasca* (1619), and creator of the great comic character Bertoldo.

Seventeenth Century

The seventeenth century is the age of gold for Commedia. The Italian comics dominate the European stage; professionalism and the actress are now universal. A star system reigns, making up for a certain tiredness of ideas and redundancy in the Commedia itself. This is the phase of Commedia as a trade, but there is still a great deal of spirit, and new variations are constantly invented. The spirit is well illustrated by the engravings of Jacques Callot in his series the *Balli di Sfessania,* beautiful and very famous images of Commedia characters, although the character names written under each image are often mistaken (which may suggest that Callot invented them). The French engraver has left us additional visual testimony of great documentary value, such as his *Pantalone, Innamorato,* and *Scapino.* Of special interest is his representation of the *girotondo* (similar to the English ring around the rosy), which is included in the collection entitled *Capricci* of 1617. A company of masks dances in a circle; a Zanni beats time with a *tamburello* (large tambourine). In the group we recognize a Magnifico, a Dottore, a Capitano, a Servetta, and six Zanni. The image is convincing and shows us a beautiful family of masks of the early seventeenth century. The dance does not appear spontaneous; its ritualistic quality closely recalls one in the *Compendium Maleficarum* (1608 and 1626). In this book, Francesco Maria Guaccio describes a circle dance in which all backs are turned to the center: "At this point, each demon takes his partner by hand, and since everything happens nonsensically, they form a circle holding hands but turning their backs to each other, and they start dancing while shaking their heads like crazy people."[1]

We believe the allusion to a satanic ritual is intended humorously.

In the eighteenth century, Commedia becomes rococo. It becomes coquettish, fussy, mannered, genteel, mawkish, effeminate, losing its zany, masked aggression. Ever more often, an actor or actress dominates not merely the scene (as has always been the case) but the entire comedy and its plot, monopolizing the audience's attention. It is a time of decadence and reform: Luigi Riccoboni arrives to correct Commedia, and Carlo Goldoni arrives to correct Theater.

The Goldoni phase of Commedia stretches from Goldoni's departure from Venice to move to Paris in 1762 until the staging of his *Servant of Two Masters* by Strehler and Moretti at the Piccolo Teatro di Milano in 1947.

We recognize that the identification of such a phase is highly debatable, but there is a thread that unites those centuries. We name the phase after Goldoni because, despite his own wishes, he is the most important reference point and represents the beginning and closure of the period, which could just as easily be called French Commedia. In fact, we would pick out within the Goldoni parentheses the maturation of an entirely French vision of Commedia, where Arlecchino prevails over all. Not Arlecchino, in fact, but Arlequin. This is Comédie Italienne, where Italian means a certain very French style, acrobatic and arch, full of bows and curtsies, a stereotypically Italianized esprit, a vague, pathetic quality of charm, and lots of *lazzi* (with French pronunciation, *lazi*).

France sends this stale, stinking mish-mosh back to us together with a Goldoni (mercifully relocated to his native Venice) irremediably linked to Arlecchino, plus, to complete the package, a mute, romantic, desexualized, bloodless, solitary Pierrot who gazes at the moon. Zanni gazes at the moon too, but because he thinks it's a cheese and he wants to know how to get up there so he can eat it. We have still not freed ourselves of Pierrotism, but the worst of all fates has befallen Pulcinella of Naples, who has become pitifully Pierrotized. Fiorillo, Calcese, Fracanzano, and Petito, the great Neapolitan Pulcinellas, are turning in their graves.

And now we come to our own phase, the modern, beginning with the first experiments by Strehler in 1947, until today. This phase is characterized by three fundamental tendencies: the persistence of Goldoni, reconstructive kitsch, and continuity. We shall now deal with each of these in turn.

The Persistence of Goldoni

We do not agree with the equation that Goldoni equals Commedia dell'Arte. It is not only erroneous but renders very poor service to all. To Goldoni himself in the first place, to improvised comedy, and to audiences. Cultists and popularizers find a total identification between Goldoni and Commedia, and they perpetuate the damage. This would seem to be a passing problem, but from an international perspective, not only is it not passing, it is spreading like an oil spill. It is now a dated opinion, and it is difficult to dissuade its proponents because it is often the only information they have about Commedia dell'Arte. To clarify things is difficult, because they are plunged into a total abyss of information.

We therefore dwell on Goldoni to point out at least one aspect of his work, a peculiarity of his method that should serve to make clear his irremediable detachment from improvised comedy.

Goldoni, then. The Reformer. The artist of slow but unstoppable maturation, Goldoni who "killed the masks," or rather who made them grow up, and with them Italian theater as a whole, as well as—why not?—the European theater of his era.

The Venetian lawyer could no longer stand the bad habits and simplemindedness of the theater of his time, and practice led him to formulate a principle of change in a single word: verisimilitude. The theater was no longer creditable, while in his opinion it absolutely should be. Whether wrong or right, he proceeded with his reform in search of the truth, and we may indeed say that he succeeded. He succeeds not because verisimilitude shows itself to be a winning principle, but because his principle is also the motor of his comic intuition, his talent as a great practitioner of theater. Goldoni certainly doesn't use the word "psychology" when he explains his ideas, but the really extraordinary thing he does is to confer the psychological uniqueness that is in every human being onto his characters. He calls this "character."

I am not a historian of theater, but we are attempting here to develop our discourse on Goldoni in the same way as the rest of this work, both technically and poetically at once, which is to say, aesthetically. We shall concentrate on the difference between mask and character, between traditional theater and Goldoni's reform. My point of view is that of one who practices theater and studies it from and on the stage, who wants to understand and decipher theater's symbols, meanings, means of communication, and relationship with audiences.

To stage Goldoni today may mean facing a choice: should it be treated as the last expression of the historical Commedia dell'Arte or as the first expression of a new theater that has nothing to do with improvisation?

We believe that there is continuity between Commedia dell'Arte and the comedy of Goldoni, and that this continuity is declared by Goldoni himself in his memoirs, his writings, and his comedies. The very fact that Goldoni "surpasses" the use of masks, as is often asserted, is a complex matter, because you cannot surpass what you do not know, something that is not part of what you are. Goldoni, bored with masks, wants to create characters. Thus the difference must be sought in the two terms "mask" and "character," according to Goldoni's conception of them.

By "mask," Goldoni means "fixed types," which appear throughout Commedia. We know that Commedia dell'Arte is based on four fixed types: the Old Man, the Male/Female Lover, Servant, and Capitano. Goldoni indicates his own choice of four, defining them as *the four masks,* but his findings are different: Pantalone/First Old Man, Dottore/Second Old Man, Brighella/First Zanni, and, with different names that mostly all end in "ino," the Second Zanni. Goldoni pointedly ignores the Capitano, but he then proceeds to invent a number of haughty cavaliers who in one way or another carry on that mask. He does not regard the Lovers as fixed types, but he reelaborates them and treats them as characters.

This is already a preliminary picture of the interweaving of tradition in Goldoni's proposed reform. He tolerates some of the masks for reasons of prudence and marketing, while others already known to audiences are just fine as well, except that he reelaborates them with the liberty of a comic poet.

By "character," Goldoni means "unique type," a nonarchetype, unrepeatable. And the unique and unrepeatable must never again turn up in later plays. As in nature, accepting the principle of equality between human beings, the thing to do is to pick out in each person that detail, habit, defect, or good quality, and also that person's particular way of carrying the habit, defect, or good quality, which distinguishes every human from all others, original and unrepeatable.

Therefore character, in Goldoni, does not signify the surpassing of the mask but its evolution. Goldoni abandons masks but redefines the concept of masks according to his new criteria, which open the doors for the psychological theater of the future. The masks have been shed, the mask has been removed from the face. The psychological mask, internal but recognizable and definite in performance, is asserted instead. Two centuries later, Pirandello will define this as the "naked mask," emphasizing with this very suggestive term its exaggerated type—which Goldoni attacked but never quite overcame—and the psychology of the character as what constitutes its uniqueness.

In the conclusion to the preface to his play *Il Teatro Comico*, Goldoni gives us some precious information. He says,

> To adapt myself to tradition and enter into the good graces of the company and above all the mask actors, I first introduced them on stage in their own clothing and with their own faces, then later in their costumes and masks. This seemed nonsense to me, however, so now, in this reprint of this comedy, I have assigned to each character a character name, keeping their mask name for the rehearsal scene within the play in which they represent their mask character.

We learn here that in an early version Goldoni had presented the actors onstage in their real identities. He calls nonsense a practice that is still regarded as rather daring in our own day. Theatrical convention, the stage fiction, requires constant respect; it is a question of the credibility of the work of art as such. Goldoni senses the incongruence that comes from too casually tossing out tradition. Putting the actors onstage in their personal clothing, who then go to work on rehearsing a mask sketch, simply jumps over the characters that, technically speaking, are situated in between nontheatrical reality and mask. At this point, Goldoni has theorized them and ignored them at the same time. So he does the right thing: he invents characters equivalent to each real actor, including the character of himself, the comic poet, who becomes Orazio, a sort of mixture of the company's producer (Medebach) and Goldoni himself.

Once this is established, everything becomes clearer, including the terminology that we can now permit ourselves to expand upon.

Characterization becomes the process of creation (author and actor in collaboration) of a unique, unrepeatable character, beginning from the supposition that there is an infinite number of characters available to nature and the poet.

Fixing type becomes the transformation of the human model into a theatrical character. Goldoni is an acute observer of human behavior, an ethologist *ante litteram,* a scientist of the formation of human character. He sees and understands people, he fixes them into behavioral types, inserting them into representative situations, and thus he obtains his characters. In this sense, despite our supposition of the inexhaustible number of characters, we will never arrive at absolute uniqueness, because our wish always to render the characters somehow recognizable (that is, to achieve verisimilitude) forces the author and his audience into the game of *identification*. Goldoni creates this or that character so that the spectators can think, "That's me up there! And that's so-and-so! It's him! That's him exactly! He's just like that!," a reaction that is the function and guarantee of the achievement of verisimilitude.

Enmasking becomes the transformation of the model into an archetype. The archetype represents anyone in that certain condition or situation, given as permanent through the use, actual or implicit, of the mask. The four fixed types of the Commedia dell'Arte are all archetypes. The Old Man (the Vecchio, in the subtypes of Magnifico and Dottore) represents the condition, definitive and universal, of old age, of being old. The Lover, whether male or female (in the subtypes of ingenue or adventurer) represents the condition of a person who loves and must struggle (grow, become adult) to deserve and finally crown his dream of love. The Servant (doubled into the First and Second Zanni and the female version of the Servetta) represents, through the ambivalent functioning of the create-destroy dynamic, the eternal struggle for survival. The Capitano (in the two versions of the Loser, with mask, and the Winner, without mask) represents the internal conflict between being and seeming.

Goldoni takes account of only two of the traditional archetypes: the Old Man, doubled into Pantalone (First Vecchio) and Dottore (Second Vecchio), and the Servant, in the classical organization of First Zanni—always Brighella—and the Second Zanni, who can be called Truffaldino, Arlecchino, Traccagnino, or what have you. Goldoni uses the term "Zanni" to indicate the roles themselves. In *I Due Gemelli Veneziani* (*The Two Venetian Twins*), he imposes the name Zanetto, a diminutive of Zanni, to the stupid twin, suggesting with the name his particular Zanni-type characteristic, blockheadedness, to an audience that recognizes the connotation of the name.

In the texts where he utilizes masks, Goldoni brings together his *unique types* with the *fixed types* of tradition. He thus obtains a balanced and "civil" coexistence of two effects that we will call the Mask Effect and the Goldoni Effect.

The Mask Effect and the Goldoni Effect

The Mask Effect is present when the use of techniques and expressions from the Commedia dell'Arte influences the structure and balance (the "economy") of the piece. The four fundamental points of the Commedia dell'Arte (that we shall deal with in turn) are:

1. Fixed types, or archetypes
2. Mask
3. Improvisation
4. Multilingualism

Goldoni partially holds off on the first two of these and maintains a certain linguistic freedom, permitting the cohabitation of different idioms. And improvisation? Goldoni seems very skilled about eluding this problem. The Italian comic actors of this time were all improvisers. Goldoni must play his cards very well in order to convince them to follow him. He takes away the improvisations of the many actors who form his company and assumes that responsibility for himself. He, the author, is the great improviser and he does it better than any actor, because by writing he exercises control over the verbal coherence that even a brilliant improviser does not always possess. He eliminates what lacks verisimilitude and translates into beautiful scenes an astounding variety of human chatter, argument, gossip, misunderstanding, incomprehension, secrets, confession, and reconciliation. Goldoni writes the way people speak. Thus the Goldoni Effect: in his announced and successful effort to surpass the mask, Goldoni does not take the mask away because it is false. Goldoni knows perfectly well that masks do not conceal but rather reveal. Instead, he goes beyond: he takes away the masked game of physical play—the *bambocciata*—in preference for the natural that derives from character, from a deep source. It is the invention of the interior mask, the preannouncement of today's (excessive, in my opinion) psychology.

We shall now try to detail these reflections by leafing through a celebrated comedy by Goldoni and adding "notes for a future production." The comedy is *La Famiglia dell'Antiquario* (*The Antiquarian's Family*). This play was produced at the Teatro Sant'Angelo in Venice for the Carnevale festivities of 1750 and has a second title: *La Suocera e la Nuora* (*The Mother-in-Law and the Daughter-in-Law*).

A synopsis: The play presents events in the life of the head of a household, Count Anselmo, who has lost control of his life due to his maniacal passion for antiques, about which he understands virtually nothing. His son, Count Giacinto, has married Doralice, the daughter of Pantalone. Between Doralice and her mother-in-law, Isabella, there is a war on for the conquest of the power left vacant by Anselmo and his son, who quickly reveals himself to be too clueless, too enamored of his beautiful wife, and too intimidated by his mother. In these conditions, profiteering flowers: Brighella and Arlecchino buff up worthless junk and sell it as precious antiques to Anselmo at ridiculous prices. The Servetta, Colombina, plays the mother-in-law and daughter-in-law off each other, fostering their rivalry—or rather their hatred—in a way that is frankly gratuitous. The Doctor is Isabella's "adviser" and the Cavalier del Bosco is the "male friend" of Doralice. Both of these impostors take advantage of the conflict between the two women. Anselmo has dragged the household economy, and by consequence its morality, to the brink of the precipice by spending all his savings, including his wife's dowry. It becomes the task of Pantalone, Doralice's merchant father, to set things right. He finally makes Anselmo and Giacinto delegate to him executive authority over the estate; he fires the servants, he sloughs off the advisers, and he reestablishes economic and moral order. Only one element is not resolved happily: there is no reconciliation between the two ladies of the house.

1. The play swiftly gets under way and accelerates brilliantly. Scene 1 between Anselmo and Brighella immediately suggests the further likely development that Anselmo's obsession with antiques will lead the family to ruin. His character is swiftly opened up to us, the Goldoni Effect is exemplary. Brighella gives Anselmo little nudges toward the precipice, and we know that this is Brighella being Brighella, that his method has always been one of maximum opportunism. This is a beautiful Mask Effect right at the top of the comedy. At the opening curtain, there is comedy and clarity, as with all good comedy. A conflict seeks its solution. This premise is the interpretive key to the characters who now come one by one into contact with Anselmo. The following scenes are a sort of parade of behaviors, personal stories, hints at possible developments. All the scenes are rapid, taut, musically structured; not dialogues, not conversations, but duets, trios. From improvisation to script, as the musician from ear to staff.

2. A notable aspect of this comedy is the acidic egoism of the characters. A general negativity dominates their relations. This is a leap in quality with respect to the comic tradition, which justifies everything with equivocation, such that all the characters are always to some degree "lovable." But the vital theme of opportunism is inherited from the Arte.

3. The mother-in-law is choleric and the daughter-in-law punctilious, but the father is obtuse and the son simpleminded. As for the servants, Colombina is impertinent, Brighella is ever the opportunist, and Arlecchino is untrustworthy. Thus there is no more misogyny than there is misanthropy. Further, all the social classes—aristocracy, bourgeoisie, servants—are treated with the same severe judgment. Human egoism—multifaceted according to age, sex, class, economic, and family condition—is the strong and constant theme, the *mask of action*, or in Goldonian terms, *character of action* of the three acts, in the course of which the watertight plot develops.

4. Scenes 16 and 17 of act 1 are pure Commedia dell'Arte with the splendid scene of the Armenian merchant. This is great comic theater in the grand tradition. Here we note something very interesting: the perfect functional and theatrical use of the First Zanni, Brighella. In his intention to temper the masks of the servants, Goldoni achieves a level of stylistic purity that is almost a renewal, a renovation of the masks themselves. He censors obscenity, he frees himself of acrobatics, but he perfects the meanings consecrated in their history. In the scene in question, 16 of act 1, Brighella instructs Arlecchino on how to deceive Anselmo by passing off rubbish as valuable antiques. Arlecchino is up for the game but rather scandalized by it all:

> ARLECCHINO [*sarcastically*]: You must really adore your master!
> BRIGHELLA: I tell you, I try to enlighten him, to disabuse him, but he won't have it. He throws his money away. Since he's burning it anyway, shouldn't I warm myself at the fire?

This perfectly explains Brighella, the First Zanni, who conserves even in Goldoni his fundamentally diabolical origin. But here he is, in the unfolding of a supposedly "reformed" comedy.

As for scene 17, between Anselmo, Brighella, and Arlecchino in the guise of an Armenian merchant, the potential for *lazzi* of the most classic Commedia tradition is extraordinary. Anselmo, although a new character, regally enters the pantheon of suckers of the masked art.

5. Scene 19, act 1. Pantalone delivers a *reproach*. Reproaches are typical speeches of the Magnifico of the Commedia. Goldoni does not much care for set forms of this type, but here he adapts it to his purposes. Almost amiably, Pantalone reproaches his daughter Doralice who, with cheek rather than honesty, has admitted to beating her mother-in-law's servant, Colombina. Pantalone attempts to teach his daughter a lesson, to guide her toward proper behavior. He spurs her to be wise. Classic in its form, this reproach is new in its content. The Pantalone that results is the opposite of the Vecchio of the im-

provised tradition, who, depending on circumstances, is rapacious, lascivious, tyrannical, and unreasonable. With the character of Pantalone, Goldoni mediates between old and new but also firmly carries on tradition. Goldoni loves his Pantalone, and the concern arises that Goldoni identifies too completely with this character: he is wise, honest, severe when he must be, but like all good fathers he is also too tolerant. He is the upstanding Venetian citizen, active and enterprising, a good administrator but also "one of the people." Not sophisticated, he is self-made. The Pantalone of tradition is completely different: egoistic, libidinous, stubborn, avaricious. The figure of the Magnifico, of whom Pantalone is the most famous exponent, is born as a rich old man who wants to possess the young maiden. Everything moves from this premise and every single play of the Commedia is based on it. The Vecchio will do anything dishonest to achieve his goal, and everyone else will do anything, with equal dishonesty, to prevent him. At the end, Pantalone will pay, in money and in beatings.

The Pantalone of Goldoni conserves the name, the mask, the appearance, and the language of the old one, but not the character, not the behavior, and not even the function. If the function of the Pantalone of improvised theater is to create the obstacle and release the mechanism of confusion and disorder, Goldoni's Pantalone is the one who fixes, arranges, solves knots of misunderstanding, and puts in order. The mask and the character are opposites in this case. The wise and amiable Pantalone will become a pernicious lesson for the future. In Commedia today, people are often ignorant of the difference between tradition and Goldoni, and they tend to put a Goldoni-style Magnifico onstage, but without any consciousness of the historical foundation, so that we see a cute Pantalone, rascally but really not so very bad; that is, neither a nasty degraded old man nor a sage old man, but a mere geriatric caricature, weak, puerile, and anachronistic. In reforming Pantalone, Goldoni unfolds his concept of reform. Pantalone now becomes the central role. He is reborn and thus continues but is strongly reformed:

- ☞ He maintains mask, appearance, age, gestures (although acrobatics are eliminated), and capacity for *lazzi* (as long as they don't go too far!).
- ☞ He loses lasciviousness, avarice, his function as persecutor and obstacle.
- ☞ He acquires wisdom, commonsense, tolerance, the function of resolving conflicts.
- ☞ He tempers his mean-spiritedness into wise governance, his rage into righteous anger.

Here is Goldoni's Pantalone and here, by contrast, is his clownish predecessor. To consider them according to the changed needs of the society to which they are destined is a good interpretive premise. To confuse them, mix them, use them anachronistically, is to do very poor service both to the Arte and to Goldoni, which are themselves both blameless.

6. Finale of act 1, scene of "fixing." Scene 22 of act 1 between the Cavalier, Doralice, and Isabella. A beautiful subplot in seven lines. Young Doralice, instructed by her Cavalier, consents to greet her mother-in-law before she is greeted in turn, because her mother-in-law "is older." When the older woman appears, however, Doralice immediately throws her old age in her face. This means war. The Cavalier closes the scene by saying disconsolately, "Well, we've fixed things now." The scene seems to have been added after a first series of performances. It is quite probable that the actors' contribution determined the almost perfect rhythm of this lightning-fast scene.

7. Act 2, scene 3. We have a Colombina, servant of two masters. Having more than one master is a recurring theme. A recurring theme is a Mask Effect, but we are referring here to Goldoni. Commedia dell'Arte contains the theme of excess masters as natural. A servant is a servant not only for his own master but for any master, real or apparent. By the same token, for a master it is natural to make use not only of his own servant but of any servant who might happen by. So in Commedia, to be the servant of many masters is natural and recurring. Now we turn to Colombina in Goldoni's version. She is a servant who intrigues, playing off Doralice—who proposes the double game at first—and Isabella. She does it to serve her own interests. In Goldoni, serving one's own interests is the evolved form of the struggle for survival. Colombina has a good position in the house, she enjoys the trust of her mistress, she eats every day and sleeps in a real bed; the struggle to survive of the early Zanni is now in the past. Now, instead, the prospect of gain and the rather mean pleasure in seeing the two ladies argue are the impulses that drive Colombina to her intrigues.

8. Certain scenes in Commedia "restabilize," that is, they have the function of establishing a certain level of understanding, of complicity between a reform-minded author and a conservative audience. The instinct of shrewdness, which never escapes an assiduous spectator, enters the play more as a homage to the intelligence of the audience than for its utilitarian function. A scene that is pure tradition comes as a much-appreciated spoonful of sugar to help the audience swallow all the new, reformed elements.

9. In Goldoni's reformed mechanism, Pantalone takes a step forward but comes to be "substituted" by Anselmo in the function of initial spark of con-

flict and final scapegoat. In a hypothetical zannesque or improvised version of this play, the Anselmo role would wear a mask and speak in dialect, whereas Pantalone would not.

10. Act 3, scene 5. Arlecchino's exit alters the dramatic progress, and the character thus "maintains" the mask. His flight, while dressed in Armenian disguise, guarantees the continuity of the mask. An exemplary punishment administered to Arlecchino in application of the high moral principles of the new Pantalone would constitute the death of the mask itself. The mask must survive even the most severe judgment. That's why Arlecchino exits laughing. (The laugh is, in fact, an act of justice but also of pardon. By resolving the problem, the comic actor resolves the emotion that accompanies it. If before there was rancor, now there is none.)

11. Act 3, scene 6, the arrangement of entrances and exits, maintaining the overall scenic unity. Goldoni explains that "all the characters enter and exit in this scene, and their entrances and exits constitute the scene." The rhythm is frenetic, the suspense continually reinforced, the acceleration is perfectly controlled by a script that is pure action.

12. Brighella's disappearance is entirely coherent with the traditional mask. Only the tradition of citing a proverb as a "button" on the scene is missing here, but that practice has been anticipated in his earlier line, "Since he's burning it anyway, shouldn't I warm myself at the fire?"

13. Finale scene. Pantalone resolves the crisis by applying the commonsense that apparently expresses Goldoni's views, which Goldoni would like to propose to the audience as norms for behavior. The old man is shrewd but for a good purpose. In agreement with Anselmo and his son, he takes on the administration of the household, which he will guide back to financial health, which will take some time. Pantalone reorganizes the household so that the two opposed women will never meet. He fires servants and shows the door to the advisers. He concedes a minimal allowance to Anselmo so that he may still collect medals and undertakes to teach the son how to run a family.

Like Pantalone, Goldoni is shrewd as well. In order to create something new, he makes use of an ancient mask, Pantalone, who up to now has been nothing but clownish and obscene. Now the buffoon Pantalone will become the master of good household governance, just as Goldoni is a teacher of reformed morality.

The author renounces the happy ending, which will earn him sharp criticism from the most conservative critics. But the new arrangement can't be called revolutionary. *La Famiglia dell'Antiquario* is admittedly a "reformed" comedy but scrupulously obeys a basic stage grammar that must be followed by even as courageous an innovator as Goldoni. The resolution of this comedy is exemplary of the situation in which Goldoni finds himself. All comedies are made of intrigues that finally resolve themselves. They all show a state of disorder that is finally put back in order. This comedy offers resolution both on the formal level—with moments of recognition that involve unmasking—and on the level of the plot, because the impossibility of reconciling the two ladies, which might seem misogynist, does not imply the failure of all the other resolutions. In substance, Goldoni renounces only the hypocritical pretense that everything must necessarily end happily. He renounces the reassuring finale. For his times, this was certainly powerfully controversial. But if you think about it, no Commedia dell'Arte play was ever reassuring in its "body," in its development. In Arte plays, the final "hypocrisy," extremely pronounced and played to the maximum in a way that we choose to call *comic demagoguery,* was a result of the performing company's fear that any other ending would threaten their economic survival. If Goldoni overcomes these fears, it is because he feels that the audience is sufficiently prepared to accept a linear poetic proposal that contains, along with many familiar elements, many new ones. The audience must accept the principle that the new is part of a continuum of life-theater-life. The closed circle is broken and straightened out.

Transition from Grotesque to Psychological

We will now attempt to clarify the passage from *grotesque mask* to *psychological mask.*

The first actor of the Commedia dell'Arte, working within a circular conception of time and history, develops a sort of *lay millennialism,* where everything is death and resurrection in brief, material, cyclical terms: hunger, food, evacuation, and repeat from the top. The external world is large, various, a friend in the daytime and summer but an enemy at night and in winter. The infinite is outside but also inside, where it is called hunger, love, fear, and also by the names of the seven deadly sins. In the ancient world, when a phenomenon repeats itself, it is because nature deems that it must, and that's enough. Or it is the will of God.

For the modern actor initiated into Commedia dell'Arte, this vision changes. Repetition no longer demonstrates fate but the existence of principles that undergird the workings of things. Catastrophes are replaced by difficulties. Every effect has its cause. And history, which comes from who-knows-where and goes who-knows-where, passes by here, by us, and we must try to do what we can to go where we desire to go; that is, to direct our own fates.

Goldoni is not the inventor of historical linearity, but he is the artificer of a very lucidly conducted operation to drag the actor outside his circularity, which weighs heavily on the evolution of performance and of the audience. Paradoxically, early Commedia is much closer to linearity than Goldoni's, which we can explain by the fact that as a business it immediately adapted itself to the new modern conception of time and history. The Zanni mode, even before it becomes a genre and a container of cultural signs, is an organizational model, a discipline, a method, a means for growth. Early Commedia is necessarily process, economy, competition, rereading of geopolitical space for the maximum distribution of a commercial product that, because it is art, can be sold anywhere.

When improvised theater is one century old, it begins its long decadence. It does not know that it has already accomplished what was necessary for the great leap: performance as profession and industry, show business in the modern sense. Having achieved that, it continues because people like it, and people like it because the actors are especially good.

The road was opened by the great authors. But they aren't Italian (except in musical theater, which is a different story), precisely because the Italian actors are so exceptional, able to invent and reinvent theater day after day at a pace that no one else in the market can match.

Thus we arrive at the era of Goldoni, with a Commedia dell'Arte that has degenerated into a dish that has been rehashed into every imaginable combination. It still draws crowds, but it has become an abstraction, pure convention, a social habit, display and vulgarity mixed together.

Goldoni the Venetian, like his Pantalone, reestablishes order. He shakes off the old and now empty meanings and substitutes new ones, his *characters,* his *verisimilitude,* his *credibility.* He does not entirely renounce the mask or its plots. But he perfects and reforms because he describes facts as they happen, because he bestows thought on bodies and makes them responsible for their own actions. He performs a civilizing function onstage and in the audience.

Goldoni prefers the *topic* to other starting points for a play, such as the *situation,* the *passion,* or the *person.* Naturally, he introduces all those elements into his scripts, but, judging from the way he describes the genesis of some of his comedies, he arrives at them from the opposite direction of traditional Commedia. He looks for the story, the events, the plot. The characters take form from the plot (in improvised theater, the plot takes its form from the characters, which preexist the plot and are fixed for all time), the situations develop within the plot, and the topic takes shape. The successive phase, the deepening interrelations of the initial elements, cannot take place except in movement among the actors, actors whom the comic poet knows personally, and for each of whom he conceives a *character* that he expects to be developed by the actor.

In some of our performances we have attempted to elaborate a modern form of comedy derived from traditional models. That is, what would theater be like if Goldoni had never existed? We continue to follow this path, not to negate Goldoni, but to surpass—with an acrobatic return to the past—the uncomfortable, too-tight Aristotelianism for which Goldoni is responsible.

Goldoni is great. But his teaching has not produced results up to his own level of greatness. Now that Goldoni is far away, we recognize that he was always singular.

The fact is that, from the purely comic point of view, there is no *folly* in Goldoni and there is too much *normalization.* The writer of this assertion is a Pulcinella by choice but also through his family line, as with certain physical disorders. Pulcinella is the only Commedia mask that, from his first appearance until today, has never suffered interruptions, and his evolution is completely autonomous and separate from Goldoni's reform. Pulcinella never heard of Goldoni or about any reform of theater; he has simply survived in theater the whole time.

Pulcinella is born at the beginning of the seventeenth century. He grows, he proceeds without pause along his way both in and outside theater, through infinite variations and uses. Pulcinella arrives where no genre or author has arrived before, at the "trinity" of the mask. This expression may seem blasphemous to some, but, technically at least, that's really the way things are.

We have this trinity:

The system of Pulcinella is formed of three interactive components:

1. The actor-performer, who is a professional, a worker, an actor offering his services, who, by performing a known action according to a known canon, is fulfilling his social function.

2. The actor of Pulcinella, who is the idealization of the performer according to the schema of the mask of Pulcinella. He is the actor seen by Pulcinella, a poor unfortunate forced to play the clown to earn his daily bread, but he also thinks like the audience, which sees in Pulcinella what the mask itself cannot see. These two aspects are in *comic contradiction.*

3. Finally, Pulcinella is Pulcinella.

The three coexist in performance. The system provides the occasion for great histrionic virtuosity, irrespective of any so-called Aristotelian or other kind of unity. The triune egocentrism of the Pulcinella system is powerful and overwhelming.

We cannot exclude an awareness in Goldoni himself of the risk of egocentrism present in every mask, an unpleasant tendency to which all actors are prone. For Goldoni, the comic author of an established company, working beside or at the head of the actors, the potential of the grotesque represents a sort of "creative terrorism" against good sense and realism that might explode any effort at reform. Goldoni puts the brakes on the masks and writes out their parts, even in the cases where the masks themselves have already fully invented their roles through improvisation (this is surely the case in all the masked parts written by Goldoni).

Pulcinella remains a southern phenomenon. In the south, ambivalence is substituted, or evolved, or regressed, into a three-part, self-sufficient dynamic. On his own or with others, onstage or in the street, at home or anywhere, the Pulcinella system always works.

In the north, Goldoni works to eliminate ambivalence by binding together the system's component parts, internalizing the mask and isolating the archetype in his concept of character, conferring uniqueness and asking the actor to offer his face, his voice, and his body to the character he plays according to the principle of verisimilitude.

Looking down the cast lists of many of Goldoni's plays, we note the frequent reuse of certain names for characters that Goldoni reputes to be new. Through the name, therefore, the archetype persists. This fact betrays the tenacity of the cyclical-repetitive model. Goldoni knows this very well. He does it partly for convenience and partly to serve his strategy. His culture, his education, and his formation lead him to those names and stop him there.

His mature work, before his sad final phase in France, where his freedom from the old schemes manifests itself in a stunning series of masterpieces, is a result of progressive development and, at the same time, the fruit of a brusque shaking-off of the residue of tradition.

The French period, the last for the man and the artist, constitutes a sad and humiliating regression toward "this is how they see us abroad." Can we not see in the desperate attempt of Goldoni in France to repeat his Italian success the earliest elaboration of that brand of "Goldoni-ism" that survives today, with a great stench of tourism, in many stagings of his work and the erroneous idea that Goldoni equals Commedia dell'Arte?

Our comic poet, too modern for his own time, ends his career condemned to ape what he spent a lifetime working to abolish, all because of the stupid, tenacious law of giving people what they want. From the Italians, the French want mugging. Mugging? Why? Because that's what Italians do? Beyond the Alps, this vision persists even today. First Commedia dell'Arte and then Goldoni constitute two great achievements for modern theater. The first invented it, the second perfected it. The Revolution in Paris shut down Goldoni's practice, canceling the pension he received from the now useless king. A sad tribute to Goldoni, who had a far newer and more progressive vision of society, a far more "democratic" vision, than anything the revolutionaries dreamed of.

Would the brilliant French theater of the nineteenth century have been the same without the example of that perfect theatrical mechanism, *Il Ventaglio* (*The Fan*), which Goldoni wrote during his dark years in Paris? As worn out as he is, with his *Il Ventaglio*, Carlo Goldoni, the lawyer and Venetian, writes the first *pochade*. A hundred years will pass before anyone writes another.

Reconstituted "Kitsch"

The mask is the vehicle of the false myths and aberrations that today deform the idea of Commedia dell'Arte. A shocking accumulation of clichés, kitsch, and simplifications gives us the image of a flea-market Commedia, where everything is cheap, where buyers and sellers, who performs and who watches, form an indistinct, chortling, carefree mass. There is a pretense of "Italianness" of a sort which reflects no actual Italian, because it is a pastiche of clichés of the *bel paese* created in other countries, reimported, and reused with disturbing thoughtlessness by certain current (both Italian and not) "commedia actors," producing an effect that we do not hesitate to define— we are restraining ourselves here—as a cultural muddle.

Europe offers a heap of these cultural syntheses; each nation has its own type. There's the somersaulting rascally bum Arlecchino (with lots of spaghetti and Mafia jokes); Carmen all hairy armpits and thighs yelling "olé olé"; Monsieur Dubois grumbling with his baguette; Mr. Smith with his bowler, umbrella, and *Times;* the beer-guzzling German; the Portuguese singing the fado; the cowardly Belgian; the Dutch girl with the wooden shoes and the bonnet; Greeks who are still fighting in Troy; and Swedes who give out the Nobel but never receive one because they're too porno. All this has been seen over and over in variety shows and then passed on to television playing to the lowest common denominator. In Italy, this vision of the countries of the world suggested dance numbers and sketches to variety show performers during Fascism, throughout the war and after, until its extinction in the early 1960s. We can describe these neither as characters nor as sketch-comedy caricatures, because the latter were original, often brilliant, creations of variety theater comics. Nor can we call them cultural symbols. What people would seriously recognize themselves in such idiocy? They are elementary syntheses of our reciprocal enclosure within cliché, banality, and racism; syntheses of reciprocal ignorance. These syntheses, however, serve to help us understand with absolute precision what a culture and its people are not. Let's return to the Commedia dell'Arte. We are seeking to learn more by studying what it is not, by listing the false myths and aberrations of which improvised theater has been the victim.

FALSE MYTHS

Arlecchino Superstar

Reimported into Italy from France, where he became a star, the wolflike Zanni of early Commedia was returned to us as affected and neurotic as a dog-show poodle. It wasn't enough to make him puerile and mincing. He had also to become the protagonist of a Commedia "frenchified" by the eager-to-please Italian comics who had emigrated beyond the Alps but were decidedly Italian from the French point of view. So Italian, in fact, that until a few years ago, Commedia dell'Arte was known in France as Comédie Italienne.

It is after all normal that improvised theater in France had to pay for its enormous success with a lot of renunciation and many humiliations. But it is not normal to accept the return of those conditions as progress. The effects not only continue, they are expanding. We feel a bit Don Quixote–esque in our effort to put matters back in order. Matters, however, are already better if we understand that putting "ino" at the end of any Zanni name renders those characters all equal. When they differ, it is only in terms of their role, either First or Second Zanni. If the character is called Scapino, for example, he is a First Zanni. If he's called Tabacchino, he's a Second Zanni. Arlecchino is a Second Zanni, no different from Tabacchino, Frittellino, Traccagnino, Trivellino, Trappolino, Bertolino, Gradellino, or any of the others. They are all the same because they occupy the same portion of the comedy. And they are not lead characters, because in Commedia the close relationships between all the characters do not leave any privileged space for anyone. Instead, everyone does everything, everybody is a lead character. Arlecchino superstar has ended up as the absolute symbol of Commedia, but this is a complete mistake, because Arlecchino by himself is not the Commedia, and Commedia can do without Arlecchino (with someone else, obviously, in the role of Second Zanni, a role that is essential, whatever he is called).

The Open Air

Neoromanticism and disinformation. The Commedia dell'Arte is born professional. It develops, for the first time in the modern era, requirements and concepts that become the functional structure of modern theater, from its minimal state, the platform stage, to its maximum, the princely theater. Commedia dell'Arte always demonstrates the wish to perform its work under the best possible conditions. This attitude is ignored or looked down upon by the romantic cult of open air, which would like to throw Commedia back into the middle of the street from which it arose, and which Commedia itself replaced with actual, built-from-scratch—imagine!—theaters.

True, many old engravings show us Commedia in the street, in the piazzas, under the porticoes, and such. But in those days there were many companies and very few theaters. Further, the artistic hierarchy, fruit of the free market, with its infinite shadings from the miserable to the sublime, provided designers and artists to document all the manifestations of the Arte, including those companies who had to make do with the street, the piazza, and even, to judge from certain images, the open country.

But every company had the ambition of playing in a theater. Not having achieved that goal did not prevent it from seeking, although out in the open, conditions as close as possible to those of enclosed theaters.

No actor "dreamed" of playing in the street. *Interpretation* is impossible in the street, where only a circus-type *spectacularization* can take place. This latter form of work merits the highest respect, but it's something else, something different.

Commedia dell'Arte is theater and should be performed in theaters or in places set up like theaters, in which—this is fundamental—the audience enters by choice, perhaps pays before entering, remains by choice, and (according to its will) applauds. There is no audience in the street, because people are there by chance, for other reasons. They walk by, they stop if they want, they don't stay. At the beginning of the show there is one group of people, at the end another, and in the meantime the group changes continuously. All this has nothing to do with tickets and knowing how many seats there are and how many people are in them.

Masks as the Expression of the Various Cities of Italy

The theory according to which the Italian masks are the expression of the cities of Italy and of the Italian people, with its gay irony, is one of the most pernicious myths undermining the position of Commedia dell'Arte as a poetic phenomenon on a universal scale. It is furthermore false for practical reasons: how can you pretend that every city has its own little type, just like its own emblem? How did the Bergamasks and the Venetians and the Bolognese and the Florentines get together to give simultaneous birth to their types and then put them together? Where did they all meet? And what about the Capitano? He's a foreigner. Or is he a caricature of a foreigner? But who made him? The Bergamasks? The Bolognese? The Neapolitans?

Venice-Arlecchino-Goldoni

Venice is not, has never been, the home country, the capital, the elective seat, or the symbol of Commedia dell'Arte. Nowadays all these things are taken as a given. How come? Because of Arlecchino. But Arlecchino is not Venetian, he's from Bergamo. He is a Zanni—a Second Zanni—and like all the Zanni in Commedia, he is a man from the mountains above Bergamo who has come down to the plain in search of work; there are Zanni in all the cities of the Po valley. And why else? Because of Goldoni. He was a Venetian who used Arlecchino successfully (though not only Goldoni, and not only Arlecchino). Venice is extremely important in the history of performance. But Commedia was slow in coming to Venice, because music and musical theater was much more important and influential there.[2] The most important cities for the Arte are Padua, Mantua, Modena, Florence, and Naples (for the south of Italy) and Paris (for Commedia abroad).

Commedia and Comedy in General as a Form of Social Protest

"Commedia as a force for class struggle." The seventies in Italy argued for this intrinsically revolutionary aspect of the proletarian classes. This fashion in thought has passed, but tenacious traces of this way of seeing Commedia remain, according to which a company becomes a sort of traveling revolutionary cell helping the people toward "consciousness" through subversive laughter. Our opinion is that Commedia dell'Arte and comedy in general have nothing to do with all that. Laughter, rather than subversive, is destructive. It does not bring consciousness, but satisfaction; it does not discover, but confirms.

The court jester is not the enemy, adversary, counterpoint, or alternative voice to his lord and the court that hosts him, dresses him, feeds him, and pays him. Perhaps he is a moral counterweight. Yes, moral. The comic moralizes, favoring order. The comic demonstrates disorder not to favor it, but to resolve it. If power represents order, it is nevertheless true that order can slip out of its control. Power can use order for error or make dishonest use of it. The clown, by representing disorder—in his very appearance, showing off an example of "disorganized" humanity in his body and clothing, followed by his gestures and words—always reminds the lord of his responsibility. Has a good jester ever made a king good? Yes? No? Is the presence of a buffoon completely irrelevant to the goal of having a good government? By answering yes, no, I don't know, maybe, who knows?, or anything else, we do not change the significance of a comic present where absolute power is exercised, where the comic reminds those who hold the world's destiny in their hands of their human imperfection, so that they won't be sucked under by it, sweeping away the people at the same time.

Modern dictators don't want to hear anything about comedy. It's well known that where there is no democracy there are few comics, and those few have a hard time even telling jokes about their mother-in-law. On the psychological and social level, laughter and producing laughter spark a process of destruction of the absolute and the serious, two important aspects of the self-image of power. The more authoritarian power is, the more it tends to be serious and absolute; implicitly, whatever is not serious and absolute is power's enemy.

Anyone who wears dark glasses when there's no need for them, without being a dictator or a mafioso, simply wants to intimidate others by imposing—through the impenetrability of his soul and his intentions, guaranteed by the inaccessibility of his gaze, thanks to the dark lenses—an image of himself as serious, unreachable, "high up," "dangerous." He never laughs and thus induces others not to laugh. If others laughed, the image would suddenly no longer be serious, and the man in the dark glasses would seem small, low, innocuous.

All democracies have armies of comic actors who make people laugh—if they are good enough—at will, in complete and total liberty. The presence of so much laughter is an indicator of social equilibrium and not of the imminence of total revolution.

The more people talk about problems, the more they laugh about them. The comic functions as a psychological counterweight to the anguish that accumulates even in a tranquil, normal existence, and a social counterweight to the thousand problems that must be faced in the context of society, whether individually or collectively. Comics therefore tend to adapt themselves to whatever situation they find themselves in, and there they carry out their function.

There is nothing wrong in this. On the contrary. A comic who aspires to resolve conflicts, to promote relief from anguish rather than to fan the flames of conflict, is certainly of great human and social value.

Aberrations

Pierrotism

In the Romantic era, popular theater reelaborates certain signs descended from earlier eras. One of these reelaborations is the spiritualization of the grotesque, the monstrous.

The champion of this passage is the Pierrot of nineteenth-century pantomime. Pierrot derives from the Commedia Pedrolino but has by now lost any trace of improvised theater, such as concreteness and the biological perception of himself.

There is an abyss between Pierrot and Zanni. In fact they represent two opposite worlds, the romanticism of Pierrot and the carnevalism of Zanni. Here is a simple comparison:

Pierrot	Zanni
Isolation	Externalization
Infinite interior: spiritualization	Infinite interior: hunger, intestinal gas
Love overwhelms his mind	Love increases his appetite
No one knows what he's thinking	He's incapable of keeping his mouth shut
He can become an assassin	He gives and receives beatings, with a vital symbolism of sowing and harvesting
Pretense of superior values	Proud inferiority

We'll stop here. This book will return continuously with greater specificity to the issue of the difference between Commedia Carnevalism and other expressive philosophies.

The contemporary consequences of this are "spiritualized" Commedia, Pierrotization of Pulcinella, pop romantic confusion in the world of masks.

Modern Carnevale
Superficialintellectualsnob.

The masks worn by participants in Carnevale festivities, inexpressive in their opulence, often have zannesque, Arlecchinesque, or Pantalonesque pretensions.

The sumptuousness of Carnevale costumes is in stark contrast with the comic normality of the theatrical mask-character. The characters are completely erroneous. The masks are decorative, antidynamic.

The fact that Commedia masks are still considered Carnevale masks comes from the custom in the period of historical Commedia, especially the seventeenth and eighteenth centuries, of concentrating the performance of comedies, virtually all dell'Arte, during the Carnevale period of the year. This associates Commedia masks with the period in which they most frequently appear, in particular when they contribute to establishing the generally comic atmosphere of the festivities. It's quite natural to make this connection.

We have arrived at the other mistaken equation: Commedia dell'Arte equals masks equals Carnevale, or Carnevale equals masks equals Commedia dell'Arte.

A less superficial cultural fact probably plays a role in this misapprehension. Commedia, with its *carnevalesque* philosophy, develops material that belongs to the ancient pagan festivals of the rites of spring. The philosophical base of Commedia is the same as that of these festivals: seeking atonement to usher in the season of rebirth, which is salvation, the continuity of life. In improvised theater the Magnifico represents Winter that refuses to end its cycle, that doesn't want to die, and thereby impedes the flowering of new life, the Lovers, who invoke the forces of nature. Zanni provokes a general overturning, a "spring," and the comedy itself puts back into order the normal progression of the cycle of life.

Symbolically, Commedia dell'Arte is the representation of the coming of spring, which is also the meaning of Carnevale. This connection was recognized by all and its symbols were at one time clear, because they seemed "obvious," culturally acquired. But today all of this has been lost and there remains only a superficial equation that associates two different phenomena, which become shallowly and externally assimilated.

Commedia dell'Arte as "Corporal Expression"

There exists a philosophy of the "rediscovery" of historical genres and traditions, which treats the physical body as the object of a "cult"; that is, reaching the soul by passing through the body. Fine. But once again, what does this have to do with Commedia dell'Arte?

Granted full and absolute liberty in art to do whatever you want, in any way you want, here is what happens to Commedia under the regime of "corporal expression":

1. The mask is hyperanatomical, its surface extremely thin, and it adheres to the face of the actor. The eyes are so open as to negate the mask itself. The mask is often made of paper on the spot, with an intellectualized, pompous display of simplicity, or takes the form of symbolic makeup.
2. The bodies of the actors are half naked so that the "movement and poetry can be visible."
3. The gestural dimension is intellectualized, connected to conceptual processes that come from the actor, rather than emerging from the character in a situation. The aesthetics are there for their own sake, not functional to the plot. We must observe here that functionality is a necessary condition of aesthetics, not a synonym for aridity or nonspirituality.

When we go onstage with our Zanni, our Magnifico, Lovers, Dottore, and Capitano, we feel ourselves full of meaning, of poetry, of a sense of responsibility as bringers of poetry and civil harmony through an artistic display that is difficult to create but easy to enjoy. We have no need to complicate the message to give it greater importance, because the importance of the message rests completely in the maximum pleasure it creates. There is no sense of the comic in "corporal comedy," which is in fact cerebral, despite the efforts and the convictions of its practitioners.

Infantilization

This is the most diffuse and devastating aberration of Commedia. Commedia is infantilized by:

1. Its destination, audiences of children. Thus, Commedia is children's theater.

2. Simplification of the form. Reduction of strong themes, of chaos, and of the return to order result in a charming little story.

3. Attenuation of its meanings. Carnevalesque, excessive, overspilling, "dangerous" meanings are attenuated into innocuous play.

4. Diminution, especially in the language, where diminutives and terms of endearment are thrown around loosely. Everything is "ino" in this little comedy.

5. Self-infantilization. The actor of infantilized theater infantilizes himself and tends to think of himself and his genre as "little," "this is enough," or "we do what we can."

Of all the damage inflicted on Commedia and its perception, this is certainly the most grave.

Unfortunately, another conception accompanies infantilization, that of children's theater, intended not as an occasion for formation and cultural growth of the littlest and youngest, but as the umpteenth form of babysitting. How? By adapting the performance for its young audience. Obviously, work created for adults is not suitable for the youngest audiences, but, equally obviously, there is work created for adults that suits children well. To adapt theater for children means to diminish both children and theater.

Certainly, children should be spared certain morbid, racy, intellectualistic, cryptic, symbolically overladen works, but very often adults should be spared those works as well. A *King Lear* performed and realized in its full human and poetic quality is theater for everybody. Commedia dell'Arte, zany, urgent, emergent, hard as only life can be but just as thrilling, should be performed without adaptation for any special sort of audience.

Involuntary Syncretism

We often find images, decorations, and masks in various Carnevale events and festivals of all kinds, which make use of masks and "characters" who could constitute a highly educated exercise in iconological syncretism, in the manner of certain mythological creatures. If only it weren't for the ignorance that these images manifest. We often see, for example, a Pulcinella with the body of an Arlecchino (or is it an Arlecchino with the head of a Pulcinella?).

A list of these is impossible, but the phenomenon exists and we have defined it as *involuntary syncretism.*

Syncretism, for evident reasons of the somewhat "blasphemous" mixing of parts, each of which belongs to something different but apparently "coherent," within the environment of masked parties or Carnevale.

Involuntary, for the equally evident ignorance of the material handled with a casualness that leaves no doubt of the underlying conception of Commedia: slight, charming, infantile.

Commercial, Nontheatrical Use of Images from Commedia

Pizzerias: Arlecchino, Pulcinella, and so on. Italian restaurants in foreign countries: "Restaurant La Commedia dell'Arte," "Punchinello's," and so forth. Then we have food products: pasta, tuna, olives, and more.

Ceramics for the kitchen, bathroom, and baby's room where Pierrot with a big tear towers over all contenders.

Paneling, carpeting, and so on, where Arlecchino dominates. We'll stop here.

CONTINUITY

No historian can assert that Commedia is an indefinable phenomenon that, whatever it was, no longer exists. However, this is just what almost all historians assume when they write and publish their books on Commedia. Commedia dell'Arte exists because living people perform it and see it performed. It even exists for those who review it. This is more than enough to prove its existence.

It exists in terms of continuity with respect to tradition and to the past. The fact that not everything possible is known about Commedia dell'Arte, its techniques, its aesthetic, its innumerable variations, is in the natural order of things.

Continuity is expressed today in two ways: reconstructive and continuist. We identify with the second of these. To reconstruct means to remake only that one thing, the way it used to be. To continue means to proceed according to principles but with full liberty of invention and elaboration.

As a presentation of a method and expression of a mentality, this book is our contribution to the continuity of Commedia dell'Arte.

Poetic and Aesthetic Particulars of Commedia dell'Arte

MODERNITIES

The modernity, or modernities, of Commedia dell'Arte derive from the *professional mentality* that is at the origin of the genre. Even before becoming a *form*, Commedia is a *project* aimed at providing the economic sustenance of the practitioner. The fun can now be organized, systematized, and sold. The theatrical work is a product, merchandise. The necessities that follow the first idea and those that immediately follow upon success—proliferation of other companies, free-market competition, the search for audiences and sponsors, the establishment of the calendrical theater season and the theater space—impose solutions that determine and fix factors relevant to the form that Commedia is gradually assuming. These solutions confer on improvised theater a sort of permanent state of development that permits it to move into all places and seasons, with a strong effect of *constant renewal* that in some cases is strikingly advanced.

The principal modern aspects of Commedia are:

1. Organization of the company. Perhaps an adjective should be added to the definition of Commedia dell'Arte: *fraternal.* The Padua contract of 1545 is considered the first certain documentary evidence of the existence of the Commedia dell'Arte, a sort of birth certificate. But it's too perfect to be the first. The Italian comic Mutio worked in Spain in 1538.[1] We don't know whether Mutio and his associates performed according to the terms listed in the contract of the Fraternal Compagnia signed by Ser Maffio and his company, but there must have been some written terms if they were able to plan a tour, and those first rules must have been inspired by the idea of performing, producing, and selling theater professionally.
2. Sexual equality within the companies through the "superior intelligence" of the female roles. The cultural justification for this rests in carnevalism, the comic reversal that puts the woman in place of the man in decision-making positions. But the relational effect is realistic and observable within the companies themselves, where women and men have equal importance and professional dignity. The social effect, apparently radical, is achieved through

the principle of constant renewal derived from practical rather than ideological factors.

3. The professional mentality and its effects on the formation and evolution of modern performance. The search for the ideal performance space, one that is equipped, protected, that guarantees the best possible conditions for performing and the audience's reception of the performance, will rapidly lead to the establishment of the first theater spaces, huge rooms adapted and equipped for performances, and, in a very short time, to the construction of the first enclosed theaters, the introduction of tickets, the creation of "circuits," and the nonperforming specializations, such as writer, set designer, choreographer, and musician.

4. Actor specialization and its effects. Every actor has his own mask-character that he will perform throughout his professional life. Audiences of the time could watch in action actors and actresses who performed the same character for twenty or thirty years. This practice is virtually unknown today. (Except in the case of film comedy, which once offered Laurel and Hardy, Totò, and others. At least one glorious example remains today: Dario Fo.) The actor-specialist studies, prepares, and perfects his own mask until he achieves an inimitable uniqueness. Collegial relationships evolve among the specialists, who *in concert* work out the progress of each play, their efforts coordinated by the *corago* or *concertatore,* who is often the *capocomico* (company manager, director). Techniques are formalized into a patrimony that is partly common, partly personal, and "secret." Methods developed by families of performing professionals are passed down through the generations. Rituals of stage preparation come into practice. Fame and the star system, with its attendant extravagant behaviors, become part of the tradition.

5. The eclipse of the sense of performing as a form of begging, along with the related human and social conditions of the medieval era that had been reflected in the dramatic situations and characters performed. Zanni, though ragged and blundering, is not a mendicant or freeloader; he is a worker in search of a job. Though he creates disasters, he does not do so maliciously but rather with the best of intentions of a proud and honest worker. Zanni is a real Stakhanovite of catastrophe; he doesn't ask for help, he manages on his own.

6. The city. The effects of working in cities are franticness, hurry, constant closeness and contact with others, psychological solitude (important in the mechanism of misunderstandings), and the impossibility of finding physical, spatial solitude. There is always someone watching and listening; there is always someone there.

7. Secularity: neither popes nor kings. The usual ambivalence composed of self-

protective prudence and respect for the audience. Today this principle appears very advanced, along with that of equality between men and women.

8. Improvisation as continual cultural updating. The actor speaks the language of the public, using the culture of the public. We know from experience that it is impossible to improvise fluently in a language different from one's own. It is impossible, for example, to improvise in verse, with rhyme and meter, in a language one doesn't dominate. It is impossible to improvise "in" a past culture that we no longer feel as natural and cannot share with others. How could we improvise in Latin, medieval Italian, or on lost trades, arts, and customs? Thanks to this obviousness, we are able to comprehend that the historical disappearance of Commedia is not because the social significance of the fixed types has lost relevance, because fixed types have always spoken the language(s) of the audience (the fixed types are also universal reference points: young and old, servants and warriors have always existed, and we can say with assurance that they will always exist, as will their themes, which are love and fear, possession and death). Commedia, which has never completely disappeared, experienced a collapse of interest and diffusion in the period of great social and cultural change subsequent to the French Revolution. The new theater writers wore down Commedia, which became incapable of renewing itself. In reality, Commedia's lesson not only resisted but fused itself into a thousand new forms. All the contemporary comic genres in the Western world derive in part or in full from Zanni comedy. Commedia entered the pens of the best theater writers. Shakespeare is not immune to its influence, Molière—despite himself—is Commedia, Gozzi enthusiastically continues it, and Goldoni is its illustrious victim.

9. The conflict between being and seeming, with the introduction of the problem of self-image, first manifested as concern for *honor,* then for *decorum,* then *dignity,* and today *image,* all part of the same problem. The mechanism of exaltation-frustration derives from this problem, especially through the Capitano and the Lover characters.

CIRCULAR, LINEAR, UNIVERSAL TIME

The cyclical, magical and natural, repetitive perception of time coexists in Commedia with the linear, historical, and consequential perception of time. The *cultural base* tends to conserve messages fixed in preceding centuries, such as the cycles of nature and its continuous return, and with it Commedia's repetition of the same characters and their problems.

Plot in itself is "historical" and linear, and the topics that offer subject matter to plays are contingent. The efforts of characters to resolve their problems are based on empiricism, with traces of the scientific method.

Each character taken separately corresponds to different conceptions of time. Servants and Old Men are circular; Lovers are linear. For the Capitano, we have to design his own individual perception of time. He lives all alone in a fantasy world, in the center of which tower his muscles, courage, charisma, moral and physical strength, and his status as a winner in all things. These are indisputable realities in his world. The *fantastic realism* of the Capitano is not only the sick fantasy of a poor, frustrated man but also the universality of his time. Universal time blends past and present into an epic unity, where every gesture, every word, where every smallest thing takes place on a universal scale. It is a bit like the epic of children's play, where a barely audible rush of breath, emitted with great intensity, can become the roar of a huge crowd in a stadium. The Capitano is just like that, as is the time that he expresses and that surrounds him. His every instant is eternal. The great, supreme Capitano, who from the smallness and meanness deep inside him and the sense of inferiority he dare not confess, can draw forth the particular mode of survival that confers upon him a vision of the world and the universe as an infinite, inexhaustible resource. Precisely because they are more ruinous than everyone else's, his catastrophic falls paradoxically demonstrate, above all, his indestructibility.

The circularity of the other grotesques is strictly connected to their carnevalism. They are *forces of nature* and can only express themselves in a cyclical way, inflicting, through their being and acting, an identical function in effects and events. Everything comes back. History, that most bourgeois of all phenomena, is made by the Lovers. Overcoming their moments of disorientation, folly, and torment, they push on, they go forward.

This mixed time of Commedia dell'Arte is the surest indicator of its "bridge" position between ancient "circular" and "modern" linear thought. The temporary intruder is the Capitano, who is thus perhaps the most gratuitous and poetic entity in the entire system.[2]

CARNEVALISM

The philosophy of Carnevale manifests itself in Commedia and the masks in these ways: the triumph of Winter, the revolt of Spring, the edible universe, reversal, and the final beatings.

The Triumph of Winter

The Old Man resembles Winter, which represents an immobile time that resists the movement of things, the only milieu in which to perpetuate his existence. The King of Carnevale, however, has two faces, both perfectly expressed in Commedia:

- ☞ The Magnifico: the King of Carnevale as egoist and "time-stopper," with pretensions of immortality, to the harm of others
- ☞ The Dottore: the King of Carnevale as the enjoyer and dispenser of good times with his flowing abundance, symbolized here by his giant belly and his logorrhea (that is, his continuous blabbing)[3]

The Revolt of Spring

The Lovers await the crowning of their dream of love, but they are put to the test. The plot is a rite of passage, a sort of "final exam." Having passed it, they will have earned or won their union, and they can now "live happily ever after" (this last condition is never shown onstage).[4]

The Edible Universe

Through the festival, Carnevale utopia provides a universal image, a tangible body for a biology-based perception of self and the surrounding world. The world, the whole universe, is edible, everything can be drunk and eaten, everything is tasty, juicy, and abundant, even inexhaustible.

The Dottore is the maximum representative of taste, smell, diffuse sensuality, gastronomic expertise, the capacity to swallow. His is the Reign of Good Times. Zanni is the most enthusiastic of all the eaters. For him, everything tastes good and everything is worth eating. In his vision of the world, everything goes spontaneously into his mouth. He is a happy subject of the Reign of Good Times.

Reversal

Everything that conflicts with an ideal world is abolished, above all hunger. Next to be abolished is the most important social obstacle, hierarchy, class difference, which impedes access to abundance. This "abolition" has its maximum expression in the symbolic reversal of all social and natural laws. The world turns upside down: fish fish for the fisherman, the hare hunts the hunter, the idiot shall be king and the king will work the fields. And so on.

In Commedia, reversal passes through the contingencies of the plot, in which the characters act out of necessity. They do not know they are expressing symbols, but they develop them implicitly: Zanni or Pantalone or the Capitano, dressed as women; Pantalone and Zanni marry one another; the Servant women command; the Lovers go mad or accept to be dressed as servants, or they momentarily change their sex; the Magnifico pretends to be a great seducer and tries it out with everyone; Zanni dressed as Magnifico gives cruel orders to his master, who is dressed as a servant. The world upside down brings with it all possible utopias, which would be unimaginable and unspeakable as conscious possibilities.

The Final Beatings

Palingenesis must be introduced, the principle of the rebirth of souls into a higher form of life. In Commedia, this takes place by bringing nemesis into the action. Justice is administered here with the cudgel, the cane, the *batòcio*. Bad news for any backs who try to prevent the coming of Spring.

There are neither judges nor tribunals in Commedia dell'Arte. Justice manifests itself as a logical consequence of the facts, as one fact among others, necessary and punctual. When everything is once again put in order and Spring has reaffirmed its rights, the comedy is over. Chaos, utopia, folly all come to an end. We return to order and the serious concerns of life.

Taboo and Its Handling

Commedia never squarely confronts the difficult issues, nor does it ignore them. It deals with them, it manages them. It obtains comic catharsis by showing—always in a mediated, shifting, but absolutely clear way—everything that is difficult, prohibited, dangerous, and capable of provoking anguish in normal daily life.

At the origin of this skillful handling of taboo there is undoubtedly the shrewd ability of comics to discuss everything without offending the law, morality, or religion. This providential prudence translates into a true scenic and comic poetry that has the ability to make the public see, understand, and even experience what, technically, has neither been said nor shown. Some phenomena were taboo in Western society of the past and are no longer so, such as homosexuality. Other phenomena remain taboo, such as cannibalism. Others are not true taboos but are nevertheless themes that must be treated carefully, such as infidelity and death.

Handling taboo, in Commedia, requires a psychological comprehension of the audience, a comprehension that has a powerful poetic impact. The taboo-object is never utilized as a central theme, but enters the story as a dramatic or comic complication. The most frequent taboos are incest, homosexuality, infidelity, cannibalism, murder, and death.

Incest

One complication could be that of a Magnifico who woos a beautiful maiden who is none other than his own daughter, Isabella, who has become unrecognizable by disguising herself. Obviously, no sexual relations, no incest, will take place. But the possibility has been raised and a catharsis should be produced because of having publicly and comically shown the existence of the possibility.

If Pantalone then woos a young beauty who is in fact his son Flavio dressed as a woman, two taboos are brought into one and dealt with at the same time.

Homosexuality

It must have been known to all that there were homosexuals everywhere, even among those who enforced the rules against such practices. Still, the theme was—and still is, in part—very delicate and unacceptable. But Commedia actors made, and still make today, abundant use of it.

The most commonly used method is transvestitism. When a character dresses as a member of the other sex, he or she does it out of compelling necessity. The misunderstandings that follow from individual or multiple transvestitism contribute to plot complication but above all offer numerous irresistible opportunities for ambiguity.

Consider, for example, the Capitano who dresses as a woman to be able to enter the rooms of the Lady he desires, the beautiful young wife of Pantalone. Pantalone then comes on to this gorgeous newcomer, but the Capitano, who has come in hopes of seducing Pantalone's wife, cannot reveal himself and must play along—within limits—with the game imposed by the Old Man.

The Capitano is aware of the misunderstanding, the Old Man is not. Naturally, if Pantalone is insistent, it is because he thinks that "she" is a beautiful woman. But because she is in fact a man—and the audience knows it—and Pantalone carries on with his merciless courting, we must accept that a man can be aroused by another man.

If we imagine that, in an identical situation, Pantalone is also dressed as a woman to approach his prey without upsetting her, and that the Capitano, dressed as a woman, enjoys that feminine assault (since she is a woman and he a man), the hypothesis of homosexuality is complete. The homosexual relation never actually takes place, of course; instead everything becomes clear and the homosexual utopia vanishes.

If Flavio the Lover, disguised as Cavalier So-and-So, and Isabella, disguised as Cavalier Thus-and-Such, happen to bump into each other by mistake, they may end their initial angry display with suddenly softening hearts, having noted "something strange, sweet, tender" in the other. For Isabella it will be strange, curious, but for Flavio it will be upsetting, because he is feeling such sensations toward another man. This also is merely theoretical, because the recognition scene will follow, and everything will turn out logically, showing our heroes to be "sane," neither homosexuals nor tempted to infidelity.

Infidelity

Cuckoldry is not, properly speaking, a taboo, but it is a very delicate topic. And eternal. Perhaps the history of comedy is the history of infidelity, if not of all of it, certainly a large part of it.

Cuckoldry has to be handled properly as well. In our *canovaccio,* Pantalone permits an impressive traffic of men inside and outside his wife's room. One is a music teacher, another a tutor, then a plumber, an electrician, and so on. All are happy to offer their services for free, which immensely pleases the Old Man.

In general in Commedia, the old men are "horned," cuckolded. The wife of the Old Man is always young and beautiful and the third or fourth wife. This young woman, as beautiful and charming as a Lover, but with a very different, more materialist and opportunist character, has married the venerable old man's money rather than the man himself. For the old husband, she always has a headache; for the Capitano, she always has something quite different.

In Commedia the Old Men are always fathers. Their children are always, to greater or lesser degree, Lovers. We never get to meet the mother of these children, the first wife of the Old Man. She's not there, she doesn't exist. The two reasons for this reside in the dramatic and comic function of the Old Man in Commedia:

1. In a world without the possibility of divorce, the Magnifico or the Dottore must be widowers and free to remarry, in order to trigger the comedy of the older man promised in marriage to the young maiden, from which the young Lovers must free themselves and put the Old Man back in his place.
2. Or, the Old Man is now remarried. His new wife is very young, very beautiful, and very filled with life. There are thus present all the necessary condi-

tions to develop the theme of the necessary, constitutional cuckolding of the Old Man.

In both cases, the Old Man fulfills his destiny as a punching bag. In the second, he cannot avoid the additional one of being cuckolded.

Cannibalism

The theme of hunger—constant for the servants and occasional for the Capitano—is subject to continuous variation and the search for "limits."

In the improvisations we conduct in our school, we often see groups of famished Zanni who try to resolve the problem by biting into their colleagues. But their aim is off. Zanni is not a cannibal. The very idea, in fact, is disgusting to him, despite a gradient of "taste" that permits Zanni to make distinctions. The Old Men are completely disgusting, the Capitano is indigestible, and his associates are too stringy and bitter, but Zanni may find Franceschina quite "appetizing" and vice versa.

The taboo of cannibalism is a promising theme and a great occasion for comic and cathartic solutions. If, for example, some sleeping Zanni, promiscuous as cats, "launch" the subject of hunger while sleeping but dreaming actively, they might undertake to stuff a roaster chicken, in which the chicken in question is actually one of their fellows, who is himself dreaming of being a fat chicken and therefore cooperates with and even directs the preparation of the recipe. The Zanni go so far as to eat their fellow, but we know that they actually want to eat a chicken, and the chicken, consciously and proudly, wants to be eaten. The ambiguity produces relief from the unspeakable. Then it is dawn, a rooster crows, waking the poor ravenous Zanni, who abandon their dream activity to run after the impertinent and tempting rooster who interrupted their tasty collective dream.

Homicide

Homicide is present whenever a character is convinced of having killed someone, or when others are convinced, or whenever there is the suspicion that someone has killed someone else. Only, and always, the audience knows how things really stand: that is, that no one has actually been killed. No one killed anybody, and no one is dead. It's all been a mistake, a misunderstanding.

Death

Death is present in Commedia in various ways. It is *a symbol* that accompanies the behavior of the Old Men. They, rightly, do not want to die; therefore they impose an extraordinary regimen on themselves in order to live many decades in a few minutes. They hope to become immortal by outrunning death. It's all in the behavior. Death is never named. The conversation is always about something else.

Death is a terrible *misfortune* that happens to all, but only if they (the dead) never appear onstage. The truly dead, in Commedia, are already dead before the curtain rises. Or if they really have to die during the show, they never appear. They die unseen. Whoever appears onstage, even if only for a moment, is immortal, at least for the course of the show. The continuity of the fixed type is transmitted even to the most occasional characters, the various porters, policemen, con men who pass through, characters of ephemeral immortality. Commedia does not allow for suffering after the happy ending.

Death also appears as an actual *character,* a figure who speaks, walks, has her own behavior, a character, a "psychology," a look. Whether a woman or, rarely, a man, Death is always elegant, even fashionable.

The most comical character in the play, almost always a Zanni (especially Pulcinella), who is always the most unfortunate, is destined to meet Death. He will of course be able to rely on previously unknown resources to save him from that extreme encounter, such as diabolical tricks that suddenly flash through his mind, strokes of genius, "psychological" intuitions, or chance discoveries of a weak point in Death. Our Zanni gets away and Death has a new experience.

ANIMISM AND FETISHISM

If Zanni moves an object, for example, a rolled-up ball of paper, the object is moved by Zanni only when he touches it. However, once it starts rolling on its own, the object takes on a will of its own. This, at least, is what Zanni believes.

He doesn't bother theorizing this fact, his sensations pile one upon the other as circumstances develop. Thus he might decide to send the paper to someone by having it roll to its addressee.

Zanni may believe that the ball of paper has its own initiative if it stops before getting to its destination, if it changes direction, or even if it returns to its sender (there may be a hill that the paper cannot climb). Zanni tends to attribute a life, a spirit, to everything that brings him into contact with nature and its phenomena. Zanni is himself a phenomenon of nature.

No Commedia mask thinks philosophically or religiously about what he is doing. But he reacts to everything that happens. One of these reactions, which is systematic in Commedia, is *animistic* in a technical, secular sense, the same kind of animism experienced in the first five years of life of man as well as in many animals, such as dogs and cats. The ball we play with is playing with us. We throw it, sure, but it's the ball that goes into the street. The servants are the most animistic characters in Commedia. Grotesques in general are animistic. The Lovers are much less so. They situate themselves on a higher step, because they are *fetishists*.

The Lovers have reached the symbolic level. The objects that belong to them signify them. The object that belongs to the beloved person is so representative of that person as to actually be preferable to the original.

Obscenity

Obscenity, in the language we are developing here, should not be confused with vulgarity. By obscenity, we mean a joke expressed theatrically, made into spectacle, having reference to the sexual act, the genitals, or to disgusting or scatological aspects of physiology.

We do not consider defecating and vomiting to be equally obscene. Defecation is a joyous accomplishment, not only a necessary gesture that we all have in common but a creative act. Defecation is the only creative and artistic act that is within everyone's reach. Vomiting is a regretful accident; it is being unwell. It is not only not creative but is the violent interruption of the creative act, which at its peak becomes defecation. Vomiting interrupts a cycle, keeps it from completion; it violently regresses to an earlier state when we were hungry. That is why it is so repugnant. That's why we never find funny *lazzi* about vomiting. Obscenity par excellence is based on the images and dynamics of all sexual practices and all the forms and functions of the genitals and all the other erogenous zones of the human body.

In Commedia obscenity exists when:

1. The obscene act is involuntary. The audience sees obscenity where the characters are totally innocent, absolutely spotless. We thus witness the formation of an audience of pigs with filthy minds, laughing at things that the masks are completely unaware of. In this way, the comics establish a powerful complicity with the spectators, who cannot now back out, having already joined in, by laughing, with the system of allusions that underlie the involuntarily obscene actions. This complicity can be protracted by maintaining

the "innocence" of the people on the stage and the "dirty-mindedness" of the people in the seats.

2. No realism or pretense at realism, or verisimilitude, is employed to achieve the goal. The obscene *lazzo* is always composed of gestural "machines," the parts of which stand out clearly, although these distinct parts must never be in direct and continuous contact. If Colombina walks by and Zanni, to greet her, raises his *batòcio* (short wooden club) hanging from his belt, the effect in the scene is that Zanni is greeting Colombina while, for the audience, Zanni is flaunting his erection at Colombina. In this case, the audience laughs at the obscenity without feeling uneasy, because no realism has been employed to obtain the effect. The actors have made a mechanical gesture meaningful with an allusive object that is something quite different from what it seemed to be in that moment; the *batòcio* is Zanni's weapon. The props are characters in themselves which, "performing" an innocent gesture, give the impression of "performing" another less innocent one.

3. The proportion of the *lazzo* itself and the elements that compose it are never "natural"; everything is always enormous, or microscopic, or it is somewhere else, or it is an idea, a suspicion.

4. No obscenity is produced with the intention of being obscene.

Vulgarity is obtained when:

1. The obscene act is intentional from the character's point of view.
2. There is realism in the obscene *lazzo*, physical contact, or a believable gesture.
3. The proportions are "natural."
4. The intention of the actor to be obscene is obvious.

SURVIVAL

From its earliest appearance to its ultimate historical ramifications, through its difficult period of survival at the margins of the world of spectacle, and even today during a period of "rebirth" (or rather, of reaffirmed continuity), Commedia dell'Arte has presented and continues to present the same comedy over and over again, the same story, the same plot, and to develop the same themes. This obsessive historical-aesthetic repetition testifies very clearly that onstage the same ingredients are cooked again and again and again, no matter where the kitchen and who the chef.

Given its sincere refusal to claim an absurd and improbable "originality,"

Commedia dell'Arte must have some secret, some particular ingredient or aroma if, through high highs and low lows, it has managed to persevere longer than any other phenomenon in the history of Western theater.

The fascination of Commedia dell'Arte does not reside in the story told per se but in the way in which the story is told. This means that the artistic influence of the performers (together with all the other collaborators in the performance) is absolute, total. Ability, brilliance, eclecticism, skill in poetry and drama, comedy, and everything else; it all has to be all poured out every moment by the comic artist. Put in such terms, it's frightening. Can a comic player concentrate so intensely and without mediocrity, always at the highest level? Perhaps not, but the task is to try.

It is evident that the concept of survival involves not only the character but also the character's interpreter. They share the terrible responsibility of always finding a solution to the problem, the problems, the exponentially multiplying problems, at that instant, in the very moment when they manifest themselves. They both must survive the threats of the Capitano and the distraction of the audience, atavistic hunger, the incomprehension of the critics, the refusal to laugh of the man with the mustache in the third row, left, and the fear of having to make everyone laugh more and more all the time. Commedia exclusively demonstrates the art of survival.

An Arte comedy can be synthesized like this: in the first five minutes, everything is fine until the birth of the triggering problem; then, from that problem, the first act develops in a crescendo of complication. The second act continues the crescendo of complications. The third act carries the crescendo forward to a point of excess we might call the "threshold of bearability." By now we have come to the final five minutes, during which, with the same facility with which it all began, it now dissolves. Whoever must be happy becomes happy, who must be chagrined is chagrined, and there is a grand finale, free and joyous, wherein the audience is invited to the wedding, which will take place during a fourth act that has never existed.

Complications make the comedy, "normality" does not. It is only necessary for us spectators to know that the characters are all quite normal individuals. We do not see them under normal conditions, but we deduce their normality thanks to a thousand hints in their behavior. Every type is the bearer of a specific condition of the permanent emergency of survival:

1. The Old Men are connected to their physical being, to possessiveness, and to the immediate realization of specific projects. Their hurry to get what they desire is the urgency to live a lot in the little time that remains to them. For

the Old Man, his long life is all behind him, at his back. Before him there is a very risky future, there is little, there is almost nothing, an almost nothing that will become eternal nothing in the very next moment. His use of his authority as paterfamilias is tyrannical, unjust. He uses power claiming to be driven by a sense of duty, when his goals are completely egotistical and irresponsible. The Old Man doesn't want to die, he grabs on to things to hang on to life. He is no two-bit miser, he is a great survivor. All this is never made explicit in the play. It is never discussed, because the great poetry of the character resides in the evidence of this and the ability of the audience—aided by the skill of the performer—to intuit, to understand, to write in its own head what is not written in the script.

2. For the Lovers, love is something ideal, great, immense, and eternal; that is, in the moments when everything is going well, more or less. These moments are rare pauses in the intrigue that puts the Lovers at the center of the action. But the action seems always to want to separate them, to say no to their love and their union. The time of life conceded to them—which for us is the time of the play—seems to offer them nothing but constant struggle against destiny, chance, the father, disagreeable surprises, new arrivals, the third, fourth, and fifth glitches in their plans, the messes created by their servants. When there are no external obstacles in their way, the Lovers create them with their own means: suspicion, jealousy, cerebral speculation that always leads to misunderstanding, to the mistaken interpretation of facts or even tiny details.

3. The Servants must always resolve the problems, their own and those of the others. Any servant is always the servant of all potential masters. Anyone who is socially superior to him may call for and expect his service. With casual ease, all the masters in the world unload their own inabilities onto their servants. Zanni, who is not intelligent, finds himself with the urgent and permanent need to be a genius. And he pulls it off, always, and each time for the first and last time. Because each time is an episode unto itself, unasked for, unsought, dumped into his life from who-knows-where and who-knows-why. Thus, in one act of genius after another, our Zanni gives life, fishing it out of the depths of the universe, to Chaos, to that immanent disorder that gives birth to the wished-for order sought by all, which sanctions the end of the comedy. Zanni makes and unmakes continuously his own affairs and those of others in order to escape them; to save his back and his ass; to satisfy the unsatisfiable; and finally to eat, sleep, and perhaps even get married. Zagna equals him completely. The Servetta survives better, with less urgency and fewer disasters but with an equal craving to escape. She is more intelligent than Zanni and Zagna, more analytical, more able to carry out plans.

This does not make her into a superwoman, but it gives her a position of predominance over the other servants, of whom she is the effectual chief.

4. The survival of the Capitano depends on his fundamental problem, which is that of wanting to appear to be something that he is not, because what he really is is unacceptable, unpresentable, irremediably shameful. He is a complete disaster, cowardly and ignorant, but he wants to and must appear to be a big, strong, fierce warrior, not lacking in culture and spirit. In fact he is the opposite of all that. His behavior compels him always to be an impostor. He either lies, presenting himself under a false name and title, or he does not lie in name but does so in substance. Fear and shame dominate his being.

Artistic survival is also manifested in Commedia. No matter what happens during the performance, no matter how the audience reacts, no matter what we think about the show we are performing, or what we think of our own skills, whatever news or event may have excited or upset us before going onstage, we must guarantee that we:

1. Maintain the mask
2. Maintain the credibility of the character
3. Perceive the internal behavior of the audience
4. Control and artistically make use of movements within and by the audience
5. Take artistic advantage of errors, accidents, surprises
6. Remain absolutely convinced of the excellence of our work
7. Persevere in the "game of going higher"
8. Maintain our objective of maximum amusement and satisfaction of the audience
9. Achieve collective and personal success

Is there also a principle of survival for the audience, the spectator? It would be easy to make jokes in response to this question. If there were such a type of survival, it would have to be understood in two senses: survival as an attentive, involved spectator during the performance; and survival as a spectator committed to persevere, to continue to be a spectator, to continue going to the theater. The survival of this spectator is very important, because the survival of theater itself depends on it. The public still bestows its presence on the theater. Without wanting to get into the incredibly complicated confluence of causes that distance spectators more and more from the art of the actor, we should still make a few observations.

Theater audiences have been severely tested from the postwar period to today, having been forced to witness theater change from *enjoyment* to *responsibility,* from something plain and clear to an indecipherable rebus.

In addition to this involution of the theatrical spectacle begun by the intellectual narcissism of the generations that "relaunched" it fifty years ago, there has been the abnormal invasion (abnormal for its variety, quantity, and format) of forms of entertainment that we can no longer define as competition, because the term assumes, if not equality, at least the sharing of a market. Today, however, theater is outside any market worthy of the name. Or should we say that the theatrical market is the network of discotheques, stadiums, and television studios?

The vicious circle now under way leads practitioners of theater to consolidate the idea of theater as the last shore of high and profound forms, which only plunges theater, even happily low-grade theater, ever deeper into the abyss of nonexistence.

The Structure of Improvisation

DEFINITION

We need to define the form of improvised comedy and its component parts. Our observations are based on the historical material of Commedia scenarios, especially on the collection called the *Favole Rappresentative* by Flaminio Scala, and on the direct experience of our school and our shows, which we think of as creative experiences of planning and production leading to the testing ground of our performances. Part of our experience involves applying historical information to our regime of research, experimentation, trying out, and innovation.

Our approach to an apparently rigid form and structure, historically given "now and forever," is that of one with the firm conviction of the value of creativity that is organized rather than left to pure instinct. It may seem paradoxical, but "pure" creativity, which is not organized and directed toward a project, is "short," limited, made of flashes, splashes, spots, and impulses that are destructured or unstructured. Without a solid body, creativity left to itself cannot stand, it is neither legible nor recognizable and therefore cannot be put to use. It has value only as a free outburst for whoever produced it. By structuring creativity, giving it a name, a form, and constituent parts, the impulse acquires meaning, function, and an audience-directed goal.

It goes without saying that the artist must enjoy himself, but the enjoyment of the artist must remain a private matter. On the other hand, it is imperative that the audience enjoy. This can only be obtained through a perfect awareness of one's own expressive means, which must lead back to a *name*, a *form*, and *constituent parts*, that is, a structure.

PERFECT FORM

The minimal schema that we define as perfect is beginning, development, and finale. Commedia dell'Arte never proceeds in an indefinite way. Everything must be clear and chronological. Any "returns" must take place only through narration or by summary or description, or perhaps through dreams and visions that the various characters develop to achieve the triple goal of developing the plot, aiding its comprehension, and producing *lazzi*. All traditional Commedia pieces are subdivided into three acts and develop as follows:

Act One

Everything is going just fine. This positive situation will be restored at the end. For example, two lovers prepare for their wedding, everything is ready, everyone is getting along, everyone is happy.

The first important difficulty presents itself. For example, a misunderstanding between the two old men concerning the marriage contract leads to a breakdown in the marriage preparations.

Amidst desperation, anger, orders, and counterorders, the plot machine gets under way with complications, confusion, and quid pro quo, which develop as the act comes to an end.

Act Two

Complications develop throughout the act.

Act Three

Complications continue until the prefinale. The prefinale is a situation that still lacks resolution, but the resolution can be foreseen.

The finale offers resolution and happy ending. Everything is very rapid, following in perfect order.

The coda involves the farewell and triumphal procession. This is not part of the Commedia proper, but may prolong itself for quite a while as part of the whole spectacle.

A perfect form is the first and fundamental structural element of Commedia. Such a form immediately confronts the problem of predictability. However, all Commedia is predictable, because the immutability of the perfect form "instructs" the public and prepares it to receive exactly what it expects, which is exactly what it has been promised. Thus predictability is a problem with respect to neither the form nor all the comedies derived and derivable from that form. But there is a problem of predictability with respect to the *action,* the execution. Therefore, it is first necessary to confirm the general form in all its subdivisions and then "throw off" or "confuse" the spectator while the action is under way in the present moment of the performance.

The smallest part of Commedia is the *gesture* and the largest part is the entire *commedia* itself: both have a tripartite form. The *three-part cell* is the minimal component structure of Commedia and is identical even as the components grow in proportion and duration. A gesture, a *lazzo*, no matter how quick, must be composed of a beginning, a development, and an end. The scene begins, develops, and finishes. Thus the act and thus the play.

All relations are built in *symmetry*. Two examples: (1) A scene of great happiness between the lovers as they anticipate their coming wedding must correspond to an equal, contrasting scene of desperation regarding the impossibility of realizing the wedding. (2) The planning of a robbery which two *zanni* work out in elaborate detail, anticipating a positive outcome, will be followed by the same sequence of actions, except with catastrophic consequences.

We also find symmetry in stage movement: two characters who want to make sure that no one is spying on them will proceed from a position of extreme vicinity to its mirror opposite, as distant as possible from each other on the stage, and then return to their original position. In gestural symmetry, two *zanni* walk cautiously and both use the same "cautious" walk. Symmetry produces a *predictability effect*, which can be difficult to manage. Thus predictability must be broken, split.

Lazzi, digressions, gratuitous incidents, and other inventions can camouflage symmetry enough to conceal it entirely. Unconsciously, symmetry continues to function positively, guaranteeing clarity, and therefore must not be renounced. Aesthetically, it is treated, manipulated, made unpredictable and surprising. The actors require symmetry as well: the extremely regular path that we follow, no matter how camouflaged, is clear in its rhythms, and that permits the actor to improvise without losing control and the coherence of the dramatic situation.

The formal ambivalence of Commedia is the contemporaneity of the dramatic action and the spectacle (the show). Naturally, the two almost always coincide, but they should be thought of as two interacting parts rather than as "the same thing." The story narrated in the Commedia is a sort of container of characters, situations, and surprises, and these things in turn become opportunities for displays of bravura by the actors, which the audience enjoys. Certainly, the story itself, with its moments of high drama and suspense, is itself a spectacle, but the modes of execution are that of a show within a spectacle or that of the spectacle itself.

There are moments in the execution that have nothing to do with the unfolding dramatic narrative. An inevitable example is the grand finale or coda, which includes farewells, thank-yous, encores ad infinitum, *lazzi*, songs, and demonstrations of various skills. In this situation, comic demagoguery is unleashed, which allows actors to indulge in a whole series of shameless displays of false modesty: "We're so sorry if we bored you," "We really don't deserve all your applause," "You are the most wonderful audience in the world"; and then there's the applause of the actors for the audience; a *lazzo* that seems to happen by chance; kisses, embraces, flowers; another musical number; more applause, and so on.

But there's still more. Exploiting the "accident" is a great comic practice. A comic actor makes a virtue of necessity as a basic principle, which means that he transforms any unplanned stage occurrence into an opportunity to perform. A slip, an object that falls, a moment of distraction (a "gap" in memory cannot exist in improvised comedy), a wrong entrance or a forgotten entrance, late entrances or early exits by spectators, watch alarms, and, last but not least, cell phones: all these actions and factors, which cause desperation in "internalizing" actors, are instead pure dripping fat for the good comic actor, an implacable opportunist and committed externalizer, the digger-up of the most hidden secrets of the collective spirit. Accidents, surprises, and antidramatic events are so interesting that these imponderables are sometimes invented on purpose.

Here is a classic: The Doctor enters for a brief monologue that in tone and content is coherent to the fable or story. But the brief monologue grows long, and both the tone and content sail away. The colleagues—fellow actors, not the other characters—behind the scene begin to lose patience and make discreet noises, coughing, shuffling their feet, and so on. The Doctor—the character, not the actor—gives no sign of awareness of the problem he has created but turns their noises to his own advantage, for example, by beginning a discourse on "coughs through the ages." Little by little, his fellows begin to appear and demonstrate their consternation to the audience; with masks raised on their foreheads, they make gestures to suggest, "What's going on? He's lost his mind! We don't understand." Thus little by little a huge struggle grows between one mask and the other actors. As it takes shape, the audience realizes that it's not for real, it's all set up, that it's a joke, but as the joke grows and draws laughter from the audience, it also descends toward tragedy.

The Doctor won't give in and obstinately keeps on talking to the audience while his fellows, for example, tie him up and stick him in a chest, or something like that. This is because the Old Man wants to demonstrate that he is superior to all and that the others don't even exist. When finally his fellows carry him off, the last thing the audience sees and hears is the desperate face of the Doctor still talking, and no one can stop him (the only thing forbidden the fellow actors is to gag his mouth). Once offstage, the story can continue, but a great moment of spectacle and comedy has been offered with profound confirmation of the "I don't want to die" feeling of the Doctor. He faces a death symbolized by his forced exit from the scene, which demonstrates the deep poetic foundation of improvised comedy.

System of Relations

Structurally, in its perfect tripartite and ambivalent form, the Commedia dell'Arte is a binary system of relations between parts and components that are composed of modules. The actors make use of *schema,* which are the *generic,* the *canovaccio,* and the *scenario,* all of which are part of the *repertory.*

The system of relations is the interaction between the characters, all of whom are active and of primary importance. Original companies were formed of specialist-actors, each embodying the craft tradition of his or her character. No specialist would be willing to be an "extra" (of which there were few and were roles taken by young company members in training or others picked up on the spur of the moment) or play a minor part. This situation inherent to the Arte imposed a requirement to construct intricate, complex stories, which involved a moving vortex of entrances and exits that made all characters seem virtually omnipresent without crowding the stage. In this way relational and professional requirements affect formal relations. Moving within this system of relations, the actor keeps track of the plot and his or her own relationship with every other character, both in absolute terms (a servant is always a servant, a master a master) and in relation to the play's action. Each character may enter into contact with and develop situations with all the others.

The system of relations is constructed to keep the audience informed about the situation, so that it can always understand what's going on. At the same time, the unfolding story can never be clear to the individual characters, because their vision of events is always partial and mistaken. The audience can see both the objective situation and the erroneous, limited one of the characters.

Parts and Components

The parts and components are the characters, animated by motivations and placed into situations and into relations among themselves.

Binary Organization

The entire system of relations is two-sided. Every character generates double roles or couples of roles: the First and Second Zanni, the First and Second Old Man, the First and Second Lovers. Even the solitary Capitano forms a couple with his servant.

When a character enters into contact with a character of different nature, they combine. A scene between two *zanni* will depend on that particular comic couple. Every *zanni*, however, can enter into relations with any other character, producing not so much a duet situation but one where everything moves two by two.

Within the crowded and shifting situation, the couple is always isolated. For example, everyone is looking for someone else, but no one finds the one he is seeking. Instead the characters have mistaken encounters with others but one at a time; that is, they meet up two by two. An action based on error, misunderstanding, or mistaken timing, with respect to the intentions of the characters, provides for a series of structurally well-organized "face-to-face" moments. A situation like this can be realized with continuous entrances and exits or with phased, asymmetrical appearances, making sure to avoid the sought-after encounter. The cause may be darkness or behaviors orchestrated to generate outcomes hostile to the hoped-for encounter. For example, I turn to where the person was, but that person has bent over to pick something up. "Chance" generates error, the actors organize it with absolute precision, and wherever an erroneous "face-to-face" occurs, they can improvise, enriching the scene. All the exchanges, even the most frenetic ones, contain—they must contain—binary sequences; the sense of a "crowd" results as a rhythmic and situational effect.

In three-person situations, we can easily locate the dual organization. For example, Flavio and Isabella want to communicate with each other, but something (distance or strong emotion) impedes them. Zanni becomes the medium who, running from one to the other to the point of total exhaustion, establishes their contact, develops their communication, and provides for the agreement between the two. But each time, Zanni-Flavio or Zanni-Isabella is the active double. Certainly, the third character exists and is important in the story, but the momentarily excluded one does not determine the *action*, which is always what is happening in that very moment, the present.

In mass scenes, binary organization manifests itself through the isolation of a character who relates to the whole group and vice versa; thus we obtain a sort of chorus-versus-comic hero relationship.

There are two principal motives for binary organization: improvisation by the actors can be controlled only by using the simplest possible organizational structure, which is the binary, whether by doubling, in couples, or as a duet. The second motive relates to the audience's primary need, which is to understand everything at all times, even the most intricate turns of the plot. Binary organization always keeps the situation clear. When wild and frenetic rhythms develop, the audience can still follow comfortably.

Modular Composition

Modular composition involves the prefabrication of all the parts or elements of the comedy; not that of a given comedy, but of all possible comedies that can be staged with the infinite recombination of prefabricated elements. The first and most evident manifestation of modular composition is the use of the same masks in all comedies, the application of the principle of fixed types, which are modules. The same masks, the same problems, the same developments. Two lovers in heated conflict due to jealousy constitute a module; wherever there are lovers, there is jealousy. Thus the module of conflict of jealousy is prefabricated and can be inserted, with any necessary adjustments, into any commedia. Whoever is responsible for the sufferings of others will be picked out and will receive his hailstorm of beating; this too is a module. The victim of the beating will be the Magnifico or the Dottore or the Capitano or a Zanni or more than one, but the module exists; it need only be hooked into the specific comedy.

Other modules are the *schema*, the *lazzi*, and *set forms*.

By using modules, improvisation works out well, its quality is high, the audience has the impression of credible spontaneity as though the number were born in that very moment, and the effect combines with formal exaggeration, which is the manifestation of true theater, guaranteeing a good overall result.

The *routine* implicit in the fixed, recurrent schema of comic theater has always been held to be its principal defect. Granted, routine can exist not for formal or structural reasons, but because of defects in the individual artist or company, which is not able to renew itself. However, the accusation of routine against Commedia itself cannot be justified. Curiously, but not too curiously, the exact opposite exists. In our opinion, the serious modern psychological actor is the clone of an "ideal" model, totally artificial, which we find identical in all cultures and languages. In this "perfect" world, even the two sexes are incredibly identical: the same appearance and the same voice, a deep chest voice, of course.

The comic actor relies on modules and other preconstructed parts because he or she cannot sacrifice the formal coherence, which, once guaranteed, frees the actor to continually seek new solutions, which is the very being of art, of being an artist.

For us comics, the fact that two performances of the same serious psychological play are completely identical is certainly no proof of originality or of uniqueness; on the contrary, it all appears terribly routine to us. The fact that the majority of serious psychological plays are completely identical, despite huge efforts at originality, strikes us as truly disturbing. It is thus scandalous for us to hear ourselves accused of doing the same thing, because even if the things we do are always the same, we always, *always* do them in a different way. This writer has been doing Pulcinella for years. Whoever has seen our show *Life, Death, and Resurrection of Pulcinella* can appreciate, in repeated viewings, the same surprise effect he or she felt the first time. It's the same the second and third times, because people return to us for strong, healthy laughter. They come back repeatedly.

This continuous movement, this incessant reinvention of the play, is possible thanks to the structural support of the comedy form, which is all modular in some way. The clown, the Macchietta (comic-sketch character) of the great tradition, and the modern cabaret performer are all modular structures.

Schema

The historical schema are *canovaccio, scenario, commedia, repertory.* Flaminio Scala's collection of *Favole Rappresentative*[1] offers us a schematic solution that we will illustrate by presenting in detail one of his scenarios, *La Creduta Morta* (*Love Is a Drug*), in the version edited by Ferruccio Marotti for Il Polifilo press. The numbering of the scenes is our own.

La Creduta Morta (Love Is a Drug)
Commedia

Situation

There lived in Bologna a gentleman of good family, endowed with virtuous manners, who had a daughter and wished to marry her well and happily. He determined to match her with a person from another city, equal to himself in the merchant trade.

But the young lady burned with love for a young man of her own city named Orazio who, as well as being her equal in wealth and nobility, loved her in return and longed to have her for his wife. Seeing her father's wishes to be the only obstacle to achieving his desires, Orazio made an agreement with the young woman that he would give her a somniferous draught, which would make her appear to be dead, so that she would be buried in the family tomb, with the outcome that will be seen.

Characters

Pantalone (Old Man)
Laura, his wife
Flaminia, his daughter, believed
    to be dead
Arlecchino, household servant
Graziano, a doctor
Isabella, his daughter
Orazio, his son
Franceschina, a servant
Pedrolino, a servant
Servants
Flavio, lover
Capitano Spavento
Numerous policemen

Props

long rope
a costume for Orazio
many lanterns

Setting

Bologna, Italy

Act One
Night

1. ORAZIO, FLAVIO

    Flavio tells his friend Orazio of the great grief he feels about the death of Flaminia, for whom he felt such pure affection. Orazio expresses compassion for his suffering. In grief, Flavio exits. Orazio speaks of his love for Flaminia and explains that, out of love for him, she is pretending to be dead. At that moment,

2. PANTALONE, GRAZIANO, SERVANTS

Pantalone arrives with servants, returning from accompanying Flaminia to the tomb. They make elaborate greetings to one another. Pantalone goes into his house; Graziano exits with his servants. Orazio says that he regrets the grief felt by Flaminia's father. At that moment,

3. PEDROLINO

Pedrolino tells Orazio that everything is in order and explains what must be done with Flaminia: Orazio must bring her to his house. Pedrolino shows him the rope and other tools he will need to remove Flaminia from the tomb. At that moment,

4. FLAVIO

Flavio arrives. Upon spotting him, Pedrolino goes into the house. Flavio, grieving, weeps outside Flaminia's house. Orazio comes forth to console Flavio. At that moment,

5. ISABELLA, FRANCESCHINA, LAURA

Isabella comes out of Pantalone's house with Franceschina, who is carrying a lit lantern, and Laura, who goes with her only as far as the door and then reenters. Orazio asks Flavio to accompany Isabella to her house and exits. Isabella reveals to Flavio that she is in love with him. Flavio consoles her sweetly; when they arrive at her door, they knock.

6. GRAZIANO

Graziano thanks Flavio, who exits. Then Graziano expresses his compassion for Laura, who has lost her daughter. At that moment,

7. CAPITANO SPAVENTO

Capitano Spavento, in love with Isabella, sees her with her father. He considers what to do and finally resolves to steal her away. He puts his hand on his sword, begins an argument, seizes Isabella, and leads her away by force. Graziano and Franceschina yell for help. At that moment,

8. PANTALONE

Pantalone hears the noise and arrives, and

9. LAURA

Laura hears the noise and arrives.

10. FLAVIO

Flavio also hears the noise and arrives. Graziano tells how Isabella, his daughter, has been kidnapped. Flavio runs off in search of his beloved. The others remain. At that moment,

11. PEDROLINO

Pedrolino, scared, arrives. They each ask him, "Have you seen her?" He answers yes, thinking that they are asking about Flaminia, and says that the police are chasing him by mistake. Graziano despairs. At that moment,

12. POLICEMEN

The police arrive, out of breath. Graziano tells them that he is the father of the missing girl. The police tell him they have no business with him. At that moment,

13. FLAMINIA

Flaminia, fleeing, yells, "Father, help!"

14. POLICEMEN

They chase after her. She exits with the police behind her. Graziano and the others say that it must have been the ghost of Flaminia. Scared, they go into their houses.

Act Two
Night

1. ARLECCHINO

Coming from Flaminia's tomb, he says that he found it open, and that he found clothing and other things there, and that he took the clothing. He discourses on his master's miserliness, saying that he buried his daughter at night to save money. He expresses his gladness at having found the clothing. At that moment,

2. CAPITANO SPAVENTO

Capitano wants to hear what people are saying about the kidnapping of Isabella, so he starts a conversation with Arlecchino. Neither understands what the other is getting at. Capitano exits. Arlecchino thinks Capitano is a ghost. He removes his own clothes and puts on the clothing from the tomb, leaving his own onstage, and exits.

3. ORAZIO, PEDROLINO

Orazio, desperate at having heard what Pedrolino told him about Flaminia, sends Pedrolino off to look for his beloved and remains onstage, desperate. At that moment,

4. ARLECCHINO

Arlecchino arrives. As he is dressed in Flaminia's clothes, Orazio thinks it's her. They have a scene together. Finally Arlecchino reveals himself. Orazio, thinking him a ghost, flees. Arlecchino remains. At that moment,

5. ISABELLA

Isabella arrives, having escaped from the Capitano. She sees Arlecchino and thinks he is her brother Orazio in disguise. She asks him for help, calling him by her brother's name. Arlecchino is amazed at this and exits. She is aggrieved. At that moment,

6. FLAVIO

Flavio arrives with a lantern. She asks for his help. After many words between them, Flavio leads her home and knocks on the door.

7. GRAZIANO

Graziano sees Isabella, his daughter, rejoices, and thanks Flavio. He lets Isabella into the house. Flavio, left alone, despairs and exits.

8. FLAMINIA

Fearful at being out at night, Flaminia expresses fear that some madman might attack her because she is a woman. She regrets what she has done. She sees Arlecchino's clothing and decides to put it on. As she is changing, she sees a lantern approaching and runs off, leaving her own clothes onstage. At that moment,

9. PEDROLINO

Pedrolino says that he cannot find Flaminia. He sees her clothing, is amazed, and decides to put her clothes on, which he does. At that moment,

10. CAPITANO SPAVENTO

The Capitano arrives and thinks Pedrolino is a woman. He tries to woo Pedrolino. Pedrolino plays along, pretending to be a woman. At that moment,

11. ORAZIO

Orazio arrives, believes that Pedrolino is Flaminia, and hides to watch. Pedrolino recognizes Orazio and to provoke his passion he continues playing along with the Capitano, encouraging him flirtatiously. Orazio loses his patience and puts his hand on his sword. The Capitano flees, as does Pedrolino. Orazio exits in pursuit of the others.

Act Three
Night

1. FLAMINIA

In Arlecchino's clothes, Flaminia reflects on various aspects of her situation. She finally decides to knock on Orazio's door.

2. GRAZIANO

Graziano cries out and then comes to the window, asking who is knocking and what they want. Flaminia, speaking sotto voce, says she wants Isabella. At that moment,

3. ISABELLA

Isabella comes to the window, asks who is looking for her, and becomes afraid, retiring inside, shrieking. At that moment,

4. GRAZIANO

From inside, Graziano yells and makes noise, then comes out in his nightshirt with a lantern in his hand. At that moment,

5. ISABELLA, FRANCESCHINA

The women, in nightshirts, follow Graziano outside. Flaminia circles around Isabella and Franceschina. When they see her, they become frightened, cry out, and run back inside. Flaminia despairs because dawn is approaching. At that moment,

6. ARLECCHINO

Arlecchino arrives. Believing him to be Orazio, Flaminia speaks amorously to him. He recognizes his own clothes but seeing a different face in them, he starts beating loudly on Pantalone's door. At that moment,

7. PANTALONE, LAURA

Pantalone and Laura come outside in their nightshirts. Arlecchino tells them that the ghost of their daughter is moving around the city. They laugh at him. Flaminia hides. Pantalone beats Arlecchino, making a lot of noise. At that moment,

8. GRAZIANO

Graziano comes to the window, angry that he cannot sleep. Arlecchino asks him to be a witness to the truth of what he told Pantalone and his wife. Graziano confirms having seen Flaminia's ghost, then comes into the street. Pantalone makes fun of him and goes back into his house. Graziano sees the clothing of his son, tells Arlecchino that he's a thief. Arlecchino denies having stolen the clothes. Graziano throws his lantern at Arlecchino and goes back inside. Arlecchino flees.

9. FLAMINIA

Flaminia laments that she has caused so much trouble.

10. PEDROLINO

Pedrolino arrives. Pedrolino and Flaminia regard each other fearfully and then reveal themselves. She says that Graziano forgot to lock the door when he entered his house. Pedrolino exhorts her to go in. She enters to reveal herself to Isabella. Pedrolino remains onstage. At that moment,

11. ORAZIO, FLAVIO

Orazio enters with Flavio, telling the story of Flaminia and of having seen her with the Capitano. He sees Pedrolino. Believing him to be Flaminia, he speaks amorously and complains that she flirted with the Capitano. Pedrolino apologizes, then reveals himself, telling the whole story. At that moment,

12. ISABELLA

Isabella enters, fleeing.

13. FLAMINIA

Flaminia enters behind Isabella.

14. Graziano

Graziano enters.

15. Pantalone, Laura

Pantalone and Laura enter.

16. Arlecchino

Arlecchino enters.

17. Franceschina

Franceschina enters. The story finally resolves itself. Orazio marries Flaminia and Flavio marries Isabella.

We have presented here the Seventh Day of *Teatro delle Favole Rappresentative* by Flaminio Scala. We based our play *Love Is a Drug* on this scenario, staged in 1995 by the Oxford Stage Company. In the English version, we staged the events narrated in Scala's exposition. Scala, on the other hand, begins the comedy by immersing the Lover, Orazio, immediately into the deception under way, at which time Flaminia is already believed to be dead. The subject has all the necessary elements of a normal beginning. Evidently, Flaminio Scala carries out his own little "reform" in the *canovaccio* but explains the setup for the action in the exposition section that introduces the plot.

In our Oxford version, the scene described in the exposition is staged with a particular sort of pantomime, in which everything is action but not mime. Sounds, words, exclamations, both intelligible and not, become the *sound of the situation,* which is the *sound of the characters.* The person whom Pantalone considers to be equal to himself in the merchant trade becomes a Mysterious Stranger, unnerving, beautiful as a statue, terrifying as a demon, with an androgynous white mask with harmonious, classical features, which horrifies rather than calms. The list of characters names unidentified Servants. From this indication we created evocative, nocturnal *zanni* and *zagne.* On the other hand, we did without the Policemen. There are very few props described, fewer than are actually called for in the scenario. The props mentioned in the actual text are completely necessary.

The first act is descriptive, introducing the characters and situation. The second and third acts develop the convolutions of the plot. *Love Is a Drug*— performed in two acts—does not follow all of them, because the play might last up to four hours. We deduce that Commedia actors, using *canovacci* of this type, must have entertained audiences for at least three and a half hours, not counting intermissions. Tastes and culture have changed a great deal since the sixteenth century, but the art of comic improvisation and the reaction of the public to high-quality actors cannot have changed very much.

Scene 11 of act III is the prefinale. The subsequent finale happens very quickly. Scala knows that the actors begin to ignore the *canovaccio* as the play approaches its end, so he adds virtually nothing except to indicate possible *lazzi,* which the actors can use if they like or invent their own if not. From scene 12 to scene 16 there is a vortex of *lazzi,* with very little real story development but much opportunity for the actors to "act out." Only scene 17 fixes the true ending of the play, but here as well the plot is so concise that the actors will take the opportunity to let go, and let go they do, with an abundance of comic demagoguery, as the audience applauds.

La Creduta Morta/Love Is a Drug had an extraordinary success throughout seven months of performances. Our brilliant actors, who joined their splendid, solid, English training to the specifically Italian training they received during the preparatory phase, brought all the vitality and modernity of Commedia to light, demonstrating that it is rigorous but not rigid, organized but not closed, creative and not disordered, and as deep as the source of the laughter that it provokes.

SITUATION

This is the circumstance the audience doesn't see, that precedes the beginning of the action. For the actor reading Scala's *Favole,* the situation functions as preface and prologue. Watching the performance, the audience is able to deduce the facts of the situation from the action (including the dialogue). The situation often describes crucial factors that cannot be shown. For example, Pantalone gets a woman pregnant and then abandons her; or we might learn of a man or woman who is about to die or dies because of old age or sickness or an accident or by murder or for some mysterious reason. It is unthinkable to present situations such as these onstage.

By fixing its types, Commedia dell'Arte renders its characters already born, already fully grown adults, and they are immortal. There is neither birth nor death in Commedia. Thus, the normal human condition, the same as that in which the spectators find themselves, is described in the situation, in the preceding circumstances that are narrated, cited, alluded to, reported, intuited, or supposed in the comedy itself, but never presented. Whoever appears onstage is "born" before the beginning of the comedy and will never die within the comedy.

Canovaccio

An outline of any situation, even the most minimal, but also the entire story, organized point by point, each of which describes in essential form what takes place.

Scenario

The succession of scenes that form the complete story of the comedy. The scenes are described in *canovaccio* form, giving the actors only the plot, their relationships with one another, their expressive opportunities, and the reference points upon which they base their work.

Commedia

The finished, realized work. A traditional commedia is divided into three acts.

Repertory

The collection of stories (*fabulae*), including the comic (commedia), the poetic (pastoral, woodland, or marine), the heroic, the tragic (tragedy, *opera regia, opera reale*), and the mixed, which forms the reservoir of the offerings of the company. Normally, companies remained in one piazza (location) until they had gone through their entire repertory. The standard repertory consisted of seven comedies and three other plays, which could be either serious or poetic.

The "Fifty Days" of Scala's *Teatro delle Favole Rappresentative* present a sort of ideal repertory for the number of titles and the styles offered, with forty comedies and ten tragic-poetic works in the following order: XLI:

Tragedy; XLII: Mixed—with a tragic, pastoral subject; XLIII: *opera regia;* XLIV: Heroic; XLV-XLVIII: *opera reale;* XLIX: Pastoral; L: *opera regia.*

What about today? Our effort to contribute to the continuity of improvised theater takes into account the historical schema, especially with regard to professional and specialized contents. We do not feel obligated to maintain the subdivision of Commedia into three acts. We tend to prefer two acts or a single act. Audiences today are less tolerant than audiences in the past, and it is difficult to provoke their sense of wonder. When they feel they "get" what's going on, they tend to grow bored and drop out of the relationship with the performers. They refuse to engage in the necessary complicity between performer and audience; they "disconnect." Audiences today are captivated by either the very highest quality of rapport with the performers or by aggression, which can be linguistic, visual, or due to effects—sometimes outrageous—that are delivered by high technology.

By their culture and training, actors today cannot improvise from a *canovaccio* except as soloists. When working with others, they must have a role that is precisely written out and directed by someone. That's fine. But Commedia cannot do without improvisation. Therefore the *canovaccio* must be worked out during the creation of the show, as preparation and provocation for the actors.

The modern comic poet should work with actors he or she trusts (from the point of view of the actors, of course, they must trust their writer). *Canovacci* of various types aimed at understanding characters and situations can precede improvisational work based on the scenario itself, with the scenario in this sense meaning the complete layout of the comedy before it is fixed into dialogues. From the dramaturgical development work among the actors, director, and comic poet, there results the final text, whose drafting is the task of the comic poet (who can also be the director or one of the company's actors).

The degree of authority held by the individual performing the function and traditional role of the author is a practical-professional and even human problem that must be sorted out by all the collaborators in the process. This often depends upon the importance of the author at the moment when the work is generally agreed upon. It is certain, however, that the great authors of the history of Western theater—upon whom theatrical historiography almost totally depends—worked in this way.

THE SET FORMS

Historically, set forms means the *generics,* for the most part solos, and passages and themes adaptable to all comedies. The Arte actors possessed a reservoir of generics as part of their individual repertoire, as well as *lazzi* for couples in elaborate, complex situations.

People unpracticed in the trade or those just entering it confuse improvisation with the idea of unlimited liberty. In truth, the set forms accord perfectly with the requirement for "certainty" of the professional improvising actor.

In our case, wanting to surpass the too-generic or generalizing historical term, adopting instead the expression from bel canto, we embrace the principle of set forms as a structure of ideas and a reservoir of perfected solutions.

Set Forms by Character

Magnifico: scolding and cursing. Monologues with which the Magnifico affirms his authority or lashes out against whoever has wounded him.

Dottore: tirades and blather. Monologues aimed at affirming the intellectual superiority of the Dottore over the other characters and the audience.

"Blockhead" Servant: malapropisms and misspeaking. Tirades made comic by the incomprehension of the other characters but perfectly logical to the audience.

"Crafty" Servant: schemes and witticisms. The exposition of more-or-less criminal projects; expressions, proverbs, sayings, witticisms intended to justify in terms of "good commonsense" any act that is not out-and-out reprehensible.

Servetta (female servant): greetings and harangues. The Servetta, the future *soubrette* of all variety and revue theater, must—it is her function—always be captivating, charming, playful; she is a great expert in comic demagoguery and makes abundant use of it, especially when greeting the audience in an elaborate way and winning consensus with little moralizing speeches with which nobody could disagree.

Lovers: declarations, arguments, laments, seizures of joy, derision, states of being head-over-heels. All the weaponry of the contrasts of love and the high-and-low anxieties and uncertainties that derive from it.

Capitano: the Boast. The boast is—along with the blather of the Dottore—the definition of the form par excellence, the great moment to solo, the site of maximum existence of the character. The Capitano's boast is a grotesquerie of elevated conceits and low egoism, altruism and narcissism, high culture and tavern brooding. It is the most updatable, modernizable of the set forms, and it is the most autonomous. In fact an entire solo performance can be built on it.

Set Forms by Situation

Naturally, there are an incalculable number of situations that can be made into set forms. We will indicate a few as examples.

The serenade. All the characters can find themselves needing to carry out, or needing to have carried out by someone else, a serenade. Zanni can manage on his own or have his friends help him, among whom there may be genuine specialists, who are usually First Zanni. Lovers and Old Men rely on the musical efforts of their servants, or participate in the execution, or await the effects of the serenade on its beneficiary.

Courting. Commedia is all wooing, with results that vary according to the situation. The Old Man woos the young Lover who rejects him or the Serva, who may try to get some benefit from it. Zanni and Zagna or the Servetta may be part of a comic couple often formed at the beginning of the comedy in an encounter that combines eroticism, joyous timidity, and animal ritual, such as the courting "dances" of pigeons. The Capitano and the Lady give life to "adult" courting, with great erotic tension necessarily held in check but spectacular all the same (they may consummate, but far offstage).

Even the Old Man may be wooed, but by whom? By anyone who finds it in their interests, and therefore uses artifice. For example, having to divert the Old Man in order to block his scheme to marry Isabella, Zanni may flirt with him while dressed as a woman. Or the Old Man, dressed as a woman because of some plot device, may be implacably courted by the Capitano, who will do everything in his power to seduce "her."

The interzo. That is, a scene between two characters that is counterpointed by a third character.

The hailstorm. Whoever is responsible for causing trouble to others must pay—always. In Commedia, with a few exceptions, there are no courts, trials, and judges. But justice always triumphs. The hailstorm of beatings will always find its way onto the shoulders of the guilty party; this is often a prefinale, a rain that promises to germinate the beginnings of a new life, although symbolically it is the end of the life of the one who has borne the hailstorm.

The perfect victim is the Old Man, who is consciously responsible, although convinced of his own good reasons, for the sufferings he has inflicted on the young people and the servants.

Capitano is also responsible for causing trouble for others but is not entirely aware of it; he is too taken with himself to understand whether and for whom he has created problems. The hailstorm does not punish only the responsible party but also the stupid, because in the world of permanent survival, stupidity is a grave fault and must always be punished.

The *zanni* are also subject to beatings, from both their masters and their equals; in the case of servants the punishment is only a part of what they "deserve"—deserve every moment, always and no matter what—because the other part is the prize, which can only come at the end. For the servants, whether they have behaved well or badly, there is both punishment and reward. All this happens in Commedia without any sort of moralizing; it is merely necessary, a part of the movement of things.

The practical joke (burla). Just as Commedia is not moralistic, it does not engage in "kidding." We would like to permit ourselves a digression on the *burla,* the practical joke, its meaning and use, to understand how and why Commedia is not, nor should it be, a mannered world of kidding jokesters; where survival is at stake, there is no time for joking unless it has a function, a usefulness that serves the various strategies of survival.

Practical jokes play a part in Commedia; they are certainly a set form, but the characters are never entirely aware of it, with the exception of the *Infarinati.*

In Commedia the practical joke is absolutely necessary, because the collapse of due respect provoked by a well-done *burla* can change the course of things, and the course of things must change. Before analyzing how this works in Commedia, let's take a closer look at the practical joke as a behavioral phenomenon.

The *burla* takes place preferably, most often, and most intensely and violently in situations in communal life characterized by coercion and limitations on individual freedom: prisons, barracks, boarding schools. It also occurs in schools and workplaces, during group travel, and wherever groups of people are required to stay together, such as weekend outings and ticket lines. This passage can be noted on a social level as well: wherever there is less liberty, less wealth, less culture, people make fun of one another more often. As we distance ourselves from such situations and conditions, making fun of others tends to attenuate until it reduces itself to a sort of purely verbal, respectful, and even affectionate test of how "game" a person is. When the setting is decidedly democratic and civil—whether sincerely or hypocritically—making fun of others disappears. Is making fun of others or conducting practical jokes therefore a sign of incivility, of cultural scarcity?

We think so, in real life, because everyone deserves respect and the *burla* substitutes respect with ridiculousness, which is its opposite.

This is the point: in order to carry out a joke against someone, you must first decide *not* to respect the victim, who will be humiliated, lowered, momentarily deprived of his own dignity and due respect. The object of this attention must deserve the joke and the humiliation; he must be in some way guilty.

Thus, whoever plans the joke raises himself to the level of judge-executioner; he judges, emits a sentence, and executes it. Whoever is the target of this playful attention must be guilty of something, convicted of contempt, and as soon as possible must pay the penalty.

The *burla* is an execution—we may even call it a summary execution, because it is not preceded by anything that resembles a trial—a capital execution, because it is intended to destroy not the person but his image, the image that the person has created of himself, that he believes in, and for which he claims a right to respect. Although symbolic, while being material, this death penalty inflicted on the image, which leaves no physical sign, has all the qualities of irreversibility. Still worse, it can be repeated, multiplied, varied, and reiterated especially through the sheer torment of its being repeated for all to enjoy.

But what was the crime of the condemned man? Roughly speaking, the categories of deserving victims of a *burla* are, in first place, the shitheads (*stronzi*). All the others follow after that: whoever tries to place himself too high, whoever possesses too much, whoever has an excessively evident peculiarity (too skinny, too fat, too tall, too short, as well as too elegant, too zealous, too lazy, too patient, too impatient, too much a braggart, too fearful, and so on), and also whoever is stupid, dense, slow, *coglione*.

All these things must be paid for. Paid to whom? To the restricted circle of those who frequent the victim; all together they form a little autonomous community where means of coexistence and rules are formed. The more prolonged and forced the coexistence, the heavier and more multifarious the rules.

Naturally, there are those who are immune to the attentions of practical jokers; they are the normal ones, the ones who enjoy recognized authority or superiority within the group. These are almost always the practical jokers themselves.

How does a little community of mutual acquaintances regulate the infraction of a rule? If the infraction is grave and compromises relations, naturally the continuity of the community itself is lessened. But if the infraction is tolerable, the most adequate and effective punishment is to be made fun of, which has, furthermore, the elastic characteristic of being returnable. The continuous exchange of practical jokes can constitute a modus vivendi of small communities of friends. Plus there is an age of life most inclined toward such jokes, adolescence, of course, young manhood and womanhood; and there is a gender that requires it more, the male, which is always ready for butting.

Why can certain behaviors, certain human characteristics, certain external aspects of a person, be judged as faults to be punished within a small community of friends, even though there is nothing illicit or destructive about them? Probably intervention is required wherever a detail distances a subject from the general rule. To banish the subject from the group would be disproportionate. So the person therefore must be put to the test.

The *burla* punishes traces of distancing from the standard, but at the same time it measures the degree of distancing and, sometimes brutally, recalls the one who has distanced himself into the embrace of the standard. In order to protect itself from the danger of disintegration, the community must be homogeneous, and to be homogeneous it must make its rules, its standards, be respected.

When the person condemned is a classic shithead, he expects to be made the object of practical jokes; he knows that a lesson will be taught to him. In fact the shithead (who knows he is one, as this awareness is a universally recognized characteristic of shitheads), with his behavior, beyond attempting to obtain what he wants, provokes his friends to action.

In all other cases, the victim is ignorant, unaware of his own failings; he learns at his own expense, he discovers, with the realization of the *burla* and its humiliation, that he was not following the rules of the community. He has no other choice but to correct himself, or leave the community, or strike back in kind, or tolerate, go along with the joke. If this person is incorrigible, as in the case of an impenitent shithead or a hopeless dunce, then he becomes forever the systematic, ritualized target of the others, the example and the reference point against which all the others learn to regulate themselves.

Those who are to a greater-or-lesser degree dedicated to the practical joke tend to defend their function as being terribly amusing. They willingly suppose that the joke in itself is beautiful and funny and therefore must be appreciated, even by the victim. Naturally, no victim can enjoy being the object of such a joke; anyone who goes along with the joke is clearly a person blessed with self-control or devoid of a capacity to react, but he can never claim to have enjoyed the joke. No person even marginally normal can enjoy humiliation; and even an innocent practical joke is always humiliating, which explains why innocent jokes do not exist.

Thus the *burla* is necessary among acquaintances, whether compulsory or not, because it serves to conserve equilibrium in interrelationships.

When the group lets loose with everyone against everyone, for example, in water fights and pillow fights, the OK Corral expressed in this way constitutes a collective cleaning-out, an outburst that zeros out all previous accounts, so as to start over with a new standard accessible to all.

What about the solitary practical joker? What purpose do his jokes serve? What problem do they resolve? Here, the discourse departs from our own purposes, but there is an aspect of fundamental importance to understanding the meaning of the limits of our discourse: the solitary practical joker is a maniac. He must resolve problems that are absolutely personal, he is sick, perhaps with a sense of inferiority that obligates him to lower and humiliate everyone and everything in order to reestablish an acceptable sense of proportion. In our world of masks, all pieces of a rigorously human-collective mosaic, there is no place for solitary pathologies.

Nowadays, practical jokes can assume global proportions. Orson Welles inaugurated the mass practical joke in 1938 with the famous live broadcast of the invasion of earth by Martians. The victims of the joke are anonymous if taken one by one, but taken altogether they are the public, the people. Why did Orson Welles make a practical joke against the people? What crime had the public committed? We suspect that they were guilty of credulity.

On the household level, the telephone joke already existed, and it continues to rage and goes step-by-step with the practical joke of ringing people's doorbells. In this case the victim can truly be anonymous. Here, the practical joker finds amusement in imagining the face, which must look so stupid; if the joker speaks, he says things to elaborate a "complex" joke; he brings out the stupidity of his interlocutor, who thus remains punished.

Candid Camera is still today perhaps the most merciless of democratic *burla*. Extended to almost the entire social community, the *burla* humiliates and then rewards with the famous fifteen minutes of fame. Certainly, it makes us laugh, but the scientific, carefully organized humiliation of innocence provokes a pungent sense of shame and anger in this writer. Perhaps it's all made up, constructed. In that case we viewers are as much the fools as the victims of the joke.

We might suppose that the only democratic form of joke is the joke on one's self, to make fun of one's self, to demonstrate self-irony, which is reputed to be a highly intelligent form of civility, sociality, and—who knows why?—tolerance. I lower myself such that you might raise me up; this is certainly a bit sad, more demagogic and less Christian than it may seem. Can a practical joke be gratuitous? We think not. It is always necessary to lower in order to raise up. And we must raise up.

In Commedia, all this is strictly linked to the system of relations, to the behavior of the characters, to their emergencies. The culture of the *burla*, very strong and diffuse in the Middle Ages, is already strongly attenuated when the *zanni* make their appearance. No jokes, then? Let's not be silly. We simply have to locate them correctly. Let's see.

To beat the Old Man is not a practical joke against the Old Man but a repressive and punitive act; it is a matter of blocking, stopping his project, for example, to marry Isabella, or to punish him for having considered it and at least partly put it into action. That much is evident. But the hailstorm doesn't come raining down just like that, after a moment's decision, or because the idea simply came to someone's mind. It requires an organizational apparatus that may last through all three acts of the Commedia. The hailstorm hits its target because the character has been put in a position to receive it; to place the character in those conditions means having acted toward that goal. Those actions have all the characteristics of a complex and well-worked *burla*.

Seen in this way, the *burla* would no longer be what it is, because there would be no awareness of constructing the practical joke; and in effect, constructed in this way, it is not a conscious *burla*. But the comic actor "thinks" the joke and then makes the comedy. The *burla* is a content and, like all contents, it goes inside something. The audience recognizes it easily, because everything is there: the artificers and a victim who deserves it; the elaboration of the plan; the realization of the plan; the execution; the desired effect, or rather punishment of the "guilty one," the interruption of his "criminal plan," and the return to the natural order of things. In Commedia the return to order is always to love among those who love one another and should love one another; temperance in the aged; discipline in the servants; and the voyage toward new adventures for the Capitano. This normality, as we know, can be found only in the first and last minutes of every comedy, because normality (which is perfection) is not theatrical.

The fixed practical joker exists in Commedia; it is the character of the Infarinato. He is the brilliant official *castigamatti*, the systematic practical joker, the sower of jokes that put others to the test and make examples of them; wherever he is, someone—who deserves it—will become the object of a practical joke.

Flaminio Scala's Pedrolino mask never misses the occasion to tease his neighbors. The Calabrian Bajazzu (from whom derive Pagliaccio, Pallasso, Payaso, Paillasse, all names that have nothing to do with *paglia* [straw], but rather with *baja,* which means mockery and making fun of someone) owns up to the tendency implicit in his very name and applies it with a certain cruelty.

Commedia, however, does not admit the *burla* as an amusing joke for its own sake; it must be necessary. The *burla* is always cruel. Very. *Mors tua vita mea* (your death, my life). This is the meaning of the *burla* in improvised theater. There is no time for joking around, survival must be assured immediately. If survival can be guaranteed by inflicting a humiliating joke on one who merits it, then let the joke be done. But our practical jokers will seem like wolves, not poodles; tigers, not kittens; devils, not schoolgirls.

On the topic of the rage for tail-wagging, lovable little Arlecchini who tease playfully, we prefer to pass over in silence.

Set Forms of *Lazzi*

In general, this form is any *lazzo* prepared with acrobatic sleight-of-hand techniques. An acrobatic *lazzo* can be neutral before being put in place. A somersault, a cartwheel, a backflip, and juggling of three, four, or more objects are all dynamic, nondramatic actions if observed during their technical execution outside the comedy, but also within the comedy if their application is not justified by the situation. The actor is trained in acrobatics and in juggling and has studied these practices neutrally, that is, without dramatizing the techniques; he has used his body, reflexes, and abilities to succeed technically.

If we take a front somersault and think about how to stage it, we have an almost unlimited number of possible placements: the character receives a kick in the behind and is projected forward onto the ground, executing a somersault in the fall; he will do this while *launching* the mask toward the audience in the moment of receiving the blow, which triggers it, and making an imaginary question mark spring out of his head as in a cartoon, as though to say, "What's happening to me?" Then he will fall disastrously, that is, by "interpreting" the somersault, which in itself is perfectly executed, without trouble or mistakes for the actor executing it. The same somersault can be effected to avoid an obstacle, to grab something on the fly, or for a thousand other reasons, interpreted each time. Just like a word that can be expressed with an infinite number of meanings and shadings, the same applies to a gesture learned beforehand.

Where ability in the manipulation of objects is added to this, the techniques can be juggled according to the same principle as that applied to acrobatics; the objects fly, expressing a chaos that is maintained by the perfect control of juggling technique. Technique, neutral in itself, is camouflaged by dramatization, which prevails. Proceeding on to the prearrangement of *lazzi*, these are always perfectly organized and structured: there is a motive, a consequence, and a conclusion.

CLASSIFICATIONS

Classifying the characters can be extraordinarily helpful to the immediate composition of complex behavioral solutions. Naturally this phase has nothing to do with any idea of simple formulas for obtaining good results without too much effort or study. The final result must necessarily be more complex and profound; but the impulse, the stimulus to search more deeply that derives from recombining these modules, is strong and exciting, especially for the comprehensibility that immediately permeates all the work of elaboration of the character and its use, even improvisationally, before an audience.

The value of the classification of the characters is a means of enriching by inclusion, by the addition of culturally recognizable suggestions, identifiable or intuitional, which have great evocative force. The actor applies them consciously and elaborates them with his talent.

Analogical Classifications

The Ages of Human Life

Biological

Adolescence/youth:	Lovers
Adulthood:	Servants
Middle age:	Capitano, Ladies
Old age:	Dottore, Magnifico

Symbolic

Infancy that discovers and experiments:	Zanni
Age of initiation, adolescence:	Lovers
Sensual, carnal youth:	Infarinato, Servant Girls
Fullness of adulthood:	Capitano, Ladies
Jovial old age:	Dottore
Aged old age:	Magnifico
One foot in the grave:	Tartaglia

The Doctrine of the Humors

There are aspects of past cultures that, due to the striking suggestiveness of certain images, words, or expressions, continue to be part of our lexical and even behavioral baggage, even though we know those cultures have been surpassed. That is the case with the *doctrine of the humors,* described by Hippocrates (460–377 B.C.E.), but already existent before him, which held on until the eighteenth century of the modern era.

The language of this doctrine seems elaborated purposely to describe the passions, what we might call a theatrical language.[2] And we have a duty not to resist its fascination.

When we refer to the characteristic behavior of someone, we speak of *temperament.* When we are in one psychological condition or another, we distinguish the conditions by calling them *humors.* To be in a black humor or have a sanguine temperament are expressions from the defunct doctrine of the humors that no longer has scientific validity, but they are still in use in colloquial speech.

The humoral body is an aggregate of liquids, the humors, and the solids that contain them. Vital phenomena are born from the action of these liquids. The humors are blood, which is the material of our body; phlegm; yellow bile or choler; and black bile. The equilibrium of the humors constitutes *crasi,* or good temperament; disequilibrium is *discrasia,* bad temperament, the excess of one humor with respect to the others.

An excess of blood, hot and humid, produces a sanguine temperament: happy and jocund, simple and pleasant.

An excess of phlegm, cold and humid, produces a phlegmatic temperament: lazy, a friend of leisure, slow to react, passive, gentle.

An excess of yellow bile or choler, hot and dry, produces a choleric or bilious temperament: impulsive and ardent, brave and fallacious, audacious, strong, fraudulent and shrewd; a great eater.

An excess of black bile, cold and dry, produces a melancholy temperament or black humor: silent, insomniac, timid, reserved, studious, avaricious.

The equilibrium of the humors creates the perfect temperament.[3]

Commedia dell'Arte is born and develops during the period in which the humoral doctrine holds full sway. But the arrangement of the humors in Commedia, although apparently obvious due to the presence of the Dottore and illnesses—always presumed, with the exception of the maladies of love—that afflict the various characters, is difficult and little developed.

On the level that we might call scientific, only the tirades of Graziano (that is, of the Dottore, who often calls himself Graziano) develop themes drawn from the science of that era.

Symbolically, humors and temperaments suggest momentary states rather than permanent orientations. Choler can overcome anybody in Commedia; the way of letting it boil will differ. Commedia in its totality can be considered sanguine, at least in the meaning of "extroverted" that we normally give to the word, but also bilious, which entails becoming uncontrollably and dangerously impassioned with things. While blood flows a bit all over and splashes continuously, phlegm may have trouble finding a place for itself: Lovers, perhaps, who commiserate in certain situations, passively abandoned to perverse destiny? Certainly, but only for very brief moments. Blood immediately rushes to the head and something strong, whether hot-humid or hot-dry, must be done, anything but remaining for long in the passive and unpleasant *paciugo* (mushiness) of cold-humid. The Lover, further, often shows saturnine behaviors, that of a hypochondriac, and a black humor, the fault of course of love, and these sentiments can be shared with the self-defensive actions of the Magnifico.

But action is action: bile and blood go to work right away.

The analogy of characters to the four humors is difficult but beautiful. It can give splendid results in specifically studied situations by a poetic recombination of those liquids that the science of the time mixed and dosed with great seriousness.

We have therefore four humors or liquids of the body, each indicating a basic temperament. We can create these analogies:

Sanguine temperament:	First and Second Zanni, Servant Girls, Infarinato
Phlegmatic temperament:	Lovers in states of passive abandon or self-commiseration; Pulcinella permanently
Choleric temperament:	The Capitano and the Dottore
Melancholy temperament:	Lovers and the Magnifico

Animality

Associating characters with animals, "animalizing" them, is a traditional practice, but often highly dubious. In our research we have experimented with many solutions, including that—which is after all normal—of the non-animality of the characters. Still, the practice of using animals as reference points has always been very helpful to bring out that "certain something" that is not quite human in the presence of all the masks.

Certain animals recur in all the improvisations; others turn up only rarely, while others are completely unknown to the actors. We have arrived at a module, which we offer here more as a suggestion and methodological example. The fauna are clearly Eurocentric, with the single exception of the chimpanzee.

Primitive Zanni and Zagne:	Chicken
First Zanni, evolved:	Fox, marten, weasel
Second Zanni, evolved:	Cat, chimpanzee
Pulcinella:	Chicken
Servant Girl (Fantesca):	Cud-chewing grazing animal (cow, buffalo, goat, sheep)
Servant Girl (Servetta):	Dove, pigeon, pheasant, hen, sparrow
Infarinato:	Poodle, parakeet
Pantalone (Magnifico):	Turkey, vulture, beetle (cockroach)
Dottore:	Pig, mastiff
Tartaglia:	Several types of owl
Capitano:	Rooster, peacock, stallion
Lady:	Peacock (peahen), mare
Flavio:	Purebred dog or cat
Isabella:	Purebred dog or cat
Cavalier:	Purebred racehorse
Amazon:	Purebred racehorse

The Realms of Nature

These symbols possess powerful expressive content, effective in motivating improvisation and interpretation. The dynamic identification of the realms is easily recognizable as a quality of a character. All the shadings and variations on the theme of realm of nature can be immediately put to use and be of value on the level of expression and interpretation.

Animal:	Servants and Capitano
Vegetable:	Lovers
Mineral:	Old Men

The Elements of Nature

Just as for the realms, with the elements we have a module of great expressive effectiveness. Realms and elements of nature refer back to extremely important artistic experiments for art, such as the study of perception between imagination and evidence, as is seen in the work of the painter Arcimboldo. Let's classify the character types by the elements.

Earth:	Old Man
	Concreteness and stability. Heart of stone. Hardness. Sententiousness. He is as silent as the tomb and has one foot in the grave.
Air:	Capitano
	A balloon. He gives himself airs. He flaps however the wind blows. He arrives blown by a good or evil wind. He goes with the wind. He gets by, thanks to the four winds.
Water:	The Lover
	The source of life. As fluent as his gestures, as his language. Tears like dew or rain. Unmoving. Stagnant. Agitated. Misty. Waxes and wanes. Tempestuous. Bottomless.
Fire:	Servant
	Deep combustion. Embers under the ashes. Flowing lava. A sleeping or erupting volcano. Fire and flames. A fire of straw. Will-o-the wisp. Stove, oven, furnace. Reduced to an ember.

Materiality

Following are examples of materiality, an emotional condition expressed with the dynamic of a nonelemental material:

Zanni: Too tired to go on and "reduced to a rag," the character appears to be a worn-out scrap of cloth physically. His voice, pronunciation, and ragged lexicon reinforce this condition.

Lovers: When relations become strained between them, their behavior becomes icy, resembling the crystallization of water.

Dottore: Explaining a recipe in which he describes butter melting in a bain-marie, he seems to melt as well—his expression melts; his words melt; his pronunciation emanates that lovely warmth, that bain-marie, and that Maria. The actor is carrying out a dynamic identification.

Magnifico: Everyone wants his money, and he rolls up like a hedgehog; he becomes spiny. The actor reflects spininess in the actions and behaviors of his character.

Capitano: Scared to death, he flees gaseously. In a gaseous state, he invents a great exit for his character, "scattering himself."

The Seasons

Naturally we insist on appealing and useful symbolic associations even if they are dubious. In the case of the seasons, the association is a poetic provocation. In its apparent obviousness, it affirms and confirms carnevalism, the natural philosophy of Commedia:

Spring:	Lovers
Summer:	Servants
Autumn:	Capitano
Winter:	Old Men

Love

All the characters in Commedia love. Each one does it in a recognizable and characteristic way without ambiguity or the possibility of confusion with the other characters. The four archetypes above already possess all the requisite characteristics of love, which each mask develops by applying them to specific situations. Let's look at love type by archetype.

Lovers: Idealized love, the beloved person is more to be dreamed of than "touched," the physical presence of the beloved person can actually be an obstacle if in that moment the lover adores a fetish, for example, a letter. Passion, anguish, jealousy, capriciousness, fights, reconciliations. Adolescent love, blushing, pounding hearts. The Lovers' gestures come from the aesthetics of classical statuary: pure, perfect, heroic. The breast is the dynamic center of gesture, of heroic behavior. For love, the Lovers can undergo any torture, any sacrifice, even—this is the ultimate that a Lover can give—any humiliation. Out of the desperation of love, the Lovers go mad: if the beloved dies or marries someone else, madness is certain. But when a misunderstanding is cleared up (because it's always only a misunderstanding), healing is immediate and love returns reinforced, sealed by the suffering withstood.

Old Men: Libidinous love, longing for the lost ability to love, a presumptuous regurgitation, pious illusion, but low love, very low. An old lover is a rapacious wolf, sexually aroused, possessed by the demon of lust, even though by now in his life it's all only in his head, because nothing is left of his ancient sexual potency. Just the same, love is love, and the tangle of the whole play almost always arises from the out-of-place love of the Old Men.

Servants: Playful, dynamic, healthy love; heart-pounding that doesn't exclude sexual excitation; psychophysical enthusiasm. The love of the Servants is expressed onstage through rituals and courting between male and female, and an energy develops that allows us to imagine explosive amorous encounters. Sometimes he collapses due to excessive work or too many masters, but she doesn't pardon him his failings. It may happen that the Servant Girl leaves her Zanni, casting him into desperation: she does it unexpectedly and only not to have him in the way as she maneuvers a very delicate situation. But what does he know? Zanni, out of desperation (and only because of that) can try suicide. Zanni's suicide always resolves itself positively with the abandonment of his intentions, thanks to sudden and providential reversals in the situation, but the attempts at suicide are occasions for great *lazzi*.

Capitano: Titanic love; planetary love. Great battles and great loves are part of his heroic baggage. He's a type who stops by to visit Jove, beats him at billiards (the planets are the balls), has sex with Venus (and Juno as well, while Jove is busy lining up a particularly difficult shot), and then comes back to Earth. His female equivalent, the Lady, is equal to him in every way. Together, at the expense of the Old Man, her husband, they constitute a perfectly functioning erotic couple. She conducts all the games and he is entirely happy with that arrangement.

Food

"You are what you eat" is never so true as in Commedia. How and what do the characters of Commedia eat?

Magnifico: Little, very little; leftovers, remains, crumbs. Nothing fresh: rancid, moldy, dried-out, degenerated food, but never much of it. If he had a refrigerator, he would keep it turned off and leave the food outside, propped against the refrigerator itself, an economical use of an appliance.

Dottore: A great gastronome, both connoisseur and chef, the Dottore considers great quantity and high quality to be perfectly equivalent. This suits his placement in Commedia dell'Arte, because the actor who plays this role has the same convictions with regard to quantity and quality.

Zanni/Zagna: Eat whenever they can, little and often like wild animals. For Zanni, food is almost never ready or good for cooking: it is alive, it moves, it must be captured. Flying insects are good, as well as bodily parasites and those in their clothing, which are at hand in abundance. Zanni's body is a veritable hunting reserve. He is a complete ecosystem and would be self-sufficient if it weren't for the small size of the creatures it contains, which are not enough to provide for survival.

Flies are a great help to him. In Commedia dell'Arte, there exists no *lazzo* of the fly; rather, there are numerous *lazzi* for every single fly, not to mention *lazzi* for mosquitoes, fleas, lice, cockroaches, bedbugs, moths, mice, rats, and chickens. It's up to the actor to invent them. When Zanni eats something cooked, it's always small, the fruit of small thefts. On the extremely rare occasions when he eats as much as he likes, he risks suicide, death by indigestion. In *The Last Will and Testament of Zanni*,[4] the "dying" Zanni prepares for the great passage:

per avi' pieni i budei	to have my belly full
de gnocc e sbrofadei	of gnocchi and *sbrofadei*

Servant Girls: Often and well; nibbling, because they are cooks and responsible for buying food and running the kitchen, but also due to their winning shrewdness.

Infarinato: Gluttonously, onanistically. By stealing, scheming, conning others. Or simply by serving himself. A great finger-sucker (his own, spattered with food, obviously).

Capitano/Lady: Sensually. True, great gourmands. Timbales, meats, cheeses, wines. The Lady grants herself this because she has money and servants, the Capitano because he scrounges. Food and sex in great quantities and the best quality. Lucky them.

Lovers: Very little, very fresh. Vegetables, not because they are vegetarians, but because vegetables are bloodless and refined, whereas there is something truculent and vulgar about meat. Sweets and rosolio cordials in moments of genuine sensual folly. When the Lover is gloomy (which happens often), he or she completely forgets about the very existence of food and feels no hunger. In any case, Lovers never experience actual hunger; that's for servants, for *zanni*. At the most, they may go so far as to feel a gentle pang. Eating is, in general, a vulgar affair. The verb itself, *mangiare,* is one that they would never pronounce. Fasting and anorexia are characteristic of the Lovers, or on the contrary, either for love or hate, the bacchanal.

Astrology

We consider astrology to be a highly evocative and playful cultural expression, necessary in that it is fun and very close in certain aspects to the game of characterization used in the craft of acting, and thus a quite useful discipline.

We do not believe in astrology as science or art because—as far as has been determined—the constellations are only what we are able to see from where we are positioned. The traditional astrological viewpoint of the constellations does not actually exist, and their influence has never been demonstrated. Nevertheless, the mechanism of combinations that lead to the definitions of the various characteristic personalities is highly evocative from an artistic and poetic viewpoint.

We have attempted here to give an attribution, sign by sign, according to traditional interpretations, of the principal characters of Commedia.

Aries	Second Zanni	Instinctive, Brilliant, Disastrous
Taurus	First Zanni	Attentive, Crafty, Irresistible
Gemini	Infarinato	Imaginative, Standoffish, Practical Joker
Cancer	Lovers	Tender, Oversensitive, Passionate
Leo	Lady	Possessive, Dominating, Excessive
Virgo	Servant Girl	Charming, Vivacious, Spicy, Intriguing (weaving intrigues)
Libra	Lovers	Narcissistic, Refined, Perfectionist, Susceptible, Capricious
Scorpio	Fantesca	Untiring, Carnal, Invasive
Sagittarius	Dottore	Authoritarian, Presumptuous, Jovial
Capricorn	Magnifico	Reserved, Stubborn, Indestructible
Aquarius	Capitano	Volatile, Vain, Grandiose
Pisces	Zagna	Simple, Sensual, Unpredictable

Symbols

The symbols exercise is endless. As an example, we describe here the symbolism offered by Italian and French playing cards.

Italian Cards

The four suits of traditional Italian playing cards, diffused throughout the Mediterranean basin, are *denari* or *ori* (that is, coins or gold pieces, the equivalent of diamonds), *coppe* (that is, cups, the equivalent of our hearts), *spade* (that is, swords, the equivalent of our spades), and *bastoni* (clubs).

Diamonds: We associate this suit with old age in the sense of stability achieved and economic tranquility; more symbolically, as a money chest, where great wealth is deposited, as a necessary condition of the plutocrat. Pluto, the god of wealth but also of the bowels of the Earth, presides over his treasures, sees to their conservation, and in this we recognize the Magnifico-Earth. Descending ever more into the bowels of the symbol, we find him digging a pit that is his tomb and the hiding place of his immense treasures accumulated throughout his long life, ever deeper until we arrive at hell, the greatest of all treasure-houses, the realm of Pluto himself.

Hearts: This suit alludes to pleasure achieved but above all to desire, the anticipation of pleasure, even more sensual than pleasure itself. The cup, furthermore, is to be taken as a symbol and sign of authentic femininity, full, both container and contained. Hearts pertain to female Lovers and Servant Girls. Male Lovers assuage their thirst at the cup of love.

Spades: Symbol of heroism, the spade is also a symbol "of itself," and therefore ostentatious. It also stands for exhibitionism and vainglory; luminosity, importance, distinction; swaggering, conceitedness, and "don't you know who I am?" qualities of Capitano and Lady.

Clubs: The club—a war club or mace—is a symbol of animality and sensuality without complexity. It is an object that brings immediate resolution without mediation. A *low* weapon for giving and taking blows, it is also a decisive object in nonviolent situations, usable for leaning on, reaching things, pushing away, moving things, cracking nuts, scratching one's back, and hiding behind. Simultaneously a symbol and parody of power, it is also a phallic symbol. It is Zanni.

French Cards

Used throughout the world, French cards have four suits: *diamants* (diamonds), *trèfles* (clovers, or clubs), *coeurs* (hearts), and *piques* (spades). With French cards, the symbolism changes direction. They cannot be associated as the Italian cards can with the four archetypes of Commedia dell'Arte. Instead, they lend themselves to describing the four types of behavior of the Lovers:

Diamonds:	Domination by pride
Clubs:	Domination by affection
Hearts:	Domination by passion
Spades:	Domination by torment

Jazz

Jazz is the artistic discipline with the most analogies to Commedia. There are many fundamental points in common:

- ☞ Popular origin and diffusion
- ☞ Individual possession of the artist's own *arte;* the artist as master responsible for his or her *arte,* whether as a soloist or in concert with colleagues
- ☞ Specialization
- ☞ Recurrence of instruments similar to the recurrence of types
- ☞ Improvisation on a theme based on the improvised choice that the artist makes, dipping into his or her reservoir of knowledge and experience, which constitutes the artist's "state of consciousness" at the moment of the improvisation

☞ General schemes and modules of improvisation

☞ As a principle, in jazz there is no "ugly" sound or voice and no ugly harmonic, melodic, or rhythmic solution, just as in Commedia, in principle, there are no "awkward" gestures, ugly voices, or incorrect sentences; nor, in either discipline, is there "too much" or "too little," aesthetically speaking.

☞ In jazz as in improvised comedy, an accident becomes an opportunity, as the artists direct whatever happens next.

☞ No performance identical to another

☞ The audience must have fun, must be happy. Certainly, this is true for jazz and Commedia and for improvising artists in particular, who are acutely aware of the need to please and make audiences feel good. Jazz and Commedia are sensual.

We'll stop here with jazz, but the subject merits a thorough study.

Cartoons

The modern North American cartoon series is, in our opinion, the modern expression closest to Commedia. Take any cartoon, the first that comes to mind, say, *Popeye.* It has fixed types, recurrent behaviors, perfectly recognizable characters; *lazzi* or gags; standard situations; fixed schema. Another, say, *Roadrunner:* same thing. Another, *Tom and Jerry:* same. You can continue the exercise on your own. Certainly, these cartoon series are not Commedia itself. The most important analogies are those, very difficult to describe, that concern *lazzi.*

Cartoon gags and Commedia *lazzi* often coincide surprisingly in their dynamics. For example, in their excess: when a character falls from the top of a skyscraper, he makes a huge hole in the street, then comes out of the hole beat up but carries on; and a moment later he is perfectly reconstituted and more energetic than before.

In Commedia, the epic gesture can represent a perfectly equivalent action. *The Zanni Skin Komedy* is a theater piece that combines Commedia, cartoons, and comic books: it is set in a megalopolis and the protagonists are two *zanni* skinheads, similar to members of urban extremist or marginal groups. The two skinheads in the story travel throughout the metropolis, destroying whatever there is to destroy; they beat people, they attack women, all with the almost infantile ingenuousness that characterizes all *zanni* and their contemporary equivalents. Offering a muttlike charm and a *lazzi* style that bring a whole monstrous city to life from the very bottom, from the underground, the actors use nothing but their own expressive methods and perform in an evocative cartoon style.

Another analogy between Commedia and cartoon is the indestructibility of the cartoon character, which is identical to the mask. The characters in cartoons are masks because they are archetypes: *the* rabbit, *the* coyote, *the* mouse, *the* duck, or *the* sailor in the case of Popeye, and *the* woman in the case of Olive.

The absurd as a comic progression is present in Commedia and cartoon in the same way.

The *psychologies*, in their dynamic and expressive use, are social and stereotypical, not individual and particular. The psychology of Donald Duck is not his own except when combined with his image, because it has been conceived and constructed by observing and transcribing innumerable varieties of that type of behavior, where innumerable variants stand for many different people.

In conclusion, when the author of these lines puts on the mask of Pulcinella, he becomes a colleague of Donald Duck.

Sport

Many analogies can be found between Commedia and team sports. Soccer is one of the most popular sports in the world and an excellent example for a comparison of Sport with Commedia.

From the perspective of someone completely foreign to the two forms of play, the first element in common that jumps to the eye is repetition. If we watch ten different Commedia plays and ten different soccer games, we outsiders find that all twenty are repetitive. More or less the same things are said and done onstage as on the field, in the seats as in the stands. And that's not all. What follows presumes that the comedy is well played and that the game has players who can score.

Commedia dell'Arte	Soccer
They always dress the same	They always dress the same
They always have the same name	They always wear the same number
The play the same story over and over	They play the same game over and over
The gestures are always the same	The moves are always the same
The audience expresses pleasure in a set way	The crowd expresses exultation in a set way
The audience always has fun	The crowd is always excited

Every time they redo the same thing involving the same external appearance, they develop that certain thing in a way that makes it new at the moment of execution but equal to the preceding time and the next time.

The audience shows that it already knows a great deal, it understands rules, systems, and probabilities but not the result of the present moment, which is unfolding and keeping the audience excited, or at least interested.

Furthermore, the audience always appreciates the performances: if good, they award praise; if bad, they castigate.

There are spectators who refuse to become excited but enjoy the show however it develops and turns out.

We outsiders recognize that in the stadium, as in the theater, enjoyment comes from the application of a system of rigid rules that generate surprise.

Theatrical Classifications

Integrating the Commedia characters into categories drawn from other theatrical eras and related disciplines can be illuminating for better understanding the masks. But the comparisons must be logical and historically valid, based on specific knowledge of exchanges of influence between genres and disciplines.

Origins

Knowing the cultural origins of the types, characters, and masks adds authority and individual specificity to improvisation. Experimenting with hypotheses about mixed and multifaceted origins can fuel and enrich results.

Magnifico

The aged father of Latin comedy and the same character in humanist comedy are unquestionably useful sources for the definition of the Magnifico.

In Ruzante's play *Bilora*, he is already a fully formed character, named Andronico, in his fundamental human qualities: he is old and wealthy and "acquires" for himself a young woman at the expense of her natural and (legitimate) man. Andronico ends up killed by Bilora, an end that will never befall the later Magnifico (except in the form of a thorough beating).

In Commedia the Magnifico is a merchant and the social reference is omnipresent, but above all he is a libidinous old man attracted by a younger woman.

A Magnifico-Winter, who wants to "stop time," so as to survive at all costs, who wants to avoid the arrival of the spring that will kill him, and who must be sawed, burned, drowned, torn to bits, and destroyed to make way for new life, is a very clear carnevalesque symbol that dates back to the very origin of the figure.

At the beginning, the young woman plagued by the Magnifico was a Zagna played by a man in a mask. It was eminently grotesque and a farcical comedy. With the arrival of actresses, the love of the old man for the young woman becomes truly impossible and the plots, due to the increased number of actors, become more complex.

Magnifico's attachment to money is obviously drawn from the real world of the merchant, completely immersed in a practice and philosophy of life in which money is the absolute, principal reference point and the goal of all action.

If money characterized and still characterizes the development of civilization, Magnifico is a synthesis of the history of civilization, or at least of the history of money. From the coin to the credit card, Magnifico accompanies the evolution of money from something physical to something virtual; from a recognizable, tangible object to an invisible concentration of enormous wealth; from something sensual to something sublimated. He is all these things, much more than a mere miser.

Dottore

The Pedant of humanist comedy cannot be considered uniquely the predecessor of the Commedia Dottore. They both have pedantry in common, the wish always to teach something to somebody, but this does not mean that they have the same function in the comedies in which they appear. Their respective functional positions are decidedly different. The Pedant is an educator and is in service to a master. The Dottore is a master who has others at his service. The Pedant appears to be a subtype in the history of the character of the Dottore, an invention of "recovery" subsequent to the original character and one which generates a somewhat watered-down version of the original Dottore, who in our opinion was born from a rib of the Magnifico and from the need for a balancing comic counterpart to the merchant.

The Dottore is the "other" old man, the *spalla* (that is, the partner in comic repartee) of the Magnifico, or his double, or his rival, antagonist, friend-enemy, associate-competitor. Like the Magnifico, he is the father of one of the Lovers and he is also subject to falling in love with impossible or inappropriate objects of desire such as a Servant Girl or a female Lover. And he pays all the inevitable consequences.

The Dottore makes a "claim" of great knowledge. But is it really true? Like the Capitano, he is a braggart, a "boaster" of knowledge, *a charlatan.*

The charlatan is the true model for the Dottore. He "flaunts" his knowledge to others, confident of their ignorance. He knows how to convince, how to charm, and even how to make people afraid.

The Dottore, who is all knowing with particular specialties in law and medicine, tends rather to intoxicate his listeners with words than to weave intrigues. His tirades, his endless speechifying, the soliloquies that characterize his long scenes, are acts of verbal, phonetic, linguistic, vocal, and respiratory virtuosity, based on the double talent of a great improviser and one who picks up things by ear (because he isn't truly learned). He twists, reels and unreels, and immobilizes his listeners, who fruitlessly try to get a word in edgewise, with the unique and absolute goal of proving that he is right. And then? Advantages: concrete and economic, contractual clauses in exactly the terms he wants, weddings agreed upon according to his wishes, his children sworn to behaving just as he says, everybody doing just what he wants, including an audience that laughs.

The Dottore also has origins in Carnevale. A lay version of the king of Carnevale, he is the representation of excess, overdoing everything: his speaking, his gestures. His body is excessive, enormous, gigantic, fat; he is capable of ingesting an excessive quantity of food; he is excessive in the exhibitionism of his rages.

The Dottore is not evil. On the contrary, he is a major sensualist and when he inveighs, he does it to find the words of greatest effect, and they bring him a supreme pleasure, in net contrast to the severity of his invective. Whatever he says is only to demonstrate that no one can put it the way he does. Certainly, for Zanni just as for the daughter or son of his colleague-competitor the Magnifico, he appears overwhelming. But the audience can see perfectly well that he is a big but innocuous old sow, an affectionate father, and a sensualist. He is definitely not "innocent"; he is an extreme egoist and is unquestionably responsible for the dramas endured by the younger characters, and he has to pay for that. However, he is very sharp about evading responsibility and sending ahead his "friend" the Magnifico, who will pay, harshly, for everything.

The Dottore is a Rabelaisian figure, not only because of his physical proportions and his formidable appetite but also because of his taste—this, extremely sophisticated—for theorizing (always *pro domo sua* [to his own advantage]) anything and everything, for schematic illustrations of phenomena that anticipate both futurism and surrealism, and for interminable and astonishing lists.

Zanni

The most ambivalent of all the masks, Zanni is born a devil and an immigrant. He is immediately both First and Second Zanni. Seized by duty and necessity but also by the wish to play, he is permanently active in a game of construction and deconstruction of relationships, schemes, messages, maneuvers, manipulations, small, medium, and large acts of survival. He *does* to achieve goals, he *undoes* to repair the mess of what goes wrong, and vice versa.

Zanni is a stupid genius: both his genius and his stupidity contribute equally to preventing him from approaching life in a rational manner. He can't do the simplest things but pulls off the impossible: these achievements are always connected to his chimpanzeelike agility and his lightning intuition, no matter how brief its duration.

If he wants to go from point A to point B following a straight line, not only will he not follow the straight line, he will never even arrive at point B. Or if by some chance he makes it there, it will be by sheer chance, by accident, by necessity, by love, but never because of his own planning and will, because his plan and will have fragmented along the way into a thousand points, each of which goes off on its own development (great is the actor who can do this completely, and great the joy of the audience).

Zanni is a disrespectful devil who is not aware of being one. On the other hand, he is perfectly aware of being an immigrant who might have to leave at a moment's notice. The result is always the same: making and unmaking, creating disasters and resolving them. Because of this, at the end he will receive both the prize and the punishment.

Zanni possesses different levels of importance, not in his role but in his relations with other characters. He may be viewed by others, depending on that level, as follows:

Most wretched level:	As a scratching chicken, the dog outside, a house cat
Threatened level:	"If I find that Zanni, I'll break his back!"
Low level:	"Porter! The trunk!"
Medium level:	"Zanni, I need your help"
High level:	"Zanni, I need your skill, your ability, your acumen"
Highest level:	"You incredibly precious man! My life itself depends on you!"

The wave movement provoked by the succession and alternation of these levels forces Zanni to reinvent continuously his position in the story; from one moment to the next he may feel himself to be useless, nonexistent, indispensable, or in danger.

Servetta

The Servant Girl (Servetta) is derived from the Zagna. Zagna is Zanni in every way except for gender. The Zagna "woman" was played by a male actor until the advent of actresses. At that point, Zagna disappeared, and the Fantesca appeared, a role that will soon be fixed as the Servetta. The Servetta is an improvement in physical, aesthetic, intellectual, and functional terms, on the Zagna:

The Zagna is ugly; the Servetta is pretty.

The Zagna is rather animalistic; the Servetta is decidedly human.

The Zagna, like Zanni, is illiterate; the Servetta can manage pretty well with both letters and numbers.

The Zagna has no overall vision of matters; the Servetta is very acute. She is the only "intelligent" person in all Commedia. By intelligent, we mean that she is capable of organizing plans and carrying them out rigorously and cynically.

The Servetta is the first important creative and professional manifestation of the actress, who owes nothing to the past (except her origins from the Zanni), whereas many of the "sparkling" female figures of many modern forms of theater owe everything to her. The characteristics of beauty, eclecticism, shrewdness, vivacity, and continuous dialogue with the audience of the Servetta will be transferred—completely detached from any dramatic function, serving for pure entertainment—into the most popular and diffuse of her evolutions: the *soubrette* of French comic theater.

Infarinato

The Infarinato is an evolution of the Zanni but in some way "recovers" the civilized quality of the servants of erudite comedy that had been abandoned by Zanni, who is decidedly savage. The Infarinato evolves from Zanni through the elaborations of the actors themselves during the period when Commedia restructures itself in response to the appearance of the actress. We might consider the invention of the Infarinato as a sort of male response to the arrival of the female, proud and unmasked.

The white of the coarse Zanni costume, which, without color, indicates poverty, becomes instead a sign of cleanliness with the Infarinato, thus indicating an economic and social evolution. The Infarinato has real, clean clothes to wear, unlike the patches and rags of the Zanni. Infarinato cleans his clothes, he even cleans himself—testifying that a leap in mentality has taken place—he sleeps in a bed under a roof and he eats every day. It is only natural that he be a zealous and "trustworthy" servant, because for him it is a matter of maintaining the enviable position he has achieved.

The mask gives way to the face, which is kept masked by the application of white makeup covering the oval of the visage. White on the face is imposed symbolically, associated with the white of his original costume; it confirms the poverty of his social status and his symbolic ghostliness. The white face is perfectly readable on a visual level and suggests elegance, thus an improvement over the original Zanni.

Explanations of the white face, such as the one that considers it to be a vestige of the character's origin as a miller's servant, a stupid clod who constantly falls into the flour, may indeed be amusing and logical in the sense that one who falls into flour will have a white face. But this is completely extraneous to the formation of the signs that mark the image and meaning of a character.

Pedrolino, the most famous name for an Infarinato character, had, before assuming the famous all-white image, the same characteristics as Arlecchino: a dark, monkeylike mask and a patched costume. The same is true for Mezzetino, another famous Infarinato type. Did they all fall into vats of flour? Did they lose their masks in there? Let's be clear: Infarinato stands for white powdered face; it is a technical term that indicates a character and gives neither direct biographical data nor keys to interpretation.

We hold that the actors who invented the Infarinato followed the path marked out by the women. Throwing away the Zagna mask—performed by men—the actresses instead exalted their own natural beauty, because they must have been beautiful, seeing as how they were actual women. Now, the famous Infarinato, developing through the efforts of numerous actors, renounced the mask as well in favor of the charm of the real face, but since it was not as naturally beautiful as that of the women, the actors needed to apply some form of treatment.

Legends such as the one of the flour should also be rejected for the following reason: Commedia is an eminently urban form. Agrarian activities have nothing to do with the stories and actions of the characters, who are merchants, intellectuals, soldiers, tradesmen, and servants. They are not farmers, priests, or noblemen. In a word, they are citizens. In Commedia, there are no millers, winemakers, farmers, or herdsmen; there are not even hunters or fishermen. Food and the other products of the countryside, mountains, sky, and sea, arrive in the city ready for eating. The nostalgia of the servants for the valleys of their homelands serves only to underline their coarse peasant origins. Such genres as the pastoral comedy, with its sub-genres set by the sea or in the forests, are highly literary in origin, a recuperation of images derived from the classical world of Arcadia, adopted first by the humanists and then by Commedia. The peasants and shepherds in pastoral works are not coarse, they don't stink; on the contrary, they are sublimely beautiful, elegant, sweet-smelling, and refined intellectuals.

The world of Commedia is the *civitas,* the city and its civilization. Popes and cardinals, kings and princes: out! Here, there is only space for normal and productive people, where we watch the actions of characters who put their all into affirming that very image of themselves.

The Infarinato, who is a character of improvised comedy to which we attribute great expressive and symbolic importance, appeared to affirm this fact by "civilizing" the servant, rendering him definitively urban, metropolitan.

The exclusion of popes and kings from Commedia is without doubt an act of prudence on the part of the comics to brake their critical impulses toward those holding power (princes, moreover, were the ones who financed the Commedia companies). The same prudence prevented them from dragging in the clergy and religion (here, finances were not in play but rather the risk of persecution).

In *Love Is a Drug* (*La Creduta Morta*) by Flaminio Scala, Pedrolino dresses as a woman out of pure pleasure, and out of pure pleasure comes the misunderstanding of the Lover who courts him, thinking him to be his beloved. Pedrolino adopts a "reason" for his conduct, which is separate from the problems inherent to the plot or from the possibility that the plot could furnish the pretext for dressing as a woman. The idea—which we have developed and tested with convincing results—that the Infarinato is often effeminate is confirmed by innumerable details such as this moment in *Love Is a Drug*. We need not list every other bit of evidence we have uncovered for this conclusion. Our work is aesthetic-methodological and neither historical nor philological. The Infarinato, for example, is very rarely in love. His "foreignness" to love with women—which will be corrected in the Romantic era with the French version and Pierrot, but in that case his love is never for a corresponding female type, and in any case the form has by then lost any trace of Commedia dell'Arte—may well suit his homosexual nature, a state that would have been impermissible for an actor of the era to confess.

The world of actors and actresses has always been a welcoming and tolerant refuge for homosexuals and effeminate men, whatever they have been called from place to place and time to time (including *checche, froci, locas, folles,* gays, and, today, transsexuals). The white of his face may assume a new significance, indicating "feminine" propensities. Substituting the dark, beastlike mask of Zanni, Infarinato takes on the white of the ancient theater mask; whether tragic or comic, the whiteness undoubtedly evokes femininity. The effeminacy of the artist is resolved through the filter of a mask that is difficult to place chromatically, materially, or sexually. A sort of "evaporation" of the Zanni therefore liberates new, modern, future-oriented messages, which would be unimaginable in the hairy, uncultured, hypermasculine Zanni.

Lovers

The Lovers belong to the world of "upset normality." They would like to love each other undisturbed, make a family, have children, and enjoy a good social position and a long, tranquil life. That's what the Lovers want. The comedy comes when these aspirations are compromised. Commedia itself grows from this dramaturgical cell.

We know the Lovers especially for their bursts of passion, their boundless love. We know them to be heroic, disposed to sacrifice themselves. They never die, naturally, but death accompanies them everywhere. They pass through every imaginable hell; during the three acts, they live through the worst possible torments, and they are often overwhelmed by madness.

Zanni madness is a vestige of Carnevale, the world turned upside down; it is *morosofico* (the philosophy of folly), the premise of all Commedia, its poetic program. But the madness of Flavio and Isabella, the Lovers, is pathological. It is a grave malady, limitless suffering. There would be no Commedia without the trick, the poetic solution. The happy ending, certainly. But there's something still better. When the Lover is mad, he or she is saved. The Lover is protected from the suffering procured by self-awareness of misfortune. In madness, Flavio and Isabella find refuge and they bask in it. Normally perfect, impeccable, they are "authorized" by madness to do and say anything, at any level; it goes without saying that they descend very low. What can you do? They're insane!

In madness, in the depth of their suffering, they discover a sort of land of Cockaigne of their souls where they feel quite well. The actors and actresses have the good fortune of playing out these expressive opportunities; they never fail to give their mad characters a few flashes of lucidity, because there, in those flashes, their lacerating pain suddenly returns to them unbearably, launching them back into the need to escape their agony.

There are basically two situations that drive Lovers to madness: the beloved person dies, or the beloved is married to or about to marry another person. It goes without saying that the second is far graver than the first, as death has at least the advantage of leaving behind a pure memory of the beloved. Naturally, neither of the two materializes; it's always a misunderstanding of which the audience is perfectly aware.

The Lovers are normal people forced into an adventure. When a journey becomes necessary, which by definition signifies danger, our Lovers arm themselves if necessary with false names, perhaps wearing an androgynous mask, and even—in the case of the female Lover—changing her sex, thus discovering that the "he" hidden inside her can fight as well as or better than a man.

In our research, we have defined the variants of the Lovers according to the situations they find themselves in. We have given them technical names according to their different natures: the Cavalier and the Amazon.

Technically, the Female Lover is an Amazon both when dressed as a woman and when dressed as a man, even though the character of a woman dressed as a man always presents herself as "Cavalier This-or-That."

Particularly exciting are the duels between two cavaliers who, with their faces covered and unknown to each other, "sense" something strange about the other. They will never go so far as to kill each other, but why can't they wound each other a bit? Everything they do is for love; even their mistakes are a great proof of their love. When everything is revealed, they are happy about the blood they spilled, which unites them, bonds them, and "marries" them forever.

The Lovers exist because of the existence of the actress. When a young, lovely, rich, elegant, cultured woman arrived onstage, with her great and beautiful sentiments, there came the need for a perfectly equivalent male figure, and he appeared at the same instant.

It's stimulating to imagine the Lovers both before and after the three acts shown to the audience: before, they are unbearable adolescents, later they are boring, bickering spouses. The only part of them worth watching is what we see onstage. What they don't want from life is their best part.

Capitano

It seems a purely literary exercise to attribute the origin of Commedia's Capitano to the Pirgopolinice, the *Miles Gloriosus* of Plautus, when Italy of early Commedia was largely a Spanish colony and teemed with examples of

Don Rodrigo and Matamoro. Rather than seeking the character in books, it was enough merely to look around.

The comic actors of the Arte, after having invented everything, went looking for a past to ennoble their inventions. And since the only ennobling past at the time was the Greco-Roman one, they all went looking for classical sources. This practice continues today. Pirgopolinice is far more ancient than the Spanish invaders and gives the impression that the origins of Commedia can be found in Plautus and the *fabulae atellanae,* which Commedia does in fact resemble to a striking degree. (For example, it seems that Titus Marcus Plautus performed as the character Maccus.) But between the end of the Roman world and the advent of Commedia, there is a millennium we call the Middle Ages, during the course of which there is no record testifying to continuity between the theatrical genres of the ancient world and Commedia dell'Arte. No, the Capitano is a local slob who passes for Spanish to make himself seem more impressive.

Or perhaps he's a drunken mercenary soldier who crossed over into the territory around Bergamo, as he appears in the oldest known image of the character in the *Ludi Zanneschi,* printed by Vaccaro between 1560 and 1580.

Or still more simply (in modern terms), he is the foreigner, the stranger who comes from far away speaking unheard-of tongues, who has seen never-before-seen things, and done unheard-of things. He is a boaster, a braggart, a bar hero freeloading drinks. Just look around: the world is filled with Capitani, both male and female. The comics of Commedia knew very well that they were feeding their audience not an exotic stranger (the appearance) but a local bullshitter.

Species

We have two species of characters, plus a third, which is a mixture of the other two. We define them as *grotesque* when they are masked and *human* when they wear no masks. The Infarinato is mixed, a *semigrotesque.*

The term "grotesque" derives from the wall decorations discovered by Renaissance artists who explored Nero's palace, the Domus Aurea, which the artists regarded as a succession of grottoes. The decorative motifs show figures that mix vegetable, animal, human, and fantastic elements together. These grotesque figures subsequently became very popular in Renaissance decorative art. Anything that is not perfectly human but mixed with vegetable, animal, and fantastic elements, therefore, is grotesque. They are monstrosities that provoke laughter but laughter, some have said, "without joy."

In our case, "grotesque" indicates a condition that can be interpreted as

The enema

Magnifico at the ball

Ie suis def-honnoré, ce ruffien pipereau,   Leuer le cotillon, & la chemife auffi,   Ma vie & mon honneur entre vos mains ie mets,
M'ayât difné par cœur, encores me tourmête,   Sa Dame renuerfer comme l'amour l'apreuue,   Harlequin mon amy, prenez la iouyffance,
Et fait de ma maifon vn clapier & bordeau,   Et couler fur la motte apres fa main ainfi,   Que tant vous defirez, mais faictes que iamais,
Auec cefte putain que i'ay prife à feruante.   Frâcifquine mon cœur, en ce point con fe treque.   Hôme aucû quel qui foit, n'en aye côgnoiffance

Arlecchino and
Franceschina make love as
Pantalone spies on them.

The "ring around the rosey"

A scene from
La Famiglia dell'Antiquario
(*The Antiquarian's Family*)
by Carlo Goldoni

Pulcinella and the "Pulcicrozza"

The Charlatan, seventeenth-century engraving of the painting by K. Dujardin, 1657

A "rich" performance: the judge who is interrogating the statue is Arlecchino in disguise.

A Commedia company in action (seventeenth century)

Carnevale in Piazza Colonna, Rome

Pantalone as a cuckold
(eighteenth-century engraving)

Pulcinella and Death
(early nineteenth century)

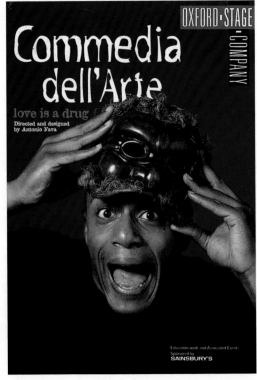

Poster for *Love Is a Drug*
(Oxford, 1995)

Pulcinella cooks
(eighteenth century)

Brighella (eighteenth century)

Giuseppe Arcimboldo, *Autumn* (1573), courtesy of the Louvre Museum

Italian playing cards

The Capitano,
drunk

Flyer by the cartoonist Clod for *The Zanni Skin Komedy*

Figure of an ancient clown,
probably Dossennus, a mask
of the *Atellan Fables*
by Francesco de' Ficoroni

Totò with the *soubrette*
Isa Barzizza

The Clown Little Pich

Zanni Primitivo. Zanni, Zani, Zane, Zan, Zuane, Zuan, Zagno, Zanin, Zuanin . . . Giovanni, Gianni, Juan, Joan, Jão, John, Jean, Hans . . . and then Zagna, Zana, Zuana, Zuanina . . . the name of everybody in one name only. Other interpretations of the origin of the name are forced or fantastical, for example, the one that makes Zanni derive from *sannio,* one of the Latin synonyms of *histrio,* buffoon, fool, comic. In the speech of regions south of the Emilian-Tuscan Apennines, the name is clearly pronounced Gianni and Gian, which are diminutives of Giovanni. The alpine-Paduan *Z* gives a dialectal pronunciation to the name but changes neither its roots nor its meaning. The name Zanni is the given name of a Commedia dell'Arte servant, historically the first of the Commedia characters, when Commedia was performed with small groups of characters who were all similar in appearance, mask, behavior, and name. "Zan" was a sort of prefix before all their names, followed by the name that characterized the individual: Zan Salciccia, Zan Fritello, Zan Tabacco, and so on. Each actor invented his own. With these characters, the first Commedia actors performed short, harsh comic stories of hunger, thievery, and fights in a shamelessly outlandish style, which they called *zannate.* The *zannate,* or zannesque comedies, staged by *zanni* actors, are the original form of Commedia dell'Arte, epitomized by these characters, who exaggerated a social type well known to the audience: the mountain people who had immigrated into the cities in search of work, shelter, and food. With the evolution of this form, due primarily to the introduction of the actress, the woman onstage, the elementary dramaturgy grows more complex, becoming comedy in the classic sense, and the various Zan become fixed as servants of various masters. By extension, used as a noun, *zanni* signifies a generic servant, the character of the servant in Commedia, any servant. The given name Zanni is thus used in plays when there is no more than one of the type, since no two Commedia characters can have the same name in a single story. The noun *zanni* is a technical term not used in performance. A master, for example, never calls for "his *zanni,*" but rather for "his servant"; if his servant happens to be named Zanni, then Pantalone calls for Zanni. An actor can play *a zanni* and might be named Zanni or some other name. Onstage therefore, we may have many *zanni,* who might be named Zanni, Brighella, Franceschina, Truffaldino, or Zan Trivella, Zan Farina, Zagna, Zan Tager, all interpreted by different actors, each a specialist in his own *zanni.*

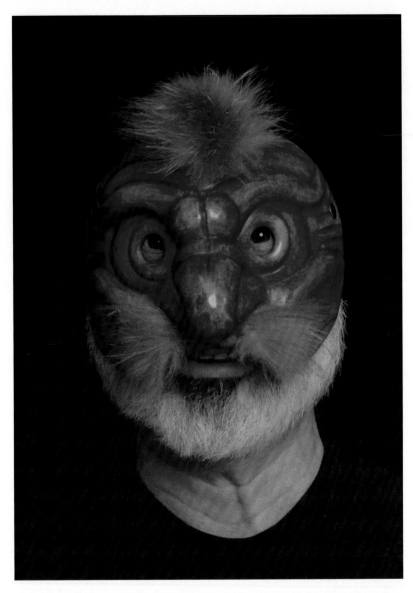

Renaissance Zanni. A mask inspired by the *trompe-l'oeil* of the *Narrentreppe* (*The Stairway of Fools*), painted by Alessandro Scalzi (known as Il Paduano [The Paduan]), in Trausnitz Castle in Bavaria. The images and situations that can be imagined from viewing the frescoes are very similar to those described by Massimo Troiano in *Discorsi delli Trionfi*. Scalzi's *Narrentreppe* may allude to the commedia described by Troiano. Our 1998 production of the mask comedy with music, *La Cortegiana Innamorata* (*The Courtesan in Love*), staged for the company Ensemble La Mascherata in Rome, was a "reconstruction" of the comedy described in Massimo Troiano's *Discorsi*.

Grand Zanni. He was baptized Grand Zanni because he is especially fit for expressing the voluminous, grand gestures of Zanni. This mask resembles the rustic, jerky, but organized and harmonious mode of the character's movement. Zanni starts off a rustic but arrives at his audience quite refined. He elaborates a sort of "gestural storytelling": all his movements explain and narrate his life, which comprises harsh experience, difficulties, and emergencies but also brilliant solutions that demonstrate how well equipped he is to face tribulation. This is all beautiful because it is full, complete, terribly necessary. The difficulty of Zanni's existence, from the point of view of the audience, represents the poetics of survival.

"Tall" Zagna. Before the arrival of the actress, female characters were played by men dressed as women. In primitive zannesque comedy, all the female characters were comic and grotesque. Zagna, the feminine counterpart to Zanni, is the formal, comic-grotesque exaggeration of the woman. The actor wore female clothing over an exaggerated female body, an effect achieved with the addition of excessive, carnevalesque accessories. The Zagna mask, similar if not identical to the male mask, and, typically, a scarf to cover the head completed the costume. The arrival of the actress, a real woman onstage, is an achievement of Commedia dell'Arte. This revolutionary event probably took place in 1560. The boom that followed is extraordinary: suddenly the feminine presence flowers everywhere. During the first period, the male Zagna coexisted with the real female Fantesca, a prototype of the Servetta (Servant Girl), until the 1580s or 1590s, when the unmasked Servetta caused the disappearance of both the Zagna and the Fantesca. The novelty of the Fantesca was the female performer and the absence of a mask, but she was traditional in using the same grotesque comedy as the masked actors in both male and female roles. The Servetta, instead, was beautiful, light, smart, and capable of scheming, solving problems, and orchestrating the most complex intrigues.

"Short" Zagna. Variation of the "Tall" Zagna

"Wolf" Zanni. In general, the term for an elongated jutting mask is "wolf." This *zanni* has wolf characteristics, and this is our mask closest to the primitive *zanni*, with a big nose and the expression of someone trying to understand what's happening. It is often endowed with a thick mustache, framed and crowned by either a real or an artificial beard. The same mask, without facial hair, can be Zagna.

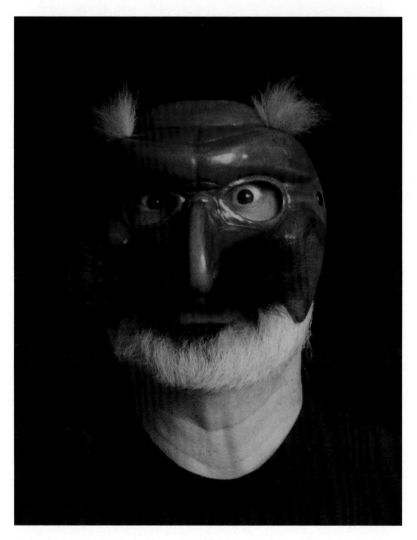

First Zanni. This mask, generically identified as First Zanni, can take on any of the names, both traditional and not, attributed to a leader *zanni,* such as Finocchio, Buffetto, or Flautino.

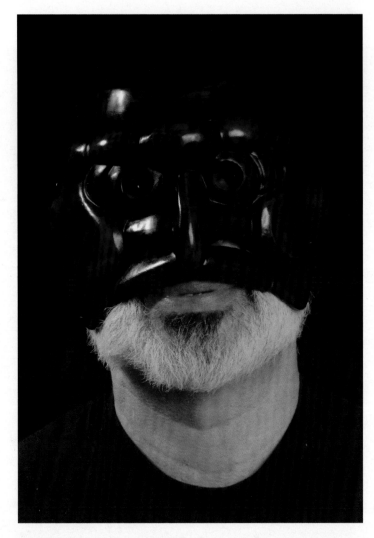

Francatrippa. One of the most ancient of the First Zanni. The name means "French tripe," implying a French stomach accustomed to being filled. Another meaning could be "free, enfranchised stomach"—a stomach into and from which anything can freely enter and exit.

Scapino. Another very famous First Zanni. The name derives from the Lombard dialect word *scapâ*, to escape or to flee. He acts and has a great ability to avoid any possible negative consequences of his action. He is therefore characteristically astute, quick to act and to flee. He is similar in every way to his more popular colleague Brighella. Scapino is an invention of Gabrielli at the beginning of the seventeenth century.

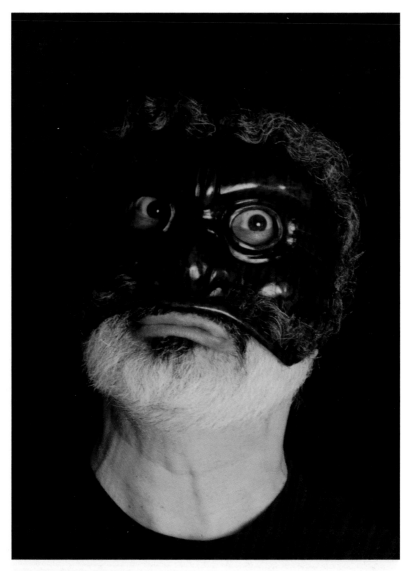

"Oxonian" Arlecchino. The name Arlecchino has been found to be a name for a devil in documents from the eleventh century. In Dante, a devil named Alichino has a distinctly comic quality. Be that as it may, the Commedia Arlecchino is a Second Zanni who acquired his name due to its "exportability"; outside Italy, the name signified an impertinent devil. Arlecchino is only one of the innumerable names given to the Second Zanni. Structurally, he is one component of the *zanni* couple formed by joining the First and Second Zanni: the sly and the stupid, the light and the heavy, the chief and his follower. Whether called Brighella and Arlecchino, Scapino and Truffaldino, Coviello and Pulcinella, or Smeraldino and Tabacchino (these last two would be a couple of comic lovers), they are always the same *zanni* pair. This mask was made for the Oxford Stage Company.

"Monkey" Arlecchino. We invented this Arlecchino with monkey traits, but the mode is perfectly in accord with tradition, which makes the Second Zanni agile, quick, and monkeylike—a servant who openly, exhibitionistically, and knowingly apes the world around him.

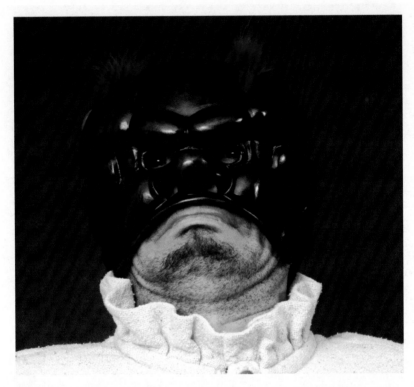

"Stone" Arlecchino. The name for this Arlecchino comes from the shape of the mask, like a pile of pebbles, rocks, cobblestones. This is an experimental mask that requires an appropriate physical presence and style of movement, which may result in a more mysterious, less sunny character.

Bagattino. A Second Zanni. The name Bagattino derives from *bagatelle,* a trifle, something of little value; the word designates a tiny ancient coin valued at one-twelfth of a *soldo.* Although the name in this case diminishes the character, he is not precluded from having sudden flashes of brilliance. In the comic universe, the dolt is always compensated with surprising skills and with energy that rises from an unexpected source, which the character himself is not even aware of. In Commedia, the wretch, the invalid, or the useless person does not exist. One who has everything can fall into disgrace (such as the Old Men and Lovers), and one who has nothing can reveal unforeseen resources.

Trivellino. A Second Zanni. The name comes from *trivellare,* to drill holes—a sexual allusion. The name has no special weight in the character's behavior. Names are always programmatic, but the characteristic that unites them all is that they are funny, that they can make the audience laugh in every situation and at any point in the comedy. In Trivellino's case, the sexual suggestion contained in the name is there purely for comic effect, since obscenity, along with disaster, is an important component of comedy. He has an obscene name for a comic character, therefore, not a comic name for an obscene character. He is a Second Zanni perfectly in line with the tradition of the servant who makes and unmakes confusion by always following the immediate necessities of the moment. Obscenity is quite present in Commedia, always by allusion and in spectacular form, factors that salvage the "innocence" of both the actor and the character he plays and demonstrate great professional skill and the ability to be daring without offending anyone.

Ricciolina and Truffaldino. This feminine mask was created for the actress Valeria Emanuele in *La Cortegiana Innamorata* (*The Courtesan in Love*) with the Roman company Ensemble La Mascherata. We chose this traditional name to baptize a Servetta mask who appears rather late in the history of Commedia, in the later eighteenth century. The structure is halfway between the Dottore mask—nose and forehead only—and a mask that covers the cheeks. The mask favors the expressive use of the eyes as the center of the character's charm. Zagna is a female mask who observes all the Commedia restrictions on female characters, according to which they may be neither ugly, nor grotesque, nor old. Truffaldino is a Second Zanni, despite the name, which, based on *truffa,* a deception, would rather seem to suggest a First Zanni. This is the walking-hurricane servant of Goldoni's *Servant of Two Masters.*

Pulcinella. A Second Zanni. One of the great masks of Commedia dell'Arte, Pulcinella—from *pulcino,* chick, and *pollastrello,* cockerel—is the most important *zanni* from the southern regions of Italy. Beyond being a great comic protagonist ever since his origin in the early seventeenth century, he is also the most important reference point for observing and understanding the historical survival of improvised comedy. While Commedia dell'Arte as an economic structure suddenly disappears after, or because of, the French Revolution, a victim of the people's hatred of the king and his minions, and therefore against the mask theater so prized at the French court, Pulcinella holds on in Naples and other parts of the south, especially Calabria. He prevails precisely because he begins to argue political topics; he sides with the winners. But if Pulcinella ends badly in one sense, he triumphs in another. He enters as the only mask-character in the new bourgeois comedy of the nineteenth century and keeps himself warm in that new setting, giving up his great passions of the past—except in exceptional cases, such as that of Antonio Petito—to become a marginal figure who tosses in occasional witty observations from the side of the stage.

This great character, however, finds his outlet in popular festivals. In Calabria, the tradition of Pulcinella is decidedly freer and more articulated. Every festival has its Pulcinella, who acts as a solo actor, narrator, storyteller, entertainer, acrobat, magician, and juggler, as well as functioning as a sort of overall director of the festival. Today, Pulcinella has perhaps too much history to be able to be described in a single way. Like Pirandello's famous character, he is one, nobody, and a hundred thousand. Whoever he may be, he is always the comic symbol of the urgency of survival, pure and simple. That's what makes him represent everyone; he couldn't make it on his own.

Two Pulcinellas.

Pulcinella as the Emperor Nero.

Pulcinella's Family. Pulcinella; his wife, Donna Zeza; his son, Pulcinicchio; and the lover of his wife, Giangurgolo; from the play *Damnatio Policinellae*.

Fosca. We are not superstitious, but adhering momentarily to the maniacal superstitions of Pulcinella, Zezza, Pascariello, Colafronio, and Coviello, in our comedies we call this character, whose identity is obvious, Fosca. In all comic tradition from the very beginning, there is a moment in which the comic hero, the antihero par excellence, comes face-to-face with her. And the comic hero always gets away. The character is almost always female and always a fully fleshed character. On occasion it may be a distinguished, important-looking gentleman.

In his life of continuous tribulation, the comic hero has become deeply shrewd, more so than he realizes, and his astuteness always saves him from death. He either convinces Fosca to leave him be, or sends her away, or faces her down, or plays her for a fool with a diabolical ingenuity that leaves our comic hero always standing at the end, ready for the next *lazzo*. Fosca is horribly repulsive and terribly charming. It is a natural instinct to avoid her, but she exercises an irresistible attraction that tempts us, makes us—who knows why?—want to know more.

Colafronio. In contrast to the northern masks, who are fixed in their roles, the southern masks combine character roles that are often quite casually determined. Colafronio, known as Cola, is often an Old Man but can also be a First Zanni.

Coviello. A First Zanni. A perfect Neapolitan equivalent of the Bergamask Brighella.

Classic Magnifico and "Oxonian" Pantalone. "Magnifico"—that is, great, grand, generous—means the exact opposite in this character, since the Commedia dell'Arte Magnifico is decidedly avaricious. But besides this extremely human defect, the Magnifico represents the highest authority in the family. He is the one who is in charge of not only the economy and the finances but also the destiny of the household and all who live there. He decides whether or not to pay the servants (he generally inclines against it, not without good reason), and he decides where his son or daughter (the Lovers) will marry, when, and whom. He thus sets in play the great drama of the Lovers, whose solution becomes the material for the three traditional acts of the comedy. "Magnifico" is therefore the technical term that indicates the character. His given name is determined by dialect and geography: Pantalone if he is Venetian; Stefanel Botarga if Milanese; Zanobio da Piombino if Tuscan; Biscegliese if from Puglia; and he can be "Pep" and something more if we make him Catalan, or a "Mc" and something more if we make him Scottish, and so on, without any change in his character, behavior, or function. The most famous and historically most common Magnifico is the Venetian one, Pantalone. The name is probably a contraction of *pianta il leone,* he who plants the lion, the symbol of the Venetian republic. Venetian merchants "planted the lion" in southern and Mediterranean markets; they conquered the world by opening plants and dominating local economies. Our Pantalone, therefore, is a Venetian merchant, a perfect example of the shrewd, cunning, vulgar, and proud dynamism of the refined, opulent, and marvelous city-state. The "Oxonian" Pantalone was created for *Love Is a Drug* with the Oxford Stage Company, 1995.

Facanapa. In our productions and our school, this mask is used as a variation of Pantalone.

Stefanello and Biscegliese. Biscegliese is the version of the Magnifico from Puglia, present in the southern Commedia tradition. He continues to exist, without a mask, until the nineteenth century. Stefanello is the Milanese version of the Magnifico.

Tartaglia. An Old Man character belonging to the Neapolitan tradition, which joins the characteristics of the Magnifico and the Dottore.

Dottor Balanzone. The most famous of the given names of the Dottore.

Dottor Gratiano delle Codeghe and Dottor Plus-quam-Perfectus. Gratiano is the most ancient of the given names of the Dottore. The forehead of this mask is "astronomical"; the lumps are laid out in the form of a constellation, symbolizing universal thought and consciousness. This Dottore is a classic Bologna-dialect Dottore with multilinguistic layers. He is a great expert in everything, "Grand Old Man," father of one of the two Lovers, and friend-enemy of Magnifico, with whom he is in eternal conflict-complicity. This mask has a minimal structure: just forehead and nose. The forehead is indispensable as a symbol of genius, the nose as the comic center of the face.

Dottore-like in everything, the character is in reality a continuation of the ancient charlatan who demonstrates spectacular but doubtful knowledge that depends on the ignorance of others, which he can always count on, because they are indeed either more ignorant than he (servants, Capitano) or too distracted by great joy and suffering (the Lovers) to notice his blunders. The audience immediately recognizes him for what he is, shameless and pompous. But he is truly, truly great in one thing: gastronomy. There he excels. He goes into exaltation, he becomes deeply moved, he slobbers all over himself while describing the recipe, for instance, of real lasagna; and he is scandalized, indignant, furious when reporting barbarous variations or ignoble practices. The Dottore is the projection of the aspirations of an entire starving population that sees in him, in his immense gut, his fat pronunciation, his language that explosively reinvents all languages, and his intestinal outbursts, as overflowing as his gestures, the realization of their most gluttonous, prohibited internal desires.

Capitano Spavento. The name suggests one who causes fear, who scares the enemy (from *spaventare,* to scare). In Francesco Andreini's version, the name is extended to Capitano Spavento da Valle Inferno (Captain Spavento from the Valley of Hell). The Commedia Capitano is the warrior, the bravo, the mercenary, the man of arms. Great in battle and great in love, he is a hero on both fronts, as well as a solitary type, for both comic-poetic and functional reasons. He constitutes part of a comic couple with his servant when he has one. He is a foreigner from far off; he has seen all the world, things no one else could have seen; he has done things no one else could have done. He speaks his foreign language suspiciously mixed with the local dialect (that is, of the audience). Naturally, he's a braggart par excellence: he boasts extraordinary adventures and acts of heroic and erotic skill. In truth, he's a simpleton and a coward, but this terrible truth, of which he is vaguely aware, must be kept hidden at all costs. He exaggerates his virile image as a winner to take advantage but perhaps most of all to conceal this hypocrisy, a source of terrible suffering. This Capitano is very contemporary, very much "our own." His entire being hinges on presenting an image of himself as glorious and grandiose. Without this he is finished, a failure, nonexistent, dead. Every effort he makes to impose this image constitutes one step toward disaster.

The Capitano, in the act of delivering one of his tirades, is a beautiful example of theater for the whole audience, for all levels of comprehension and enjoyment. In fact, the part of him that is a tavern boaster brings him close to that equivalent among the audience, but the elements of higher culture that he has picked up "by ear" raise his standing bit by bit, touching finally even the most sophisticated audience. In this sense, the Capitano is, in our opinion, what all theater should be: clear, popular (that is, for everyone), funny, sophisticated, and as complex as the character himself. The Great Tale Teller has this in his favor and another quality as well: he's a great lover. The male animal never fails. He takes joy in his amatorial gifts and so does his female counterpart and equivalent, the Second Woman, or Lady, who is young, pretty, fearless, a braggart herself (but not cowardly; on the contrary, rather aggressive), and wife of the cuckolded Magnifico or Dottore. It goes without saying that the Lady has married for money, which she loves devotedly and ostentatiously, developing her sense of status to parallel the Capitano's relationship with heroism. They both have an image problem. With his function as intruder and "third wheel," the Capitano always carries the stain of blame and his destiny is to be "unmasked." He will recover from his shame and beatings just enough to prepare a grand exit that will allow him to recover and imagine, therapeutically, a future of even greater triumph and glory.

"Oxonian" Capitano Spavento. A variation on Spavento created for the Oxford Stage Company.

Capitan Bellavita. The name is found in the Jacques Callot engravings *Balli di Sfessania*. His name suggests narcissism and hedonism. The mask has some experimental features tending in the direction of the Arlecchino Sasso. The teeth are resin.

Capitan Matamoros. His name means "he who kills the Moors," that is, the infidels, and suggests he is the defender of all Christianity, which is to say, of civilization itself. This Capitano's name is perhaps the only direct programmatic reference in improvised comedy to a religious theme. In truth, this reference has nothing to do with religion. Commedia dell'Arte is rigorously secular. The name Matamoros indicates that he's Spanish and, consequently, that he is a braggart. The Spanish of the sixteenth and seventeenth century were seen by the Italians—in a favorable sense—as fierce conquistadores and valorous saviors of civilization, due to their peculiar habit of killing Moors and infidels, the enemies of the truth. The Spanish were a model of courage, valor, conquest, and progress. The name Matamoros equates with heroic, courageous, indomitable, unbeatable defender and savior of civilization. The name, its meaning, the meaning of the character, and the world in which he finds himself and acts, remain secular.

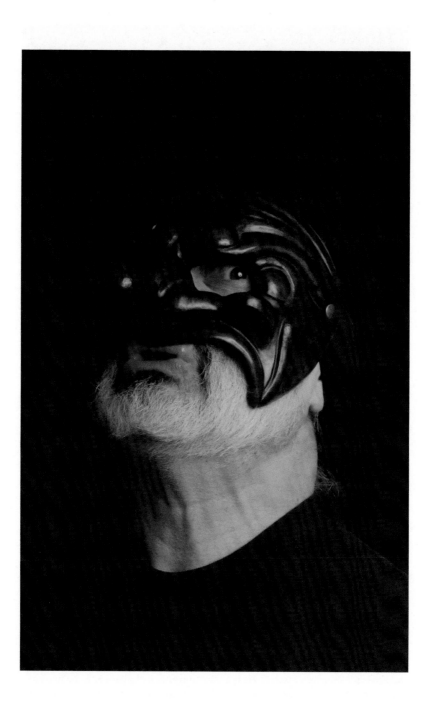

Meo Squaquara. A Capitano from Callot. Jacques Callot, in his *Balli di Sfessania,* presents a stupendously designed and engraved world of Italian—rather, Neapolitan—masks that probably never actually existed. But Callot's work is highly suggestive because of the power of the images: those figures cannot be total fantasy, because the vast iconographic documentation of Commedia dell'Arte, which claims to present Commedia as it was, never departs far from Callot's figures in their gesture and spectacular appearance. Callot's images are suggestive because of the artist's interpretation, a sort of elaboration of the evidence, in the same way as a director who asks an actor to carry out a movement in a certain way. Callot has become a model for many Commedia practitioners, but this has generated a misunderstanding: the model makes Commedia look ragged, places its performance in open air, and looks like a dance.

Certainly, there was ragged Commedia, but never by choice of the actors, who aspired to greater things. There was open-air Commedia, but only because of the difficulty of getting into a theater, which would always be Commedia's preference. Sometimes there is dance in Commedia, but it is not dance theater, and the *Balli* illustrates only danced actions. *Sfessania* refers to a way of dancing.

The name of the mask is unnerving to say the least. In Neapolitan dialect, *squaquara* means a baby girl; *fare la squaquara* means to give birth to a female baby. *Squaquarare* is the sound of boiling water. Might our Meo, or Marameo, have something to do with boiling, spilling out, pouring forth, and if so, with stomach or intestines? Hunger or evacuation? Both? Perhaps. It is difficult, either way, to imagine a character not somehow visceral. He is a Capitano and, with that name, he must be a waiting disaster and a great comic figure. Our mask is not an imitation of Callot's, though its design is vaguely Callotian. The spiral nose describes his psychophysical condition and his extreme nearsightedness foreshadows the defeat he inevitably brings upon himself.

"Phallic" Capitano Giangurgolo. From Calabria, Giangurgolo, or Gianni the glutton, is a very zannesque Capitano, picaresque, great and wretched, arrogant and servile. This variation openly declares the phallic symbolism of the long nose, a guaranteed comic effect.

Capitano Bellerofonte Scarabombardone da Rocca di Ferro. This character, created by Giulio Cesare Croce in *Le Tremende Bravure del Capitano Bellerofonte Scarabombardone da Rocca di Ferro,* a short text in verse published in 1596, is an old Capitano who inflicts his boasts on his servant, Frisetto. His boasts betray the truth that he has never really fought anybody, that all his culture comes from the tavern and the bordello, and that his historical-geographical-mythological references are randomly picked up. Patiently and realistically, the servant puts up with him and shares his own thoughts—concrete, realistic, commonsensical—with the audience. He knows what Capitano Bellerofonte Scarabombardone da Rocca di Ferro really is, a ragged, hungry, poor old man; yes, Croce made him old. The two of them together are powerfully comic-poetic and constitute an interesting anticipation of Don Quixote and Sancho Panza.

Androgino. This mask can be either male or female. This is a social mask, a personal accessory to put on and take off at will, used by the "beautiful" characters: the First Lovers, male and female, and the Second Lovers, the nonmasked Capitano and the Lady. Androgino is a mask for dissimulation and for hiding the face to avoid recognition. It is used in clandestine, embarrassing situations, in secret actions, or simply to avoid having to deal with certain others.

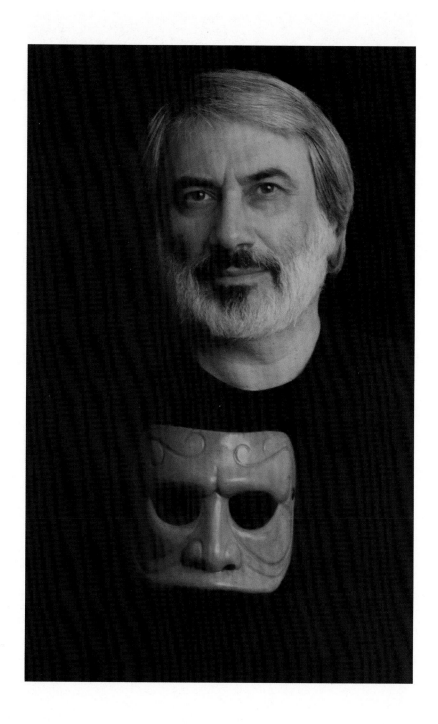

Moretta. A social mask, used for dissimulation. Only a female version exists. It gets its name from the color, always very dark or black. Part of a social costume, it signifies the social class of the woman carrying it as very high. It represents no character but merely renders its wearer incognito. It is not made for speaking and can be used either by the Lover or the Lady.

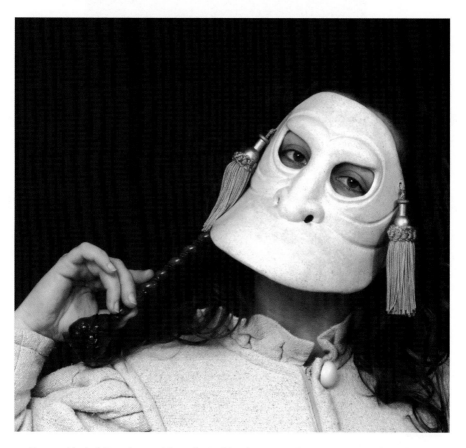

Bautta. Typical Venetian social mask used by the upper classes. It is not a theatrical mask and only appears onstage when the "beautiful," nonmasked characters must or wish to hide their true identity, following the social modes of the eighteenth century.

First Devil. In a supernatural setting, the historical-cultural precursor to the *zanni* is the devil. This devil-bird is used at the International School of Comic Acting with the name Hehllhahppehcqk in our piece set in the thirteenth century, *Il Salto del Re* (*The King's Leap*).

Second Devil. This mask forms a comic couple with the First Devil. In *Il Salto del Re*, he is named Hozthacqkehcqk.

Satiro "Gran Cornuto" and Satiri "Cornutelli." Commedia dell'Arte companies performed more than strict Commedia scenarios. A part of their repertoire was in the poetic form of pastoral comedy, with subgenres set in the sea or the woods. Here, mythological characters appeared, such as satyrs and nymphs, Triton and mermaids. But adapting to the tastes of the public, they participated in amorous and zannesque intrigues closely based on Commedia. The "great horned" satyr's name is obvious. This mask contains both classical and medieval elements and is seen by the audience more as devil than satyr. In our school, satyr masks are studied as representing beings who signify forces of nature; even when immobile they allude to certain natural and social states of immobility, with which the characters sooner or later must come to terms. Our satyr does not speak but emits very expressive and meaningful sounds. The mask shown here is still in a rough state and is missing part of a horn. Satiri "Cornutelli" are like their boss but with smaller horns.

Famiglia d'Arte Fava-Buccino. Antonio Fava, Dina Buccino, Marcella and Ferruccio Fava, May 2004

"monstrous" due to its imagery and form, in that the humanity of a character is combined with animal and other nonhuman characteristics. "Human" in this context means a character that is human only, without monstrosity or other mixtures. It does not mean that this species of character is more "humane" than the grotesque characters. All Commedia should be thought of and performed not as a "puppet show," as an aesthetic, formal exhibition, but as a human effort, made by humans and for humans. All the characters of Commedia express great humanity precisely because they struggle to overcome difficulties and pain in their quest for happiness.

Grotesques: Magnifico, Dottore, Zanni, Zagna, Capitano
Humans: Lovers, Amazon, Cavalier, Lady, Female Servants
Semigrotesque or semihuman: Infarinato

This classification reveals its importance during improvisation; knowing whether one is grotesque, human, or semigrotesque is decisive to gesture and behavior. The grotesques are more masklike and swept up in their comic disaster than the humans, who have more resources, due to the greater natural commonsense and rationality that belong to their perfect models, the audience.

This does not mean that we have two different performance styles within the same genre or even within the same comedy. Rather, we have two human species, one of which departs from the perfect model to take on similarities of decidedly nonhuman entities, such as certain animals; and the other species, which approaches as closely as possible the ideal model, trying in fact to surpass it, to be more shrewd than the shrewdest, more beautiful than the most beautiful, more anguished than the most anguished, more sensitive, and so on.

The Forms of the Comic

When discussing analogies between Commedia dell'Arte and other forms of comedy, we should speak rather of *precedents* and *consequences*. Commedia is a bridge, a passageway that unites ancient with modern comedy; it resolves the comedy of the classical era and begins modern comedy. As we have already seen, it begins the modern with a gesture that is not creative but rather organizational. The idea of the profession of the actor and of theater as a product to sell contains unstoppable consequences, which are still under way.

What precedes Commedia furnishes fundamental evidence for the development of characters and situations, as well as for the development of the idea of professionalism. The stories of love challenged by obstacles and the characters that undergo these problems are derived from humanist comedy of the Renaissance. The Lovers, borrowed also from humanist (or erudite) comedy, "summoned" by the new, feminine presence of the professional actress, enter into Commedia.

The practice of making a living by performing, the "choice of life," comes from older and longer-lasting precedents. Throughout the Middle Ages, until the advent of Commedia, the *giullare,* the professional buffoon, characterized public entertainment. He is not an actor, he is an entertainer, a performer, who amuses and surprises crowds mostly by his physical abilities. These abilities pass directly from the *giullare* to the Commedia actor, but there is a substantial difference. The *giullare* performs his acrobatic feats to surprise and thrill his audience; when the *giullare* performs a flip, for example, it is the flip itself he is showing off to his spectators, who award him with applause and other rewards in recognition of his skill. When the Commedia actor performs an acrobatic feat, he is not merely showing off the feat for its own sake but giving it meaning and a justification within a dramatic situation: Zanni stumbles and falls, and the actor executes the fall with an acrobatic solution. Pantalone is afraid; the actor playing Pantalone gives him a nervous twitch that makes the character react with a backflip.

The dramatization of acrobatic abilities clearly shows us that a leap has taken place in the evolution of performance. The ability indicates the constant preparation and competence that has existed since Roman times and throughout the Middle Ages up to the Renaissance. But from that moment, the acrobatic move is no longer a finite product, but a *base technique,* an instrument for realizing something more specific, which is the specialization of each actor's own character. The Commedia character is a container of techniques common to all artists but unique in each actor's particular way of featuring them.

The consequences of Commedia can be found pretty much everywhere. Laurel and Hardy may represent the clearest example. To begin with, they are a comic couple, a crucial, original invention of improvised comedy. Their mask is immutable, in that all their films feature, with mathematical precision, the same faces, gestures, voices, and gags, a form of *lazzi,* which belong unmistakably to the two actor-masks. Laurel and Hardy are fixed types; their archetype could be defined as the human being in search of his place among his fellows. Their character can be defined as "the loser." They have two roles, that of the *leader* and the *follower.* They are characters, named Stan and Ollie, or Stanlio and Ollio, as we affectionately dub them in Italy.

Their types can be easily identified as First and Second Zanni because their roles are perfectly indicated: Ollie is a First Zanni and Stan is a Second Zanni. They function exactly like two Commedia Zanni, since the leader turns out to be not so intelligent after all, and the follower turns out to be not as stupid as first thought. This is exactly what happens between Brighella and Arlecchino, between Coviello and Pulcinella, and between Francatrippa and Zanni. Modern versions of these exist everywhere. Ollie even *points his mask,* when, for example, after having fallen into mud, he looks the camera—the spectators—right in the eye, thus commenting on what has happened. Although the rhythms and the techniques vary, the *stares* of Ollie and those of Zanni are one and the same in their principles and meaning.

The Forms of Laughter

Here, I would like to touch on an extremely complex and profound aspect of comic artistry. To make people laugh supposes—especially on an intuitive level, as is almost always the case—"knowing" how and why to make people laugh. We also suppose that the audience "knows" how and why it laughs. We maintain that this "knowledge" exists but is, especially on the part of the audience, unconscious. But it must exist, otherwise there would be no explanation for the punctuality with which a comic makes people laugh and for the punctuality with which audiences laugh.

Fundamentally, we laugh for relief and for confirmation. Relief produces the most frequent laughter, such as the kind that follows upon a disaster happening to one of the characters. *Mors tua vita mea.* Confirmation resides in the laughter linked to the obscenity of the sexual act, to showing the genitals, and in general to the body as a sexual object. By confirmation, we here mean the continuity of physical life that comes from the comic-obscene exhibition of sex, in all its many spectacular manifestations.

There is also a form of laughter that is somehow perverse, since it procures neither relief nor confirmation but rather promotes and feeds conflict, hostility, and hatred. Perverse laughter does not belong to the comic because it does not satisfy the individual and collective need to be saved from anguish. On the contrary, it nourishes anguish; it does not reduce or zero out tensions, it maintains them. People laugh, yes, but not all together, because it is a form of laughter that divides people.

Although everyone is perfectly free to make people laugh any way they please, laughter that divides separates spectators into those in favor and those against, making one group laugh and the other grimace. The Arte comic does not play to these tendencies, which in other settings deserve all due respect. He does not participate in this kind of comedy because he is a *morosofo,* a philosopher of folly, comic folly that universalizes the defects, the pain, the conditions and aspirations of all humans, who are considered irredeemably equal despite their external differences.[5] This does not mean that comedy flattens out all topics. On the contrary, comedy does not distinguish between good and bad topics because everything can be turned to comedy. The *morosofo* is both above and below all factions, he is outside them, he sees them all from angles unknown to those who are in the midst of them. He does not see "one thing well" and "another thing poorly," because he sees them all together, as they appear to him as an impartial, pitiless, cynical *morosofo.*

The comic therefore is universal; he regards everybody individually and collectively. We therefore consider comic only that which provides relief and confirmation both in the individual and the group, or rather that laughter in which each single laugher joins together in a common laugh.

It goes without saying that there is always someone who doesn't laugh, either because he's thinking about something else, doesn't understand, has different tastes, or doesn't like that particular comic. Or perhaps he's tired and sleeping, or he may belong to one of the three categories of *agelasti;* that is, those who absolutely never laugh: foreigners, colleagues, and critics. Or the nonlaugher may be any other kind of person with his own reasons for not laughing, but not because the comic has given him a choice: either you're with me and laugh, or you're not with me and f—— off.

We do not consider divisive laughter to be comic. Instead it should be given a different name, which can vary depending on the case. Two stand out in particular: *satire,* where known people and events are made fun of, using the object's real name and imitating his physical, gestural, vocal, and oratorical habits; and *parody,* which is counterfeiting and monkeying around with something, for example, another genre or work, such as opera or *Hamlet.*

Satire and parody have in common that they depend on something "other": another genre or characters not inherent to the plot but brought in from outside, whether from the news or other real or fictitious sources. Satire and parody must always refer to something, which means that they have no formal and poetic autonomy. They are definitely comic if the overall result of the work in which they are inserted absolves the fundamental functions of relief and confirmation.

Curiously, whenever an improviser is at a loss for ideas or not in good shape, he seizes on satire and parody because these forms of direct and aggressive comedy are "easy." They are easy because they depend on what already exists, on what is already famous. By satirizing and parodying, an improviser can always come up with something. Then, having warmed up, he may enter into the living play; his character can become human and occupy its full humanity. The crutch of the already known disappears and the comic finally bursts forth. It isn't easy, but it is simple. It is the essential point of arrival of a complex process.

5	Method

Principles

Our method is essentially built on two principles. First, Commedia dell'Arte is a *genre in movement,* which has known historical highs and lows but, since its first appearance (before 1540) until today, has never ceased to exist. It is therefore misguided to refer to a single moment in Commedia's history and assert that that moment "is" Commedia and then execute an immutable, extremely faithful reconstruction of that preselected image. It is because of this way of looking at the matter that today we have a mixed bag of Commedia dell'Arte, all of it old and mannered and capable of being distinguished in various forms: "Venetian," "Goldonian," "Pierrotian," "Pierrot-ized Pulcinellesque," "street romantic," "pure-and-simple street," "infantilized," and "iconological" (especially Callotian). Most of the time, it mixes together into an uncontrolled and miserable kitsch, in which the actors, from a cultural point of view, haven't got the slightest idea of what they are doing.

We consider Commedia a genre in evolution, making its way, in movement. Everything changes along the way, adapts, is reinterpreted. At the same time, there are certain reference points that we perceive as immutable or, at least, as permanent. From these, which we call fixed points and elective points, we draw our second fundamental principle, that of referentiality: given the permanence of the reference points, each and every invention must take place within their "limits."

The Five Points

In our elaboration of a method for *realizing the work* of Commedia, its definition develops according to five points, four of which are *firm* and one of which is *elective.* We consider the four fixed points indispensable. The absence of any one of them results in an improvised comedy that is mutilated, gravely compromised in its form, perhaps even unrecognizable in its genre.

We hold the fifth point to be optional, but we feel its implementation is of the first importance to obtain a formally complete result and to provide an aesthetic stimulus for the *continuity* of Commedia.

The fixed points are:

1. Fixed types (and the system derived from them)
2. The mask (the object, the principle, and the uses of the term)
3. Improvisation (an expressive comic principle, a method of construction, a training method)
4. Multilingualism (and its derivatives: multislang, multiculturalism)

The elective point is:

5. *The aesthetic of anachronism*

FIXED TYPES

Fixed point

The fixed types, or recurrent types, are present in every Commedia performance. They are not an invention of Commedia but rather a characteristic of all forms of spectacle, especially the comic but also the dramatic, in which there are characters performing actions. Greek tragedy and comedy have "standardized" characters, given that even characters who appear one time only must resort to preexisting masks. In his *Onomàstikon,* Book IV, Julius Pollux (second century C.E.) describes the masks of Tragedy and New Comedy and dedicates a few lines to the masks of satyr plays. He furnishes a list of the "stereotypes" that must be represented anew in any tragedy, comedy, or satyr play. Periodical corrections and adjustments, with elimination of some and the admittance of others, can be acceptable, but fundamentally the list of masks was established and had to be taken into proper account.

The *Atellan Fables* appear in the second century B.C.E. in Atella, an ancient city in what is now called Campania. In Latin, they continue until the second century C.E. The *Fables* present structural characteristics similar to Commedia dell'Arte, in particular the fixed types: the "philosopher" Dossennus, the chatterbox Buccus, the glutton Manducus, the false dunce Marcus, the aged Pappus. No other types are known, but the absence of female characters is striking. We may assume that they haven't come down to us, or that the *Atellan Fables* were organized like Greek and later Latin comedy, where female characters were physically absent from the stage (with a few exceptions) but present in the story. The actors improvised on the basis of a *trica,* the *canovaccio* of the time. And they wore masks.

But the *macchiette* and *soubrettes* essential to Italian variety theater are also fixed types, without which variety would not be variety. (*Varietà* was a sort of Italian vaudeville or music hall contemporaneous with American and British forms of popular theater in the first half of the twentieth century. *Macchiette* were character sketches involving a song or comic monologue, often parodying a social type. *Soubrette,* the name taken from classic French comedy, refers to the female dancer-singer of variety theater. See, for example, Federico Fellini's early film *Luci del Varietà* [*Variety Lights,* 1950]). And the same is true for clowns, whether under the big top, in the theater, or anywhere else.

In Commedia, the fixed types constitute a fixed point and are recognized not only as a poetical but also a professional and existential truth. That is, being a First Zanni or an Ingenue or a Capitano is something that manifests itself "naturally" before it ever gets to the stage. It is an innate psycho-artistic-physical category that one cannot choose for oneself but must be recognized and accepted to achieve the highest artistic results and professional advantages.

Commedia adapts these fixed types very early in its development. The first documented improvised comedy is the one described by Massimo Troiano from Naples, in his *Discourse on the Triumphal Processions, Jousts, Displays, and Other Most Notable Things Created for the Wedding of the Most Illustrious Excellency Signor Duke Guglielmo, First Child of the Most Generous Albert the Fifth, Paladin Count of the Rhine and Duke of Upper and Lower Bavaria, in the Year 1568, on the 22nd of February.* In the Commedia performed, there appear Pantalone, Zanni, the courtesan Camilla, the Lover Polidoro, the Spaniard, the Fantesca (Female Servant), and a French servant. Therefore, the principal types and their derivatives are already present in 1568. They have passed down to us today intact. When, under the principle of "modernizing" Commedia, we hear about "new and updated types," we immediately sense the uselessness of such an operation. The new types already exist in a thousand other forms; if we add them to Commedia to update it, we are depriving the form of a fundamental characteristic that guarantees the recognizability of the genre. The result is either unnatural or something else entirely. Furthermore, the need to update Commedia by adding new types has already been superseded both historically and traditionally by the dramatic use of the fixed types, which are simply directed to new applications, while keeping the mask itself intact. For example, if we want to invent the mask of a politician, all we have to do is take the known Commedia types and put them in a new situation, so as to obtain types of politicians who are combinations of the mask and the political behavior we wish to feature. If the politician is a Dottore, we have one combination and one precise image of a politician; if the politician is a Zanni, we have another type, and so on. In this way we can both respect an indispensable structural aspect of Commedia and introduce new themes, new issues.

There are four fixed types in Commedia:

1. The Old Man
2. The Servant
3. The Lover
4. The Capitano

Introduced in this way, these types are rather abstract, pure reference points. They should be considered *absolute archetypes.* From these comes forth an entire proliferating system of characters.

This system of proliferation has its own particular internal organization, which has always existed in practice but has never been formally defined, in part because of the lexical confusion resulting from the use of such terms as "type," "character," "role," and so on as synonyms. (The confusion is still more tangled in the English language, because we use "character" to mean both the defining combination of an individual's qualities and a theatrical role. In Italian, *carattere* refers to an individual's qualities, whereas the term given to a theatrical role is *personaggio.*)

In what follows, we would like to propose a new way of categorizing the terminology of the evolutionary phases, which develop from the absolute archetype to the most recent phase of what we generally call the character, which goes by the term "part."

The terminology for classification of types:

1. Fixed Type (technical/artistic), Absolute Archetype (semantic)
2. Subtype (technical), Character (artistic), Comic Archetype (semantic)
3. Function (technical/semantic)
4. Role (semantic), Relational Function (technical)
5. Character (*personaggio*) (technical/artistic) Mask—second meaning (technical/artistic/semantic)
6. Part (technical/semantic)

Fixed Type—Absolute Archetype

The Old Man, the Servant, the Lover, and Capitano correspond to absolute archetypes. There are no others. Each one's fundamental character reflects an absolute archetype, never a *subtype, character, or comic archetype.* The above terms are never the name of a character.

The fixed type is the archetype referred to. It is the expressive founder of the family line, the explication of a particular phase or human condition, universally recognizable. Each archetype, respectively, is the human being in the following conditions:

- ☞ When old
- ☞ When at the beck and call of other human beings
- ☞ When in love
- ☞ When struggling against enemies

In this sense, when the four fixed types correspond to the four human conditions above, they can refer to either a single character in the action or to all of them, because any character can find himself or herself in each or all of the conditions expressed by the types. Or, within the specific poetic conditions of Commedia dell'Arte, we may consider the four types as functional dramatic divisions of a single reference point, the "human being," within which these four conditions have been identified as sufficient to develop all possible dramatic combinations.

Subtype—Character—Comic Archetype

The type becomes more precise by incorporating a subtype, by becoming a *character,* that is, a *comic archetype.* The subtype indicates the ramifications of the absolute archetype. No longer, for example, the aged human being but rather a certain aged Magnifico or Dottore, who manifests a certain way of being aged. Like the absolute archetypes, the terms indicating the characters are not used as given names; they are technical terms that define them and fix their number. The character is the human and sociocultural substance that allows for the poetic identification of the comic archetype.

- ☞ The characters of the Old Man are:
  Magnifico
  Dottore
  Tartaglia (a combination)

☞ The characters of the Servant are:
  Zanni
  Zagna
  Fantesca (Serving Girl 1)
  Servetta (Serving Girl 2)
  Infarinato

☞ The characters of the Lover are:
  Ingenue
  Male Ingenue (the Ingenuous)
  Amazon
  Cavalier
  Zerbinotto
  The Lady

☞ The characters of the Capitano are:
  Bravo
  Spaniard
  Frenchman
  German
  Turk

Function

The absolute archetype and, in consequence, the *comic archetype* perform a function within the play:

Old Man: Function of Persecution

A vital function in Commedia, persecution (which is neither conceived nor experienced as such by the character doing the persecuting) is represented by the apparently insurmountable obstacle posed by the Old Man (who has his own specific goals) between the two Lovers.

The Old Man, acting "against nature" (although aged, he wants to marry the young lover), must be stopped. But he is the absolute authority in the house and commands whoever lives there. Thus he can only be stopped in a "dishonest" way, either by force, deception, or betrayal.

The Old Man triggers the plot in which everything unfolds. At the end, he is put in a condition whereby he can no longer persecute. His symbolic death takes place through shaming, beatings, or the imposition of expensive cash payments.

The Servant: Function of Making-Unmaking

The Servant is the one who has to remedy the problem posed by the Old Man and all the problems that flow from the first one. In the grip of a double tension, promise of reward and threat of punishment, he tries out solutions that fail, leading to new problems. Trying to make, he unmakes, and vice versa. The accumulation thus produced leads to the maximum crisis point, the maximum mix-up, that precedes the final solution, which is usually almost immediate and very simple. The mechanisms of complication are what draw the interest of the audience in Commedia. There is always a single solution at the end, which returns us to normality. Reward and punishment, both "deserved," inexorably come to the Servant at the end of the play.

Lovers: Function of Initiation

The Lovers, young, beautiful, elegant, cultured, refined, and everything else, are inexpert in life and love each other with grand idealistic ineffable passion. The interruption in the flow of feeling between them is unbearable, a pain that destroys them, that drives them mad. But on the purely functional plane, it is a long, obligatory rite of passage, a necessary test. Having passed through it, they shall not fail to receive the prize of adulthood.

The moment of the wedding, the matrimonial rite, has always been relegated to that nonexistent "fourth act," in which the couple will be joined and the spectators invited, following the rule of comic demagoguery, a practical poetic ingredient necessary to maximum success.

Capitano: Function of Complicating

The Capitano is almost always an extra inconvenience. He may or may not know this, it may be important to him or not, he may be concerned with the complication he creates or not. It doesn't matter; it doesn't alter his behavior in the slightest. The Capitano's function has a "disposable" quality to it: once the tragedy has been unleashed and all the other functions are set into motion, he may well have no further purpose. He keeps in reserve, however, other functions, by no means secondary:

Moralistic. There is a need for a pure, totally guilty party, a scapegoat, and, fool that he is, he fits the bill perfectly.

Comic. The Capitano is an extraordinary laugh machine. We might be able to justify eliminating the Capitano because he is dramatically superfluous, but to give up his comic presence—obviously, this depends on the skill of the actor—would be a grave error of underestimating the type and his function.

The *function* is a structural characteristic and the dramatic space occupied by the type in the Commedia system. A Commedia dell'Arte without an Old Man, a Lover, or a Servant is not Commedia dell'Arte. It might be a play in the style of Commedia dell'Arte. Without a Capitano, it is a play in the style of Commedia dell'Arte or a diminished Commedia dell'Arte.

The function is connected to the meanings that are expressed by the form. In fact, function and all the meanings determine the form. In Commedia dell'Arte, form and content coincide. To give up a type means to mutilate the form and give up important meanings.

Role—Relational Function

In Commedia, some of the relational functions are those of First and Second Old Man; First and Second Zanni; First and Second Lover. A character, say the Capitano, is described with adjectives that suggest his actions and behavior and, consequently, his role—*fanfarone* (braggart), *bravaccio* (bully)—or his origins—*spagnaruolo* (Spaniard), *todisco* (German).

The role is a relational function, determining a further development of expressive variations: the doubling of the characters into the first and second variations, which enriches and complicates the system of relations in the plot.

The contributions of the individual artists increase in theory to infinity the number of character names, but they cannot increase the number of archetypal functions or relational functions or the number of roles, which seem to have arrived at their structural limits. There are two for each character, or multiples of two, for example, two, three, or four couples of Lovers; three formations of First and Second Zanni.

The role, or relational function, is the dramatic space occupied by the character in each single Commedia play.

Character—Mask

The *personaggio*, or mask, is the identification of the character. The *personaggio* can be a development, in the way that Arlecchino, Pulcinella, and Pedrolino are developments of Zanni. Or it can be a variation: Zan Frittello and Zan Traccagno are variants of the primitive Zanni. Truffaldino and Arlecchino are variants of the "ino"-type servant, a Second Zanni with a snub nose. Francatrippa and Brighella are variants of the First Zanni. Corallina and Olivetta are variants of the Servant Girl; Bajazzu and Pedrolino are variants of Infarinato; Pantalone and Stefanello are variants of Magnifico; Isabella and Flaminia are variants of the Female Lover; Orazio and Flavio are variants of the Male Lover; Graziano and Balanzone are variants of the Dottore; Scarabombardone and Giangurgolo are variants of the Capitano.

Often, these variants are such in name only, remaining identical in their external traits—granted, of course, the variations between one performer and another—as in the case of Truffaldino-Arlecchino; they are identical in everything except name. For this reason, the Truffaldino character in Goldoni's *Servant of Two Masters* has usually been called Arlecchino for many years now. This is done for purely commercial reasons on the assumption that "Arlecchino" is more familiar than "Truffaldino."

There are characters that have remained "sterile," virtually never giving birth to further developments or variants, such as the Scaramuccia invented by Fiorilli, the Beltrame invented by Bartoli, and the Sivello of Gabrielli, even though these masks achieved great fame and success during the lifetimes of their creators.

The *personaggio* or mask is the theatrical being in action, identified by a name, considered in his or her individuality, which is the sum of all preceding evolutionary phases added to the proper name and the specific external traits. Pantalone, Graziano, Zanni, Pulcinella, Colombina, Franceschina, Pedrolino, Pagliaccio or Bajazzu, Flavio, Isabella, Spaventa, Scarabombardone: they are all *personaggi,* or masks. The name is the premise and the apex of all the details that compose the personage and fix his or her individuality and identification.

The name always has a programmatic quality: it perfectly suits the character. Pulcinella is a *pollo* (chicken); Arlecchino is a devil (the hard *c* evokes a number of medieval names of devils); Brighella is a sleazy manipulator (from the word *brigare,* to con); Pantalone, the Venetian merchant, "plants the lion" (St. Mark's lion is the symbol of Venice) wherever he invests capital; Doctor Balanzone (a large scale) is a "weigher" of concepts and theories but also opportunities and situations; Colombina is pretty and flutters like the dove; Diamantina is sparkly and precious; Olivetta is pretty and tasty; Flaminia burns with passion like a flame; Orazio is full of poetry (like Horace); Tartaglia stutters (from *tartagliare,* to stutter); Scarabombardone is fire, flame, and the booming of cannons, and so on. We have thus far been unable to find a single historical name in the Commedia tradition that does not have a programmatic meaning.

Part

The *part* is what is given the actor: such-and-such an actor in the *part* of Pulcinella, or in the *personaggio* or mask, but not "in the role of" or "in the character of" Pulcinella (or some other name), as is often found, erroneously.

In terms of performance, "in the role of" is incorrect because a role is a structural phase; "in the character of" is incorrect because the character is an archetypal phase, still without a specific given name. There is not a "character," for example, of Pulcinella; rather there is the character of the dumb servant. Therefore we should say instead, "in the character of the dumb servant."

When the character takes on a name, it becomes a *personaggio* or mask, and from there, once this is entrusted to a specific actor, it becomes *a part*.

According to the requirements of each individual play being staged, with its identifying title, the role will be determined. Pulcinella, for example, may take on the role of First Zanni, even though he usually takes the role of Second Zanni, if that happens to be what he is called upon to fulfill in that particular play.

The part unleashes the mechanism of the performance. That is when the part achieves its unique, inimitable completion by being entrusted to the personality, the psychophysical particulars, and the human experience of the performing artist.

The part can also be indicated by one particular quality, for example, such and such an actor in the part of "the poor unfortunate overcome by hunger." Thus, we can have the actor Luca Cairati in the following positions:

☞ In the *part* of "the poor unfortunate overcome by of hunger"
☞ As the *personaggio* or mask of Zan Cavicchio
☞ In the *role* of Second Zanni
☞ In the *function* of the con man
☞ In the *character* of the dumb servant
☞ Corresponding to the *type*, the Servant

MASK

Fixed point

When today's actors become aware of and are subsequently drawn to Commedia dell'Arte, they seek an immediate confirmation of certain impressions (often based on clichés); they always want to know whether a certain thing is the "symbol of Commedia dell'Arte." That certain thing is almost always Arlecchino, *the* Arlecchino. We will never tire of repeating that Arlecchino is a Second Zanni, that Commedia is a system of relations and situations between characters who are all of equal importance and have no absolute protagonists. At least in principle, no one symbol represents it, because a symbol can always exclude everything else. If instead of symbols we speak of reference points, then we can allow this formula: the most important reference point in Commedia dell'Arte is the mask. The mask as a meaning-bearing object and the mask as a principle that permeates the entire expressive system.

We have isolated eight meanings of the word "mask" with respect to its significance and use in Commedia dell'Arte.

Mask as Physiognomorphic Object

This is what we wear on our face. In Commedia there are two types: a mask of *simulation,* which is the mask that characterizes the *personaggio,* that gives the *personaggio* its face (Zanni, Pantalone, Dottore) and which is his very "flesh." Then there is the mask of *dissimulation,* which is a social object, used by the nonmasked characters to conceal their identity.

Mask as Character

A number of characters in Commedia do not wear masks: the Male and Female Lovers; the Servant Girls; the nongrotesque Capitano when he functions as the Second Lover; the Second Lady, or comic Lover; the Infarinato-type servants, such as Pedrolino, Mezzettino, Pagliaccio (Bajazzu). This circumstance leads us to consider the meaning of mask as character. Independent of the appearance of the face, with or without an actual leather mask, with makeup or a dusting of flour (as with Infarinato) or any other means of characterizing the personage and transforming the actor, the *complete personaggio is a mask.*

Mask as Expressive Visage: Mobile Mask

This is the nonmasked visage of the artist, the facial qualities that he or she lends to the character, both static and mobile. The use of facial mobility is a mask because of the strong sculptural effect given to the expressions: a passage from joy to grief becomes a sequence of two allegorical sculptures, that from the visage expressing joy to that of the visage expressing grief. Explained in this way, rather than seen, the matter may sound mechanical. The actor, who can count on an infinite range of expressions and nuances—just as with the voice—justifies his sequence by its logic and the emotional effect it provokes in the other performers and in the audience. We should consider the two sculptures like two peaks, between which the actor sequences a succession of nuances, variations, interruptions, and repetitions, so as to achieve the desired effect. The public sees psychologically meaningful expressions but does not witness a psychological interpretation; it is not drawn into the "interiority of the character." Rather, the character externalizes everything. This form is opposite to psychological theater, but the meaning is the same. There is no difference in value between *internalizing* and *externalizing*, only a difference in modalities of expression. This leads to a radical emotional difference, which is that between comic and dramatic genres. Drama raises emotions; comedy resolves them.

Mask as Enmasking: Becoming the Mask

Enmasking is the elaboration by the actor, the realization of a character. The concept of enmasking is fundamental to comprehend the "transformation" that the actor carries out in his *actio*, that is, in the performance of the character entrusted to him.

Natural Mask

The physical, cultural, and psychological totality of the artist. In other words, the *style* that that carrier of the mask imposes by combining his or her own qualities with the requirements of masking in general and of his or her mask in particular. The natural mask is the physical-and-character vocation of the individual artist, the particular natural expressive tendencies of that actor, which he or she can make use of to complete the assigned mask: that particular voice, that particular face, that characteristic gesture. All these personal facts add to the cultural facts: native language or dialect, acquired languages, family and social habits, personal tastes, studies and professional training, experience, and so forth. Still further, the experiences, travails, and misadventures, such as want, or even the absence of noteworthy experiences. And it goes on accumulating. All this, part of an always original human equilibrium, enters and must enter into the process of enmasking, into the mask-system that each artist elaborates.

If we compare a perfectly individuated natural mask, accepted and developed by a comic artist, with the artificed mask of a classically trained stage artist, we feel disconcerted. The so-called classically trained artist, all booming voice (both males and females) and text (memorized; the only way), rarely (only at the director's request) uses his or her own natural mask, because all the training undergone (from three to five years, in some academy or conservatory) is designed to wipe away, to cancel all that natural expressive patrimony, the very thing that induced the young actor to become an actor or actress in the first place.

Spatial Mask

This is the congenial correspondence between the given scenic space and its constituent elements and between the masks in action and the action of the masks. Often overlooked when not completely unknown, the spatial mask is decisive for a full realization of the masking process, the play itself. The spatial mask should not be confused with the set design which, even when beautiful, is not necessarily a good spatial mask. The set is conceived to affirm or negate the famous so-called Aristotelian unities; in both cases the set (which dominates, whether spare or imposing, almost all the actual theater) is the container, the "jewel box," of the characters who move inside it. Too often, there is no relation between the two worlds; sometimes we encounter mismatches painful to witness; other times we face disparate pieces perfectly joined but without justification; mismatches that are explained in the "premeditation" of the whole theatrical work. The spatial mask, by contrast, is allowed to "grow" together with the play, at least during the first phase of development when all the approaches are tried out, amplified, or corrected, leading toward a second phase, that of finishing, where all the parts, space included, are fixed. By spatial mask, we mean the space of action constructed at the same time as the definition of the characters and their actions. The character summons and thereby frees the space that contains him. If a certain idea that comes up during the improvisation phase of the piece's preparation suggests a particular space or scenic element, those spaces and elements are set up and included. We don't put an Ionic column onstage because we like it or because it makes reference to something, but rather because the need for it arose during the "invention" of the show. This does not mean that we begin without ideas and depend on an undefined spontaneity. Not at all; the project is precise and perfectly elaborated, its parts already at the point of departure, just as much as a written text (it may indeed begin with a written text). But the project at its point of departure is used to put into action all the creative potential of the company, guided by the director, an able provoker with a good knowledge of his or her actors; a teacher, not a tyrant, who is able to keep the creative explosion within its original limits without argument or censorship. Whatever is coherent and homogeneous in a well-done play can often be ascribed to the realization of a thrilling, effective spatial mask rather than to the "correct pairing-up" of the individual parts of the staging. The kind of "matching" carried out academically at a desk, with "good taste," can look nice in a shop window; in the theater the results are flat and banal or, in the best of cases, dryly aesthetic. Proper elaboration of the spatial mask provides for the stimulating coexistence of elements that would normally be considered incompatible; it favors freedom of expression within apparently narrow limits; it contains aberrations, such as the "jumbled" effect that can come from joining incongruent elements or an uncontrolled flow of ideas.

Total Mask or *Grand Mask*

This term means the spectacle altogether. By calling this a mask we place ourselves inside a system of complex signs that must be deciphered with professional acumen to create an exquisitely, exclusively theatrical play. The mask, both comic and tragic, allows us to represent a universe, both visible and not, in a totally theatricalized form. The exaltation of the *phony*, the *made-up*, the *worthless*, but also of the *forms*, the *spaces*, the *constructed behaviors*, lead us toward a *truth of the false* that is capable, if well done, of challenging all the terribly serious theories of theater. The Stanislavsky actor appears rather schizophrenic to us, just as his opposite, the sour, detached Brechtian, strikes us as insincere.

The exaltation of the phony refuses to be frozen into a definition, for example, the theater of the absurd, where "absurd" rather dumbly stands for "nonrealistic," an ambiguous medal of honor and mark of shame, wherein theater becomes the ghetto of "alternative" ideas. Coined to force Beckett and Ionesco together, the expression "theater of the absurd" is meant to indicate a genre including the forms, meanings, poetics, and limitations of two illustrious renovators of text-based theater in the twentieth century. But the two never recognized anything in common in their work and, most of all, neither ever believed his work to be the slightest bit absurd. If we think of Beckett, the term "absurd" leads to a provincial form of the great author's work, which has cast him deep into a conception of theater as lugubrious and anguished, in which both that author and the spectator must suffer mortally. In this case, the spectator is made to feel guilty for not comprehending what is thrown at him or her (we can't always blame television for driving spectators, bored and annoyed, from the theater). But Beckett, taken as he is, is exhilarating, as exhilarating as Ionesco. Vladimir and Estragon in *Godot* are two Zanni in the great tradition. The Fire Chief of *The Bald Soprano* is an authentic braggart straight out of Commedia. Also pure Commedia is the verbal, phonetic, and human outbreak of madness of the personae of Ionesco's finales. This contagious madness makes his piece a blood relative of the verbo-phonetic madness of Dottor Graziano, or of Pulcinella, or of the mad *lazzi* of any three or four bumpkin Bergamasks driven by hunger to the cruel city.

In our universe of masks, disguises, and spectators, we have a genuine good time. We laugh, we make each other laugh, we see the comedy in situations that are not funny at all in nature, we make them hysterical so as to make them bearable. And ambiguously (or rather ambivalently) we make fun, when we can, of objectionable or tragic or otherwise grave situations without depriving them of their upsetting characteristics, by applying our mask schema to them. The effect, especially when the subject matter is particularly difficult to handle, can affirm the total mask. In *Ambleto* by Testori, making the circumstance funny is not a simple matter of "look how I can make you laugh at this," but rather a carefully calibrated intervention into dramatic material, in which the mask draws on all its meaning and functions to act with unpredictable liberty of action to create a "controlled hybrid."[1]

Grand mask or total mask, in the sense of the complete work, is the artistic result, the total work written, staged, performed, enjoyed, judged, rewritten, and so on. The object-spectacle that finds its full identification in the mask, which is born of and fulfilled in the mask.

Maschema

With the term *maschema*, we do not wish to indicate a mode of being a mask, but a demonstration of the presence of the mask. The *maschema* can be found in any action, gesture, or word that signifies, shows, and confirms the intention and the nature of the character, in its minimum recognizable form. Some examples are:

Linguistic. A particular linguistic trait that is associated with the character.

Verbal. The character uses a recurrent verbal theme (an expression but also a particular pronunciation, defect, sound, or onomatopoeia) or a system for the production of recurrent verbal themes.

Habitual. Recurrent behavioral peculiarities.

Gestural. This has nothing to do with the unpleasant tic—which is certainly a *maschema* but a corrosive, facile one. The gestural *maschema* is the recurrence of specific gestures and the means by which those gestures are performed.

Natural. The actor recognizes and puts to use his or her own natural *maschema* during the process of enmasking.

Social. We all produce *maschemi*, privileging moments when we demonstrate the image of ourselves that we wish to project: a cell phone pulled out in just the right way; a pair of dark glasses removed, put back, removed again; verbal expressions we use to enter discussions; ways we adjust our clothes; studied walks; singing to ourselves that is actually projected outward, and so on.

There are horrible *maschemi*, such as the always raised little foot of the baroque Arlecchino or the Pantalone who lifts his dressing gown with one hand. Since these images have been handed down to us by illustrators and engravers, actors now slavishly imitate them, and everywhere we see Pantalone lifting his dressing gown with his hand. These are cases of posing for a picture as well as a natural use of a piece of clothing, but when it becomes a *maschema*, the gesture nails the character in place, turns it into a puppet.

Personal. Personal *maschemi* permit us to identify different interpretations of the same mask through the use of the same techniques. The three tempos of walk for a given character may be carried out equally and correctly by both of us, but it comes out one way for me and another way for you, thus personalizing the *maschema*.

Referential. A *maschema* can evoke one of Totò's walks, a Jacques Tati hop, or a Chaplin fall.

The actor searches for *maschemi* and uses them to build a gestural, lexical, and vocal repertoire. He or she does everything possible to construct an original expressive system, putting his or her natural *maschemi* into relief to perfect and develop them; and to develop, from experience and the example of colleagues and masters, all the necessary information to enrich his or her own expressive repertoire.

IMPROVISATION

Fixed point

In the world of theater, *improvisation* generally means an interpretation invented on the spur of the moment, following immediate inspiration, without the aid of preparation or study of a text or an action.

By inspiration, we don't mean something abstract or ineffable, but an opportune choice that the improviser makes at the moment. The expert, uninhibited improviser uses a form of opportunism, comic opportunism, which is the ability to understand what to do and how to do it on the fly. Only during the improvisation and only before the audience does the improviser know what to do and how to do it. The negative connotation of the term "opportunist" should be corrected here, but in a rascally way, because the comic opportunist snatches chances from both the piece and from colleagues but always to the benefit of the final result. The comic opportunist acts like a hired gun; he or she decides in the fraction of a second, grasps how to strike, and never misses a chance: he does the *lazzo* and it almost always works. In that realm of *almost*, there is a percentage of risk. There is no improvisation without risk, no improvisation without the minimal collapse anticipated by the minimal risk, and thus no perfect improvisation. Therefore even the best improvisations can be criticized (and so we, writing these lines, beg a little indulgence, considering the risks we run).

The given theme is the minimal condition necessary for any form of theatrical improvisation.

For the Commedia actor, improvisation is a method, another form of writing, or direct writing with immediate results. The improviser writes "his" text, not literary but functional, directly onto the faces of the spectators.

Even meager or vapid improvisation is necessarily meaningful, because it always carries the artistic, cultural, and human experience that precedes it. During an improvisation, it is possible to witness sudden unpredictable outbursts of subconscious impulses liberated by the expressive urgency implicit in the act of improvisation itself. The shift and reorganization of the phases of theatrical writing from the desk to the stage, imposed by improvisation, do not imply the absence of intention or meaning. The project that precedes improvisation is identical to that which precedes composition at a desk. From the idea to the topic, from the topic to the plot, and from this to the "text," which is written if the comic poet works solo and in advance, but is improvised if the comic poet entrusts the plot—which will be further refined and expanded into a succession of facts, occurrences, possible *lazzi*, as well as concepts, meanings, poetic intentions, which altogether we still willingly give the professional name, *canovaccio*—to improvising actors, who will develop results that could never be found at a desk. These results will be ratified by the comic poet in the final draft of the work.

There are multiple advantages to this method:

- ☞ The poet produces vivid writing, resulting in credibility, good rhythm, a sense of action.
- ☞ When reciting the final text, the actor will maintain the natural quality that only improvisation can give.
- ☞ The character enjoys maximum credibility, which allows him or her to develop at will relatively normal situations as well as those based on the absurd and the grotesque.

☞ In its development, the situation has been sifted many times, so that formally, at least, it is perfect.

☞ The work is well put together and enjoyable.

☞ The audience is happy.

☞ The poetry of theater is affirmed, confirmed, and renewed.

Our method recognizes three types of improvisation: *preparatory, creative,* and *active.*

1. Preparatory improvisation: Through improvisation, the actor applies his technical and cultural knowledge, tests his own characteristics, and arrives at a definition of his own version. The themes that guide preparatory improvisation are planned on the basis of a teaching method aimed at preparing the actor for the complexity of the material at hand in its execution. At first mandatory for all participants, the improvisational themes are gradually personalized for each actor, adapting to individual characteristics as they emerge.

2. Creative improvisation: This is the process of evolution of all the systems of relation and intention contained in the dramatic project (subject, schema, *canovaccio,* scenario, as well as text). In this phase, the theme is the performance project itself. The comic poet follows, corrects, adapts, enriches or diminishes, reviews and rethinks his dramatic project in response to its evolution toward the final form of the piece, which will ultimately be fixed. Naturally, audience response may determine still further alterations and touch-ups. The comic poet decides what to alter, but his decisions must be verified by the actors. The comic poet knows that his work cannot avoid the "comic incontinence" of the actors, who have the right and the duty to proceed with the next phase, active improvisation.

3. Active improvisation: This is what happens onstage before the audience during the performance of the by-now-perfected comedy. The actor must control the *tempi* and length of the scenes, the coherence of the characters, their relationships, the events in the story, and the opportunities for interplay between performer and partner. The most desirable improviser is always the "environmental" one: his improvisations fit perfectly into that particular comedy, that particular performance. When the improviser is not environmental, there can be moments of incoherence, incongruence, gratuitousness, and out-and-out mistakes: manifestations of ignorance about this or that subject, loss of technical-artistic self-control, vulgarity, and aggressiveness. A natural tendency that must be controlled is that of the histrionic

actor, the facile improviser, often brilliant in the creative phase but dangerous before an audience, who invents spurious *lazzi,* or ad-libs, jammed into
awkward moments, justified by weak logical or dramatic connections, motivated purely by the wish to create an effect. The effect is guaranteed if the
histrionic actor is a comic opportunist, aware and intuitive about *tempi* and
audience, but his inventions risk damaging both the drama and the poetry.

As a method and poetic resource, improvisation cannot and must not be
used with the attitude of "it just came to me at the moment" but rather must
always follow a path and unfold by applying the techniques, styles, and intentions that precede and motivate it.

Given a path to be followed, no matter how complex (the story, the
events, the situation, the plot), improvisation must always follow that path.
In following, it may now and again deviate for interruptions or explorations,
only to pick up the path again later. The planned path must be respected and
followed through; the overall project may include variation, which always
remains within the right style, spirit, and taste. But no modifications or upsetting of the planned course are admissible.

Improvisation is linked to, a part of, that "something" that maintains the
solidity of the physical representation, that something that makes us say that
this is pure theater, this is not theater, you can't say that, you can't do that,
this is perfect, and so on.

By definition improvisation is unique. No two improvisations are equal.
There does exist the process of reworking a *first* improvisation toward a
definitive version to its *fixed state.* Each step in this process is itself unique
and contributes a detail, a little addition or cut in the earlier improvisation,
leading toward the definitive version. This final version is then transcribed.
Only now can the transcription lead to the final draft, which can take place
at a desk, and may indeed include significant alterations in the material
originated in improvisation. But it can never go without that "something,"
that truth, that nonliterary, fully theatrical credibility that was achieved
through improvisation, which is indispensable and must permeate the final
poetic text.

The first improvisation is an extraordinarily important moment in the
creative phase. It cannot be transcribed—not even by the wish to keep track
of it—except after repetition and confirmation, which implies development, evolution, sometimes even *in*volution. It cannot be redone. Even a
sudden "stroke of genius" cannot be re-created immediately afterward; to be

found again, it would be necessary to "scientifically" reconstruct all the internal and external conditions that lead up to it. The first improvisation liberates compressed creative energies whose mechanism can only be understood a posteriori; any improvisation can only be repeated through reconstruction, and its *tempi* are rigorously individual, absolutely impossible to generalize or standardize.

A dramatic project based on improvisational creativity must take its intentional character into account. If the actor were not moving within a system of intentions, we would not have improvisation but rather preparation or an already written text memorized and staged. (The professional environment of historical Commedia nourished a sincere scorn for actors and actresses who did not know how to improvise. It seemed simply idiotic to memorize words and gestures and then parrot them slavishly in front of an audience. It was regarded as a manifest sign of incompetence, a total lack of professionalism, and even rather dishonest—something like lip-synching. Their French colleagues, committed practitioners of the premeditated, were the target of criticism and mockery by the Italian comics.)

The improvising actor always knows perfectly when and where to improvise and how to do so because the "how" springs from the knowledge of one's own stage character, the genre, and the expressive system in which the character finds itself. Improvisation is therefore always purposeful and developed within *a system of intentions* that must correspond to the following assumptions:

We improvise what cannot be written in advance; the impossibility to anticipate a happening imposes the use of improvisation.

The literary text a priori describes the intentions of the character and makes him into a "self-describer" of his present, his past, and his destiny. By contrast, the character obtained through improvisation "produces his own life" and has no need to be described because it is already exposed and evident.

The process of creative improvisation toward a text fixed only a posteriori, is peculiar to theater and results in a live character that acts in the dramatic present, liberating intentions that are active, not descriptive, and are humanly credible in any aesthetic context.

Intentionality is a pure theatrical act in a pure theatrical form, uncontaminated by other forms, such as literature or—very fashionable today—video, voice amplification, projected images, and other effects that substitute an actor-artist with an actor-accessory.

The improvising actor always reveals his or her intention without resorting to special efforts; the result is guaranteed by *being in the situation*. For example, if Zanni wants to steal a letter sticking out of Pantalone's pocket, all his play, his words, his efforts, and the deriving misunderstanding and consequences shall be expressed *intentionally*. The audience will understand more from intentional facts than from explicatory texts and will enjoy the action much more as well.

Improvisation must never give instructions, as in moments when the action must be entrusted to literary explanations rather than actions. Rather, the words, the dialogues, and the monologues are strictly linked to the actions, behavior, and intentions. The great writers of theater stand out precisely by virtue of their "gestural" and intentional writing; they compose action, not literature, not instructions.

Multilingualism

Fixed point

Commedia's multilingualism (today called also multidialectism) translates a practical, concrete need, imposed by the linguistic realities of sixteenth-century Italy, into a powerful expressive solution. At that time, there was still no national language. Local and regional dialects—more properly, distinct languages in themselves—were (and still are today) dominant and diffuse. Virtually everyone spoke in dialects that rarely had a written form and existed within narrowly circumscribed areas. Between Florence and Milan, a traveler would have passed through as many as ten different linguistic areas: there would have been urban Florentine, rural Florentine, rural Bolognese, urban Bolognese, Modenese, Reggiano, and distinct dialects in Parma, Piacenza, Cremona, Lodi, and Milan.

The linguistic situation in Italy was as follows:[2]

> *Dialects* are languages which, for historical, political, and cultural reasons, have not become *official languages*. Within *linguistic islands*, people speak different dialects from those spoken in the wider region. At times dialects are related to the official language of another country rather than to Italian: these cases derive from ancient migrations which were often due to religious or political persecution. More recent emigrations have not created islands, but rather diffuse presences of different dialects, especially in the industrial regions of northern Italy.

Italo-Romance Dialects in Italy

Northern Italy: Piemontese, Lombard, Ligurian, Emilio-Romagnolo, Lunigian, Northern Marchigian, Veneto

Tuscan: Tuscan, Corsican

Central-Southern: Central-Southern Marchigian, Umbrian, Lazian, Abruzzese, Molisan, Campanian, Lucanian, Northern Pugliese, Salentine, Calabrese, Sicilian

Sardinian: Gallurese, Logudorese, Campidanese

Dialects of Other Groups in Italy

Ladino

Franco-Provençal

Provençal

German

Slovene

Italo-Romance Dialects Outside Italy

Istrian

Lombard-Ticinese

Corsican

Linguistic Islands

Albanian (in Abruzzi, Molise, Northern Puglia, Salento region of Puglia, Campania, Basilicata, Calabria, Sicily)

Catalan (in Sardegna)

Croatian (in Molise)

Franco-Provençal (in Puglia)

Greek (in Salento, Calabria, Corsica)

Ligurian (in Sardegna and Corsica)

Provençal (in Calabria)

Slovene (in Basilicata and Sicily)

German (in Trentino, the Veneto, Friuli)

Each of these linguistic areas can be still further subdivided into cities, towns, valleys, and mountainsides where the variations multiply, sometimes quite inventively. Within the metropolitan areas, changes exist among downtown, the periphery, and the neighborhoods. In the absence of a national language, therefore, it was unthinkable for a traveling theater company to tour with a play spoken in a single language, which would have been comprehensible in only a single area, and too narrow to support a professional level of work on a continuous basis.

To perform a comedy in an area as vast and Babel-like as Renaissance

Italy, a specifically theatrical language was required, a language of Commedia that could be understood by all. Thus the solution: a different origin was attributed to each different character, so that in the same play there is an old man speaking in the dialect of the Veneto or Milan or Bisceglia or Piombino, and another speaking Bolognese; two lovers speaking Tuscan (because the Tuscan dialect of Florence was the most noble of all the Italian tongues, the closest to Latin and the most adapted to literature, as well as the most widely diffused and closest to a national language); servants speaking a rough, comic, "alien" Bergamask dialect, or perhaps a melodic, rich, surprising Neapolitan, or a sharp, bitter Calabrese. Then there were the French, German, or Spanish-sounding braggarts and poseurs.

If there were no national language in Italy today, comic actors would no doubt opt for a unifying English speech. Why didn't earlier actors seek a similar solution? Why should the Babelic choice turn out to be more comprehensible than a single language?

Two fundamental motives, among others, guarantee comprehensibility. The first rests in the opportunity to have at least one character use the language of the audience or the language closest to that of the audience, thus assuring its understanding of the story. The second motive rests in the *verbal gesturality* of the dialects, tongues strong in sonority and expressions, languages that employ the whole body in order to be best pronounced, accented, and interpreted. Because the dialects were not literary languages (at least, they were not received as such), the words never arrive at the formation of complete concepts. Because the words are not "self-sufficient," they must be completed by gesture, action, and physical signals to the audience.

Other motives guarantee the intelligibility of the *fabula* (story), such as the evidence given by the action, always clear and logical to the audience. There was also the possibility, as diffuse then as it is now, that the spectators might have an ear for, or a thorough knowledge of, other dialects and foreign languages. Thus, the language of Commedia is multilingualism.

Some commentators attribute the origin of Commedia's linguistic multiplicity to a brilliant idea of the first actors, who sensed the solution's expressive potential. But in reality the expressive power is an effect rather than a cause. The cause remains the need to distribute the theatrical product throughout a wide and linguistically crowded area. The effect is powerful, one that becomes an indispensable fixed point, which allows us to recognize not only the provenance of the characters but also the principal characteristic of the cities they represent. The Dottore, the learned gastronome, can only be from Bologna, which is known for its cuisine and its university. The

Bergamasks who came down into the cities of the Paduan plain were real, their guttural sounds were comical, and thus was born Zanni. To *act Spanish* was a social habit of the time, thus it was natural to take a Neapolitan or Calabrian and make him act Spanish, boast and bray in a mix of authentic paternal dialect and phony Castilian mother tongue.

Today, with respect to the question of continuity in Commedia, the principle of multilingualism takes on a global aspect. Any language in the world can enter the Arte, on the same stage, within the same comedy.

Our research is heading in this direction. The International School of Comic Acting is a multilingual theatrical laboratory, where the development of Commedia dell'Arte is studied and deepened with contributions from cultures throughout the world. This is possible, naturally, in a research environment. But when developing a Commedia play with a monolingual company, it is important to work on that sole language with techniques of subdivision and multiplication, by seeking out slang within its reservoir of words and expressions, excavating the necessary linguistic variety. It is a matter of finding a multislang that permits each of the different characters to speak his own unique language, according to his or her character, culture, social position, age, needs, and emergencies.

Multilingualism is born in Commedia, therefore, of necessity: it develops as a genuine explosion of the word, a word that is inherently gestural and perfectly at home in the physical gesturality of its characters and actions. Multilingualism confirms and affirms the nomadism of the Commedia companies, which gather and disseminate information of all kinds as they bring together artists who are inherently antiprovincial and who "de-provincialize" their audiences.

These artists seize on cultural and linguistic traits of what can today be defined as European; notwithstanding the thousand references to this or that specific place, Commedia dell'Arte is never provincial and never "dialect theater." A cultural project that is both local and diffuse is unthinkable. Above all, the Italian masks are Italian because they appeared first in Italy, but they are not, nor ever have been expressions of the cities they supposedly represent. The first *zanni* plays were rigorously based in the Paduan plain or more generally in the Lombardy-Veneto region. The *zanni* were "pan-zanni." Everything was zanni-ized: love, fear, hunger, beatings. Where were the masters? In a first phase, there was no need for them, because they were omnipresent but offstage. But the development of the dramatic situations and the success of the new genre of entertainment led to the first jump toward more complex schema. The Magnifici and the Graziani appear, old, rich masters, to beat up on, to exploit, to con. They in turn beat up, exploit, and con the Zanni. Isn't it possible that the Magnifici and the Graziani arose spontaneously throughout Italy, wherever it was logical for them to appear, and that Commedia simply gathered them up and put them onstage? And isn't it still more logical that Commedia itself should decide what characters it needs, together with their tongues, languages, and social baggage?

Another misunderstanding concerns the local characters, such as Gioppino, Gianduja, Meneghino, Stenterello, Rugantino, and so on, who are in some way emanations of Commedia dell'Arte: local, monolingual adaptations of the various servants and bullies of Commedia but not Commedia dell'Arte. We shall attempt to clarify the differences by comparing two Bergamasks, Zanni and Gioppino.

Zanni	Gioppino
Declared provenance: the valleys around Bergamo	Effective provenance: Bergamask plain
Language: rural (mountain) Bergamask	Language: *zanichese* Bergamask
Presence in native area: only when on tour	Presence in native area: permanent
Knowledge of the world: complete	Knowledge of the world: hearsay
Diffusion: global	Diffusion: Bergamask dialect zone
Influence on theater history: all modern comic theater and cinema	Influence on theater history: none
Partnership: multicultural, multilingual	Partnership: local, monolingual
Particular Bergamask characteristics, other than language: none	Particular Bergamask characteristics, other than language: goiter
Ethnic recognizability: impossible	Ethnic recognizability: immediate

Zanni is Commedia dell'Arte and Gioppino is not. Zanni is a Bergamask born in a lab, wished for, conceived, and created by those who conceived and created zannesque, improvised, mercenary, *Italienne*, Arte, the *trade* of theater. Commedia needed a type who could be immediately identified with the poor fool always seeking to survive in the city, which already seemed huge, insidious, endowed with tentacles. The "immigrant" of that era, who has never seen his own native land, this comic yokel was born in the cities of the Paduan plain, in Padua or Mantua, Venice, Milan, or Bologna. If we wanted to invent the contemporary equivalent of the sixteenth-century Zanni, would we go to Morocco or the Philippines to ask them to supply us with a "natural" new Zanni? Certainly, we could make use of Moroccan or Philippine actors, but what if they turned out to have talent as Lovers, Old Men, or the Capitano, or were brilliant tragedians, or had a flair for soap opera? No, instead we would create a new Zanni with our own means, "inspired" by the new realities, by observing the models offered by the immigrants from those countries. That's the way it went with the first Zanni. The type was recognizable precisely because he was a mixture and was destined for a mixed public scattered across a vast area already called Europe. The audience was unaware of the details of local culture but capable of generalizing human and social types on the basis of widely recognized qualities. (Don't foreign tourists today want to hear their Venetian gondoliers sing "O Sole Mio"? It's useless to explain that the song they want to hear is from Naples, and that there's a huge historical-cultural-linguistic difference between Venice and Naples. It's equally useless to try to convince the gondoliers themselves that for historical-cultural-linguistic reasons—as well as for their own dignity—they should sing a Venetian song instead, say, "La Biondina in Gondoeta.")

And what about Gioppino? His is the expression of the people of Bergamo. He is homegrown. His three goiters, a hyperbole of the malady that has afflicted his countrymen for centuries (until recently), hang from his throat as a demonstration of his local authenticity. The peasant Gioppino, impossible to export, could never be assimilated into the cunning, metropolitan, and almost stateless Commedia dell'Arte.

"Masks" such as Gioppino are scattered all over Italy. They are each a compendium of local ethnic culture, and they often contain great humanity. Altogether, they constitute an impressive linguistic patrimony unique in the world. They have famous names and faces, such as the Florentine Stenterello or Gianduja from Turin, the Milanese Meneghino, the Roman Meo Patacca. Less famous ones are no less bound to strong traditions, such as Sandrone from Modena or Mingone from Bibbiano. Funny and beloved by their audiences, they are perpetuated by often quite brilliant local actors. They are "characters" not only because they express themselves, but because they adhere to a known local character type. Rather than deriving from Commedia, they are an adaptation of Commedia to a local site, a sort of reflux of Commedia.

In our vision of Commedia dell'Arte, multilingualism is a *project of recuperation* with a very original significance and importance.

For Commedia to achieve universality in the modern environment, it must utilize all possible languages. Our contribution, which began in 1980, moves in two directions: the application of multilingualism in Commedia through the internationalism of our school and the staging of multilingual spectacles even when the performing companies are not themselves international. Teaching always provides a special opportunity for multilingualism: we have seen love duets between a Catalan Flavio and a Japanese Isabella, where the noncomprehension of the words translates into understanding through the sounds, intentions, and expressive, glowing intuitions. We have seen boasting by Capitani who gather together all the boastful bullshit from every linguistic corner of the planet, and servants expressing themselves in the most obscure tongues of countries we had imagined to have only a single language, such as Great Britain.

Beyond the vaguely chance sensation that comes from these experiences, these multilingual improvisations are always perfectly logical to the situation in which they occur. This logic is especially clear to the Italians, who witness their "old" multiplicity of dialects substituted by a modern multilingualism in a absolutely consistent way.

Thus enters the *recuperation:* The original spoken languages of Commedia, the Italian dialects, were (and are) in effect *different languages,* not accents or variant pronunciation of a single national language.

Young Italian actors of today are usually terribly uneasy when called upon to speak in dialect, even their own. They feel handicapped by their lack of the complete fluency of their grandparents or certain mythical comic actors of the past, whose work they know from theater, television, or cinema. Those dialects, naturally, were perfect. But dialects are living languages in continuous evolution and mutation, just like official languages. Not only that, but Italian dialects are often spoken more than official Italian by new immigrants to Italy; and naturally they are spoken with all the errors, imperfections, interpretations, pronunciation, and the accents of their original tongues.

The contribution of actors to the "reinvention" of our languages is absolutely extraordinary and precious. After all, that was how the original Zanni spoke. He did not speak pure Bergamask but a language contaminated by the idiom of his "new land." Our new immigrants today mix their original language with their adopted one, which is not necessarily Italian. The artistic and expressive recuperation of dialects needs to grow from these new mastications, together with the process of updating. Some years ago, an engineer friend delighted us by reproducing his telephone conversation with a foreman who was running one of his projects: it was a long, complex explanation of a sophisticated technical problem, all in the purest dialect of Reggio Emilia. Obviously, the foreman knew perfectly the work to be done and its technical language, as long as it was in his dialect, as did the workers, although they were virtually all immigrants.

At our school, we require Italian actors with no dialect background to turn their "pure" Italian, at risk of monotony and excessive literary qualities, upside down and mix it with all the dialectal terms they know. Whatever the result, all the force of the mask emerges strikingly.

THE AESTHETIC OF ANACHRONISM

Elective point

Commedia dell'Arte has never ceased to mutate, modify itself, evolve, involve. The historical duration of the genre makes it impossible to maintain intact forms of perfection achieved in a given moment (such as in Japanese Noh theater or Chinese opera). Nor is it possible to maintain the accumulation of everything that has been created over the course of time by the incalculable number of actor-creators of Commedia dell'Arte.

We take from the history of improvised comedy those parts we consider useful, beautiful, indispensable, but not everything. After all, that's just how Commedia has unfolded. It seems boring and tired to repeat Commedia staging according to "philological correctness" or "historical reconstruction," as though it were something for museums.

We hold the total modernization of Commedia to be unrealistic and the updating of every element to be aesthetically incompatible, because this has already taken place in other genres derived from Commedia over the centuries. If we present an improvised comedy today with costumes, objects, and sets in the present, we find ourselves stuck in a pastiche, a modern piece with our masks added in. Commedia can never do without its past, a past that must never be censured or hidden, because it constitutes a long, rich tradition.

It is rather the *culture* of our own epoch that must be present in Commedia, for example, a real telephone would strike a decidedly strident note in one of our plays. But a Zanni who removes his shoe and uses it as a phone to ask his foot, after a long walk, "How are you, pal?" seems perfectly in harmony. We don't use the telephone; we use the culture of the telephone. Thus we are both in tune with today and faithful to tradition.

This is how anachronism should be presented:

1. Evident, visible, unmistakable, recognizable even to nonexperts. Two anachronisms must not be joined together. An anachronism produced by two elements close in time can be theatrically invisible or appear to be an error. Aesthetically, certain anachronisms are those that form, together, a sort of "historical compendium" through objects, images, and so on.
2. Diffuse. There must not be "chronological anachronisms" in a logical succession. By their nature, anachronisms do not follow logic or linear schemes; they coexist.

A securely datable background that lasts throughout the play's action provides for the individuation of anachronisms and assures that the jokes that derive can be best enjoyed by an audience. A permanent background states the time frame of the story, the historical and stylistic reference point without which anachronisms would not stand out, but would seem instead to be parts of a jumble.

6° | Techniques

What is presented in this chapter is a sort of second chapter on the method and discipline of improvisation in Commedia dell'Arte.

The Character System

Our research finds that Commedia dell'Arte techniques are rich with complex routes to follow, which we will make an effort to describe clearly. This is necessarily a reductive discourse; direct practice, the evidence of what we are talking about, is missing. But we will try to be informative just the same.

Why a system based on the *character* and not on the *type*?

There exist consecrated characters. Tradition has enriched and transformed them into autonomous systems. Commedia dell'Arte has this possibility, implicit in the specialization of the actor, the depositary of all the secrets of his or her own character, separate and independent from any single play.

We speak of a *character system* because all the characteristics necessary to arrive at a character's definition are present.

Each character constitutes a system unto itself due to its particular traits and its history, which all the diverse performers have built up, and also because of what is currently evolving.

To examine each of the characters, touching only on the best known, is a matter for a whole separate book. The Pulcinella system has already been illustrated.[1] We will limit ourselves to describing a character system for the following types: Pantalone, Zanni, Isabella, and Capitano Scarabombardone.

Pantalone
An expression of *dynamic old age.*

Pantalone the character and the actor performing Pantalone have the same expressive opportunities as the other characters and actors. The state of old age is formally exaggerated and absolutely recognizable; it permeates the entire psychophysical behavior of the character, but it never produces in the actor or his performance an equivalent limiting condition. On the contrary, Pantalone, often working in concert with Zanni, continuously finds himself in explosive situations, for both their meaning and their physical demands. Pantalone can do anything but without ever losing his old age. The actor must only be careful not to "stretch out" Pantalone's body, because, although dynamic, the old man is irremediably "curved."

Avarice is an effect of his condition of being a very old man who senses the approach of the end of his life, who is clutching at his things and money, because that's how he clutches at life.

Avarice is not a cause, however. If it were, the character would be monolithic or unidirectional or seized by mania. Only when a single comedy intends to deal with the theme of avarice does this vice present itself as the principal *maschema;* this is possible with any other quality that becomes the theme of a play. Considering the importance of the function of the Magnifico, avarice, as an absolute, permanent *maschema,* would invade all systems of relations. Avarice, however, is only one of Pantalone's *maschemi* and is not the principal one.

Pantalone's *maschemi* are:

- ☞ Nose like a bird of prey and white hair
- ☞ Long curved body on a vertical axis
- ☞ Short rapid steps, his feet following the dynamic of his Aladdin-style slippers
- ☞ Youthful, vigilant, hyperactive extremities—head, hands, feet
- ☞ Diffidence
- ☞ Avarice
- ☞ Libido
- ☞ Tenderness and severity with his children
- ☞ Tyranny with his children and his servants
- ☞ Careful concern for the advantages and disadvantages of old age: aches and pains, heart murmurs, tiredness, memory loss, deafness; capable of producing his own death when convenient
- ☞ Monologues on set themes: suspicion, reproach, cursing, avidity
- ☞ Desperation for the beatings, the humiliation, and the losses borne
- ☞ Rebirth

Zanni

An expression of the state of *permanent urgency.*

This condition is present in his every gesture, pose, action, or moment of stillness. Zanni's body follows a broken line along a vertical axis: chest out; gluteus out; lumbar vertebrae strongly arched; weight always on one leg bent at the knee, while the other is extended; the arms and hands are "ready" (in our method the hands are never stuck in the belt). His outline in silhouette would be perfectly defined in all its parts; the head, hyperactive, always checking everybody and everything: he *aims* when he looks and *launches* when he points: his long pointed nose is a periscope, a camera eye, a gunsight, a cannon.

The body of Zanni is a confederation of parts, perfectly coordinated among themselves but each part capable of disassociating from the others. One of Zanni's legs may want to run and the other not, so that they have to come to an agreement. Zanni's body is an ecosystem where many different forms of life coexist in perfect equilibrium.

When called, Zanni runs: on purpose, by chance, pushed, drawn, or only because he was called, or for innumerable other motives and dynamics. The point is, he runs.

When reproached, Zanni humiliates himself; he begs pardon, he lies shamelessly to defend himself, to save himself.

When praised, Zanni puffs up disproportionately, he attributes merits to himself that he has never possessed and do not pertain to him.

Kissed by his beloved, Zanni explodes into an outburst of psychophysical joy, uncontainable but perfectly choreographed. Naturally, she, Zagna or the Fantesca or the Servetta, when kissed by Zanni, does the same.

When assigned a task, Zanni completes it, although no one can imagine how, including himself. That *how* is the essence of his being.

Zanni's *maschemi* are:

- ☞ Either a huge nose, slightly tipped downward, or a short snub nose
- ☞ Hair either spiky or curly, but always thick and hard
- ☞ Hunger
- ☞ Fear
- ☞ Goodwill
- ☞ Unwillingness
- ☞ Easily influenced
- ☞ Incapable of being normal
- ☞ Brilliance in extreme situations
- ☞ Low, rich, spurious language
- ☞ The broken voice of someone who eats, sleeps, lives like an animal
- ☞ Horrible appearance
- ☞ Sweet character
- ☞ Urgent gesture

- ☞ Epic, narrative storytelling gesture
- ☞ Meaningful gesture
- ☞ Body a broken line
- ☞ A rich variety of walks, ways of changing direction, posture, and stasis
- ☞ His slapstick (*batòcio*)
- ☞ Aggressive and peaceful use of the *batòcio*
- ☞ Malapropism; a gestural and vocal solo in which Zanni manifests all his fundamental ambivalences: maker-unmaker, stupid-genius, alert-sleepy, crazy-sage, disastrous man-man of destiny

Isabella

An expression of *aspiration to happiness* through love.

Her body and gestures are inspired by classical art, perfected by mannerism, corrected into a *pathetic* function by using an oblique axis.

The body manifests in a pronounced way the Tower-of-Pisa syndrome, which never falls, as the nursery rhyme says. Isabella, like her lover, Flavio, never falls, but the sensation of having arrived at a crisis point is permanent.

Her body expresses youth, beauty, health, elegance, refinement, culture, passion, and heroism, but not wisdom, which she must achieve and will never achieve before the eyes of the audience.

Isabella (and with her, Flavio) is undoubtedly the most intelligent of all the characters, but her intelligence is clouded by passion, the pains of her love, and also by joy and happiness, all of which gradually wrap her up and overcome her, to the point of forcing her to live through the entire story in an altered mental state that is not intelligent at all. The consequence of this is that the most "intelligent" characters are always the First Zanni and the Servant Girls.

Isabella (and Flavio's) *maschemi* are:

- ☞ Beautiful face, splendidly made up
- ☞ Physical perfection
- ☞ Perfection of appearance in every detail
- ☞ Perfect comportment
- ☞ Passion
- ☞ Susceptibility
- ☞ Jealousy
- ☞ Suspicion
- ☞ Punctiliousness

- ☞ Pride
- ☞ Dramatic-pathetic recognition, always in extremis, of her own errors
- ☞ Absolute love
- ☞ Absolute hate
- ☞ Narcissism
- ☞ Anorexia
- ☞ Rapture
- ☞ Absence of a sense of humor
- ☞ Continuous effort at self-control that is never fully achieved (due to her boiling passions)
- ☞ Pathetic gestural dynamic, based on the systematic use of diagonals and arcs
- ☞ *Heroic* gestural dynamic, based on the display of her chest, seat of the heart and the sentiments
- ☞ The aesthetic of gesture always "kept under control" to demonstrate one's perfection, a physical trait that leads us to suppose an equal moral and intellectual perfection. Even in the most desperate situation, in the mud, in a lake of blood, overwhelmed by scandal and shame, Isabella is always perfectly "presentable"
- ☞ A personal object always in use, such as a handkerchief, fan, letter, stiletto, sword
- ☞ Grandiose, crowd-pleasing stares and expressions
- ☞ Beautiful voice
- ☞ Songlike speaking
- ☞ Elevated, poetic-literary language
- ☞ Monologues of folly, jealousy, love, hate, desperation, hope, infinite joy

Capitano Scarabombardone

An expression of an *exalted self-image* attempting to remedy a sense of shame.

From the stars to the sewer, never the opposite: the character appears at the peak of his success because he *seems* great, strong, handsome, courageous, terrible in his aspect, irresistible, fascinating, elegant, rich, generous, unbeatable in battle and love.

At least, that's how he appears to the other characters, who cannot resist a shiver in his presence, each in his or her own way. Isabella might feel, for the first time in her virgin life, a certain something at the sight of so disconcertingly male a man. Flavio immediately sees a potential rival; Pantalone senses the deal of the century; Zanni smells the odor of food and the jingle of monetary compensation. Franceschina would definitely try him and may well do so. His colleagues cannot resist feeling admiration, respect, and pride at being with his sort. In sum, he's quite the success.

And the audience? The audience sees this guy and sees that all the other characters join in admiring this new arrival, and they understand this appreciation because he, Scarabombardone da Rocca di Ferro, really does seem to be what he wants to seem. But they also see his real substance, that he's a disaster. How?

Permanent Disaster: The Capitano continuously applies a self-destructive mechanism that makes him trip on the carpet or the cobblestones; he falls on his ass spectacularly; he stumbles over his own tongue or his sword, and so on. He is the behavioral predecessor of the modern Clown, a pretentious failure.

His gestures are a hybrid, a grotesque combination of Zanni-ism, monumentality, military style, and the low tavern. The Zanni's broken line on a vertical axis, at the base of his physicality, softens in his gestures, following his ostentatious pretense of elegance.

Maschemi of Capitano Bellerofonte Scarabombardone da Rocca di Ferro (and all those like him) are:

- ☞ Big long nose
- ☞ Big mustache
- ☞ Big voice
- ☞ Boasting
- ☞ Total, unconditional fear in the face of danger
- ☞ Permanent victim of micro-accidents: stumbling, getting stuck, falling, mistaken direction, hurting himself brutally when attempting to demonstrate his skills with a sword or a lance or a club or any weapon at all
- ☞ General exhibitionism, as well as military and sexual
- ☞ Bravura: a narrative monologue of his adventures, a compendium of his being as he wants to appear, demonstrating that at least in making up tales and reinventing the world, he is truly great

The execution of the *character* as a system depends on the *modes of improvisation* and the *modes of lazzi* that belong to each actor-mask; on the *modes of working in concert,* which range from a system for putting in action to systems of working with partners. Finally, the system depends on *modes of technique,* which are the patrimony of each character, known by all artists and possessed by all. The specialist artist enriches his or her own character by bestowing on it particular colors and technical means.

The first two modes ensure control of the coherence of one's own system.

The third modality ensures the coherence of relations. That is, one cannot expect another character to behave in a way that is contradictory to that character's traits or system.

Technical means are an essential foundation, without which the performance of a character cannot even be hypothesized.

Naturally, the motor of all this is the discipline of improvisation.

Types of Improvisation

1. Dynamic mimicry: adapting to everything that happens, going along with everything that comes up in the course of every participant's improvisation
2. Epic gesture: the minimal gesture with the maximum imagery
3. Systematic misunderstanding: everything converges toward misunderstanding; a sound, a word that sounds like another, a gesture that seems to express an intention it does not have, and so on
4. The defect: either fixed (a defect of pronunciation, the body, the brain, the gesture) or momentary (a loss of a word, memory lapse, sudden inability to use an extremity)

Modes of *Lazzi*

Absurd-Logical

In Commedia, everything is real, possible, existent, and reproducible. There are therefore no abstractions, magic, ghosts, evil eye, and so on, except in the imagination and credulity of the characters. Just the same, in the world of comedy it is possible to use absurdity, as long as it is logical.

The absurd is logical when it follows something possible, when it is a logical consequence of a premise that is not absurd. For example: Zanni is seated on a chair. His fellow pulls it out from under him, but since Zanni is unaware of the trick, he doesn't fall. When he finally sees what has happened, he falls, since according to the laws of nature, he should indeed fall. The *logic* rests in the impossibility of falling before one becomes aware of being in a situation where one must fall: I fall only when I know I must fall. If the *lazzo* is well done, the audience understands the "sense" of it and laughs immediately without asking itself what happened, because the logic is clear as a lightning bolt.

If, for example, Zanni limits himself to not falling, to remaining suspended, then the matter assumes a "transcendental" meaning that is far from Commedia, from the world of comedy, from Zanni, and from the absolute truth that Commedia never fails to affirm.

An absurd-logical *lazzo* that is poorly executed or constructed or justified is absolutely incomprehensible.

The absurd-logical is, in terms of comedy, the fruit of a scientific mentality.

Double Image

Involuntary actions can generate double images, or layered images. For example, Zanni sleeps and moves in his sleep; the movement is like that of rowing a boat. The double image is that of Zanni sleeping and Zanni rowing a boat. But the audience does not confuse the two images. Within the situation it remains clear: Zanni sleeps. The double image has a comic-aesthetic function and can be used dramatically to generate or clarify misunderstandings.

Allusion

Allusion can provide for the introduction of obscenity as an autonomous form of comedy, along with other forms of mischief that can be drawn from the situation in which the characters find themselves.

Special Skills

Many situations can be made spectacular, revitalized, and turned into *lazzi* with the use of special skills. Every Commedia actor must be able to count on certain abilities beyond sheer acting with which to expand his or her expressive powers. Acrobatics and juggling are the most fruitful skills, because of their immediacy, the rapidity of execution, and their permanent availability. Another important skill is music, whether vocal or instrumental. Music boasts expressive autonomy but can be folded into the play to support any intended meaning and every possible action. The use of special skills for dramatic effect is always a possibility within a *lazzo*.

Semantic Realism

Commedia characters often take the meaning of words and expressions completely literally, in their most immediate realistic sense. For example, when two Zanni have been recruited into the army, at the order "At Ease!" they immediately flop down onto the ground, one on top of the other, stretching and snoring with epic proportions. To attempt to remedy the situation by yelling "Attention!" disseminates such total panic and chaos that the platoon disbands as quickly as it was formed.

Awareness of and Respect for "Comic Tempo"

Comic actors (and the Italians in particular) insist on achieving the correct "tempo" as an essential condition of a successful comedy: "An actor who can't make people laugh is one who gets the tempo wrong"; or, in praise, "Great, perfect tempo." This observation is generally right on the mark. Just the same, what follows from this concept is never spoken aloud. What exactly is this comic tempo? No comic actor or critic-actor or comic critic ever explains. A professional secret? Is it a matter of difficulty in expressing conceptually something that only instinct and craft can bring to perfection?

In the effort to explain, *tempo* and *rhythm* are often confused. Adding confusion to confusion, rhythm is often confused with *rapidity,* so that "having no rhythm" comes to mean "too slow" or "too long." A "good" rhythm, on the other hand, is taken to mean something fast and short.

Let's see.

Rhythm is an ordered, coherent, and proportional succession of dramatic effects (whether comic, tragic, or any other) in performance. Rapidity and slowness are characteristics of *velocity* (see below). Regularity, alternation, duration, and an infinity of other shadings, as well as excess, are characteristics of rhythm and can be chosen according to taste, style, and opportunity. That notorious state of "having no rhythm" can turn up both in rapidity and slowness, in brevity and length, because the lack of rhythm is a disordered, incoherent, disproportionate succession of dramatic effects in performance. A wrong rhythm can also come from bad contact between comic tempos, which in themselves are correct but are missed by the audience for other reasons. The reasons for this failure can be cultural, for example, a Western audience rarely laughs at even the most excellent Eastern comics, because the codes of laughter are not different, but "shifted." Another example is when a comic follows an idea of comedy that is too daring, where the tempo, the signs, and the meanings are lost on the audience at first, because the *contract of complicity* has either not been established or has been suspended until some later point in the performance. Some comedy is "before its time" and must wait months or years before the tastes of the audience have evolved in the direction of the "daring" comedy proposed.

Tempo is an opportunity to apply to a given *lazzo* (or *bisguizzo*) what we have defined as comic opportunism.

An effect is comic only when it satisfies opportune requirements, when it falls at the exact moment for its maximum efficacy, so as to provoke a chain of laughter. Too late or too early, even the slightest misstep, can compromise the effect.

Why *lazzi* don't work:

1. The effect strikes the audience already interpreted, already digested. An excess of rationality or a failure to surprise do not prevent recognition and appreciation of a comic effect, but laughter is impossible. Any sort of warning, any hint of "you'll laugh at this" that seems to "telegraph" what is coming, puts the audience on guard, and the joke always comes too late, already obsolete. Too-late effect.

2. The effect arrives *before* the conditions have matured to allow viewers to understand it. The audience senses that it has missed something but doesn't know what. What's happened is that the preparatory maneuvers, the procedure that sets up the anticipation of something funny about to happen, complete themselves before the comic tempo is picked up by the audience. Audiences note a rhythmic indication, at which they begin to "keep time" together until the comic moment and the laughter hit. By anticipating the effect, we call a sudden halt to the march, before its goal is clear. The audience doesn't understand, although they recognize that the moment has slipped by, unappreciated. Anticipation effect.

In both examples above, the mechanism that releases the laugh has jammed. That doesn't necessarily nullify the audience's amusement. The audience may be constantly aware of being immersed in the right comic atmosphere, the spectator's face may present the typical signs of laughter on standby: mouth half open, ready, alert expression, tense facial and forehead muscles, breath almost interrupted. He or she is ready for the snap, ready to burst out in laughter, but it hasn't happened yet. The audience is well disposed, but since the mechanism failed to release when it was supposed to, the expression remains suspended, and an interrogative ridge starts to develop between the brows of the spectator.

This occurs quite normally during a comedy, even in the best of them: it's part of the dialogue between the stage and the house. The intelligent, experienced comic actor doesn't place too much weight on such missed chances, because he or she knows that the audience doesn't regard it as a problem. On the contrary, it knows that it must stay alert, that everything is moving toward a laugh, even though the laugh won't always come. But the climate is intact, the fun is not compromised.

Velocity is speed. The shorter the interval between two expressive points, the greater the velocity of the execution. The longer the interval, the slower the execution. By expressive points, we mean the minimal components of the fundamental expressive instruments:

1. Gesture. Minimal component: a movement of a part of the body that cannot be further subdivided
2. Word. Minimal component: the phoneme
3. Movement. Minimal component: for example, a step

Now then, to perform, for example, a monologue with extreme rapidity in pronouncing the words and making gestures, in carrying out the movements and actions, certainly doesn't mean that the monologue is played with a "good rhythm," but simply at "high velocity," despite which it may seem interminably long, thereby ending up very "slow."

Therefore, the exact moment is a moment defined by what precedes it and what follows and to which we add absolute clarity of effect. Given a correct rhythm that has brought us to the moment of comic effect, any "going astray" at that very moment of the effect can be fatal. If all of a sudden we change tone, velocity, or duration, we can ruin the effect, or blunt it, or make it unpleasant or incomprehensible. All this can happen despite the correct selection of the chance at hand, despite applying comic opportunism.

The principle of comic opportunism is the basis for determining comic tempo and its proper execution. Instinctively or rationally or both, the actor knows these principles before going onstage. Onstage, he or she applies and develops them. From the audience response, the actor knows how to draw out and evaluate all the infinite, extremely personal comic shadings that are useful to his or her comic art, whether premeditated or improvised.

Up to this moment in our research and experience, we have identified the following comic tempos:

First comic tempo: *sense of relativity*. The sense of relativity is a "cruise-ship" level of comic tempo, it requires no particular preparation, it is applied constantly, it is an interminable "out-of-phase" quality with respect to "what should be," and it contributes to the characterization of old men, babies, drunks, sleepwalkers, clowns, fools.

Second comic tempo: *surprise*. Surprise is comic tempo par excellence, it effectively and rapidly satisfies the need of the spectator for liberation from those states of anguish that compel him to seek laughter.

The comic spectator is always voluntary. He (or she) knows, before entering the theater, that he is attending a comic play, he knows he will laugh or hopes to, and he knows that everything that will make him laugh will in some way "surprise" him. He knows in advance that he will be surprised, therefore, but he doesn't know how. On one hand, this expectation reinforces the effect, it prepares for the effect. On the other hand, it's a source of distinct worry for the performer, so psychologically complicated that it has driven many comics to abandon the Arte; stage fright afflicts the actor before the performance, not during it. There is no laughter capable of driving away this form of anguish.

Surprise happens when a comic action takes place in a moment that is inopportune with respect to the plot; it is an unexpected comic action. For example, on a city sidewalk, two lovers kiss in a transport of love. Suddenly she drops out of sight, lowered by the freight lift she was standing on; he remains, holding her wig in his hands. Funny.

Third comic tempo: *announcement*. The announcement is refined and difficult to manage. The spectator is made to know and savor in advance that something comic is soon to happen; an announcement of something comic that is itself a comic effect. The spectator laughs already, not for what is happening, but for what he imagines will happen. The art here consists in making happen what we have caused the audience to imagine, but not exactly in the way anticipated. Instead, what actually happens is even better, in that it goes beyond what the spectator imagined.

The comic effect absolutely must not turn out to be less than the expectation set up, the promise made. Fulfilling the promise just as it was made should itself provoke joy and admiration for its means and quality and in this way show itself superior even to expectations.

We know what the audience is imagining, because we ourselves prepared the expectation. The risk is to obtain a result that is merely "given" and therefore disappointing. The spectator, induced by the comic to imagine what is going to happen, "writes" the comic number in his own head, and this "writing" amuses him from the outset but is a sort of suspended amusement, a "comic limbo." The comic has to measure up to this expectation. In reality, the artist is already able to anticipate the audience's behavior rather than the opposite. The audience is here a sort of happy victim of a psychological con, carried out to its advantage. With his craft, the comic prepares the tasty treat of pleasingly "tricking" the audience; he constructs a chance for fun for it and success for himself.

Fourth comic tempo: *intentional delay.* Easy to explain: the comic prepares the third comic tempo, the announcement. When it is ready to snap, instead of concluding, the comic holds the audience in suspense for a moment, then hits them with the effect. A true act of comic virtuosity. Great (*bravi,* that is) are those who know how to do it. The audience explodes and applause is sure to follow.

Fifth comic tempo: *repetition.* This is the repetition of what was earlier achieved by surprise but on condition that the repetition be unexpected, so that the surprise is renewed. The comic effect is strong precisely because nobody expects the repetition of the same effect. Repetition can go on indefinitely, but the comic must be aware, each time, when he has arrived at the point of *too much* and stop before that point, still leaving a bit of "desire."

Sixth comic tempo: *displacement.* When, after the first repetition, the audience understands that there is the possibility of further repetitions and has figured out the process of preparation, repetition can now manifest itself by displacement. Displacement functions like intentional delay but is inserted differently. With intentional delay we have a surprise within a surprise because it's the first time. In displacement, we overturn a habit that the audience was beginning to feel comfortable with.

Seventh comic tempo: *tormentone* (hailstorm). The *tormentone* should not be confused with repetition, which is always "surprising," even when part of a lengthy series.

When it happens, it is understood that the *tormentone* will be a "traveling companion" of the action throughout the comedy, without remission.

The intention is to underline, to mark, almost to vulgarize and overweigh the comic action.

This is a slightly sadistic dimension of comedy that depends on the little bit of masochist in every spectator. The *tormentone* is hammering at a particular effect. It is neither given nor obligatory that it provoke laughter every time. It becomes a sort of "comic decoration" that can be indispensable to the unfolding of a comic action. Eliminating it in the name of "sobriety," "refinement," "good taste," or "intelligence"—or any of the other euphemisms dear to those who, for example, talk of "smiles" when discussing Totò, when in fact laughing and smiling are two completely different functions of human behavior[2]—would create an empty space, a hole, in the comic universe. A certain "vulgarity," a great peculiarity of the *tormentone,* is always there, indispensable, to remind us that what is comic is in some way always punishment, suffering, castration, a collective dowsing, flogging, a communal expiation of evils and sins both individual and collective. It is nemesis. During the comic sacrifice we laugh at the characters and through them we laugh at ourselves, excluding no one.

But with the hailstorm, we reach the sublime of sacrifice—at the deepest base of ourselves—because through the *tormentone* we laugh at laughing itself, the very need for purification, and the very impossibility of surviving without some form of catharsis.

Eighth comic tempo: *without pause* and *pause.* These two terms refer to two expressive excesses; they are not tempos but rather rhythms. It is impossible to list all the rhythms because they are personal or the result of the union of different personalities. Nevertheless, the extremes can be defined.

Without pause is a very Mediterranean rhythm. Italian comedy is full of examples: Chiari, Fo, Grillo, Benigni, Rossi. The comic occupies all the attention of the audience, without pause.

The *pause,* instead, plays on silences, broken phrases, concepts never completed, on uncertainty, on *thinking that . . . but then, not.* This is extremely rare in Italy: an Andreasi, a Valeri. On the other hand, this is almost the rule for British comics and quite common among the French. The rules of the comic tempos and the principle of comic opportunism pertain to these two extreme rhythms just as they do to any other rhythm.

We can infer that these techniques do not admit mediocrity in their execution. There is a single minimal level, and that is the *right* one. Naturally, it's always possible to do better.

Modes of Working in Concert

Improvising together, or in concert, must observe some basic rules:

1. The other, the partner, is perceived as a permanent proposal to be kept always in the highest consideration.
2. The exchange, even when it is based on a theme of opposition, conflict, hostility, aggression, is always positive.

3. The game is to grow; the development of the ideas leads to their enrichment and improvement.
4. The technique, or principle, of compromise must be achieved whenever the concert jams up.

MODES OF TECHNIQUE

These are (1) gesture, (2) machines, (3) vocalism, (4) *grommelot,* (5) objects, (6) comic weaponry, (7) disguise and discovery, (8) the "geography of the passions," (9) the mask and its correct use.

Gesture

It is impossible to describe gestures in detail so that they can be reproduced. They can, however, be "narrated" or explained. The goal of this book is not to explain how to do things. But we can still discuss the names of the various walks and postures, enough at least to give an idea of how much a Commedia actor should know and keep "oiled up and ready to go."

Zanni

All the servants, male and female, without distinction and whatever their name, use these modes of gesture. Unless specific variations are mentioned, the following apply to the Second Zanni and the Zagna:

☞ Zanni's body: he resembles a broken line along a vertical axis.
☞ Basic position: the posture of Zanni is erect but moving in place on a virtual platform that can move in space. Zanni does not move in space; it is his individual space that moves.
☞ Big Zanni walk: so-called because it uses the greatest volumes of the body; it is a relatively slow walk, ample, nocturne, clandestine.
☞ Two-tempo walk: a hopping one-two; running, flight, parading, a walk for rapid passages.
☞ Three-tempo walk: one-two-three step for each side, regular tempo, fast, cheerful, vaguely hopping; a walk for following someone, nose on the track, urgent searching.
☞ Tired Zanni walk: while maintaining the state of suspension that characterizes all Zanni gesture and all Commedia dell'Arte, here Zanni gives the impression of wanting to sleep on his feet, while moving forward. Even in this case, the walk remains strongly dynamic.

These are only a few of the principal Zanni movements we use in research and technique. These gestures come in part from tradition, in part from study of historical iconography, and in large part from direct experience and research. The gestures of other characters are developed in the same way.

Brighella and First Zanni in General
Brighella, although completely Zanni or First Zanni, features some variations that are all his own.

- ☞ Basic Brighella position: open, projected outward, belly sticking out, tending to tranquilize those present
- ☞ Brighella walk: conforms to the Brighella position in movement, in space
- ☞ Breaking jump: the Brighella walk, over a long course, broken by a little hop, which confirms his "self-awareness" and his always being "ready to serve"
- ☞ Posture of repose: weight alternately on one leg, then on the other, maintaining the lateral quality that distinguishes him

These variations are in use during his "official," social, public comportment; his normality. When the situation demands urgency, secrecy, or flight, the First Zanni returns to classic Zanni gesture.

Infarinato
For the Infarinato as well, urgent situations provoke an automatic return to classic Zanni gesture. When he does not fall into Zanni-ism, when he appears in an official capacity, his walk is effeminate, not swaying sideways but swiveling his hips forward, *a coito.*

Servetta (Servant Girl)
Common Zanni gesture. The Servetta adds a touch of foot in the high part of her step, as a gesture of feminine pride: her skirts "explode" lightly.

Pulcinella
Pulcinella's gesture is the same as that of the other *zanni* actors, but with certain complications. He is constitutionally tired, so he rarely jumps. He has constitutional aches and pains, so he "oils" his extremities, giving a sensual effect to his gesture. He suffers from corns, so he places his steps with care. He suffers from hemorrhoids, so he carries his whole pelvis forward, as though trying to flee them.

Magnifico

Old age has bent him, but he remains vigorous.

The cruise-ship walk of the Magnifico requires the whole foot, from heel to toe, accentuating the whole process, such that his step and walk design a line similar to that of the Aladdin's slipper that he wears and that characterizes him.

His step is rapid and never longer than the foot itself.

Hands and arms rigorously free. They never carry a cape or dressing gown, nothing.

He can carry out the entire Zanni gesture repertoire, according to situation and circumstance, but his back is always curved.

Dottore

On his feet, which function exactly like those of the Magnifico, the Dottore hops, putting into relief his physical and human enormity. The huge ball of lard can "zanni" with the best of them if circumstances require.

Ingenue Lovers

The step flies from one point to the next, maintaining intact the diagonality, the arcs, the torsion and counter-torsion of classic style. The Lovers privilege the tip of the toes as the first touching point of the foot, because anything low on the body "vulgarizes" them. Their gluteus disappears in their perfection of gesture and elegance.

Dark Lovers (Cavalier and Amazon)

The same classic walk, but harder, made steel by their circumstances and identity as warriors.

Capitano

The Capitano is fundamentally an evolved Zanni. He therefore uses Zanni gesture abundantly. Just the same, certain walks are his and his alone:

☞ Mountain walk: a march characterized by reaching extreme distances with his feet. The foot strikes the ground at its heel, and the whole body follows in a low arc due to a not-exaggerated flexion of the knee of the supporting leg, while the other leg is literally launched into the air, dragging behind the supporting foot until it contacts the ground with the point of the toe, and so on. As one walks in the mountains but applied here in the plains, this walk "makes a man grow."

- ☞ Parade walk: The walk resembles the vain rooster walk of the Zanni, with the addition of military vainglory.
- ☞ Muscular walk, like a sailor: Although a normal movement, the walk puts into high relief the entire musculature, even if it happens to be on the scrawny side.

Machines
Commedia avoids complicated sets. Its nomadic origins impose the maximum simplicity of design, which has become a style.

The challenge of spectacular stage design is resolved by the actors themselves, who always work out a way of arranging themselves onstage and a mode of moving together that creates structures in continuous movement and mutation, authentic human machines that can either have mere dynamic value—the minimum obligation—or can create double and triple images or other visual and rhythmic effects, a triumph of three-dimensionality in every direction.

Vocalism
Comic actors can count on their natural voice. For the comic, there is no such thing as an ugly voice, only different, individual voices. Uniform stage voices hold no interest for us. At the same time, however, the Commedia actor must control his instinctive tendency to "make voices," that is, to imitate, which results in an effect even falser than stage voices. Many of our students, although excellent Zanni and Pantalones overall, fall into the habit of making funny voices, sounding disturbingly like bad dubbing to cheap cartoons.

The actor and actress must convince themselves that their own voice is the best possible voice. They must make maximum use of it to the limit of its natural possibilities. If they need to perform a character who is old, they must join that old character's behavioral and gestural dynamics with a breathing pattern that makes the voice credible, but in no case should they ever imitate the voice of an old person. Imitating is the exact opposite of acting a character.

Grommelot
Grommelot (not "gramlot" or other strange spellings) is a term of French theater jargon derived from the verb *grommeler*, meaning mumbling, grumbling. It is not a specialty of one character more than any other but rather an expressive resource, which all artists can use, whenever the action calls for the use of mumbling, grumbling, *grommelot*.

Grommelot is a speech of onomatopoeic sounds and tossed-in intelligible words. The use of *grommelot* favors complicity between actor and audience about the meaning the actor expresses in a nonexistent language; the audience understands everything because the actor makes it all understood by the perfect application of his system of intentions.

Objects

In Commedia dell'Arte, objects have dignity as characters, they have a name, an expression, a weight, a function, and a destiny. The object must therefore be handled with and granted this level of importance. The character does not know how important the object is to the actor; the object itself doesn't know either, obviously. But the audience sees that every object is extremely important, down to the smallest pin. Two rules govern these objects:

First, the object must never be tossed carelessly on the ground. The banality, the commonness of the fall, destroys the beautiful gesture that has been intelligently elaborated to execute the action. The object can break. It can get bent. The sound it makes hitting the ground is almost always somewhat ugly. Anyone, artist or not, can toss an object onto the ground. Therefore, the object can be thrown but its life continues. For example: a character is holding a compromising object, a knife, and tosses it away to flee, but before it hits the ground, the knife ends up in the hands, the pocket, the purse, or something else, of another character, creating a new situation or simply passing continuously into successive situations as the comedy goes on.

Second, from an artistic point of view, that is, to the artist, the object is not inferior to the actor but rather has an equal value. Because the object cannot manage on its own, however, the artist's task is to build around the object whatever is necessary to confer it appropriate dignity. It is not unusual for an object to become a character. In fact, every character in Commedia makes use of an object that is that character's alter ego: Zanni's *batòcio,* the Capitano's weapon, the Lover's love token, the Magnifico's purse, the Dottore's book.

Comic Weaponry

This is another case when it is absolutely impossible to transmit "by book" techniques that are as precise and dynamic as those behind the correct, expressive use of comic weaponry, which are the *batòcio* of Zanni and the other servants; the Capitano's weapon, be it sword, club, or lance; the Magnifico's dagger; the Lovers' swords and stilettos; and the Dottore's huge book, an inappropriate weapon but an effective one. Infinite other weapons can be invented on a case-by-case basis.

The comic weapon par excellence is the slapstick, the *batòcio* (also called *spatola*, *battacchio*, and *sciuscella*). It is a wooden caricature of a sword, with two blades that make a big noise when they strike someone, but we presume that it doesn't really hurt anybody. It is the weapon of servants. Zanni makes universal use of it, both to strike and to protect himself, not only from adversaries but also from the cold, the rain, from being seen by others. It is a stirring stick for polenta, bread, and lasagna. It is a back-scratcher, a fly-swatter or other bug smasher, an extension of his arm, a phallic symbol. It is Zanni's inseparable pal; where's there's one, there's the other.

Disguise and Discovery
It is almost inevitable in Commedia that one character will disguise him- or herself as another. The characters are never aware of the disguise (unless a conspiracy is in play) but the public always is. The disguise always leaves something recognizable of the character underneath; this is for the audience, which must never doubt the truth. Suspense is lost this way, but the plot's intrigue is always too complicated and the audience must always be kept clear about what's going on.

Discovery, or recognition, is always a "climactic moment," for which reason the discoveries tend to concentrate themselves in the prefinale or other key moments in the story. They always have a very dramatic unfolding, with plenty of ooohs and aaahs, including sudden realizations, scandalized reactions, and happy solutions, leading to the finale proper.

The "Geography of the Passions"
With this term we baptize the criteria of placement of the "passions," the external expression of strong emotions, of any of the characters. This placement follows a symbolic, physiological, or other "logic" and determines the physical focal points of emotional expression. What follows here is a brief series of examples of the method the artist can apply, but there is an almost infinite gamut of shadings:

- ☞ Fear: body emptying out, legs unable to stand, allusion to intestinal collapse and loss of sphincter function
- ☞ Hate: spine, self-negation
- ☞ Love: complete opening of the whole body, giving of one's self
- ☞ Humiliation: nape of the neck
- ☞ Noble courage: the chest
- ☞ Exhibitionistic courage: the jaw

- ☞ Laziness: sense of the weight of the body
- ☞ Avarice: the whole body shrinks from all stimuli
- ☞ Envy: sideways movement of the body, of the gaze, in locomotion, in speech, in meaning; never a direct rapport
- ☞ Anger: total, spasmodic tension of all nerves and muscles
- ☞ Lust: insistent and somewhat "liquid" effort to make physical contact with all the parts of the body, one's own and others, especially in situations of public respectability
- ☞ Pride: the area around the mustache; everything tipped up, as though from a bad smell; haughtiness
- ☞ Gluttony: saliva; watering mouth; abundant salivation; the expression, from head to toe, of being one big slobbering mouth; and so on

The character can display these qualities to the maximum degree in conditions of apparent normality, when it's not obvious, when the other characters are unable to see quite what's happening but are aware of something odd, an unease, vague disgust, terror, or pleasure. It's a matter of method, not a trick.

The Mask and Its Correct Use

We will close our technical and poetic exposition by speaking about the mask and its correct use.

Whoever wears a mask, when performing the action of looking at something, must orient it by thinking of it as a single great eye. The actor must situate the center of this eye at the point of his own nose, not that of the mask. The mask's nose may be bent, strange, poorly completed, poorly made by the mask maker, poorly centered on the mask. Although it may be expressive, beautiful, well-adapted to its purpose, the mask is not necessarily balanced in the distribution of the functions of the face that it represents. So the actor must trust his own nose. Beneath the mask, the actor orients his gaze by pointing his own nose where the mask is supposed to be looking; this will give the mask the appearance of "looking."

If the actor moves his eyes around, no matter how visible they are under the mask, the effect will be seen only by the closest spectators, never by the whole audience. To the audience it will appear that the mask is looking where the actor is pointing his nose. It's infallible. That's how the mask works.

The actor looks by *pointing*. He does this by directing his own nose toward the point of attention and sticking his head out in that direction. The movement is clear-cut, precise, rapid, and *thrown*. One *throws* and *points* the mask. This procedure is constant, not relative to particular situations or emotions; it is built-in, an essential function.

In his throwing and pointing, the actor has three reference points: his partner, the object, and the audience.

In alternating its pointing among the three reference points—which vary continuously—the mask lives its life.

The three reference points can vary, but there are always three. The category of partner is singular or plural, as many characters as there are in action at a given moment; the actor must always keep them in consideration in his throws, one by one. The sum of throws identifies the group.

The object or objects, still, in movement, in a pile, tangled together; or the object as an action, a fact, an occurrence; the actor throws out a volley of looks, detail after detail, and thus builds a puzzle.

The audience is not a mass of unknowns, but a reunion of individuals, to whom the actor gives his attention one by one with specific throws of his mask.

Beneath all this throwing and pointing, the mouth and jaw move and exaggerate every possible expression and meaning to compensate for the immobility of the leather above it. The mouth and jaw move a lot but always to a purpose, always at the right moment.

The mask is a multiplier. A multiplier of things, people, events. A multiplier of life. The mask is alive and lives by nourishing itself, ravenously and urgently, on the life that surrounds it, returning it multiplied to the audience.

☞ | Notes

Chapter 1

1. Ferdinando Taviani and Mirella Schino, *Il Segreto della Commedia dell'Arte* (Florence: La Casa Usher, 1986).

2. Giorgio Cosmacini, *Ciarlataneria e Medicina* (Milan: Raffaello Cortina Editore, 1998).

3. See Albert Bärtsch, *Holzmasken* (Aarau: AT Verlag, 1993).

4. Sergio Torresani, "La Commedia dell'Arte," in *La Commedia dell'Arte Ieri e Oggi* (Cremona: Scuola Teatro, Amministrazione Provinciale di Cremona, [n.d.]).

Chapter 2

1. See Francesco Maria Guaccio, *Compendium Maleficarum,* ed. Luciano Tamburini, preface by Carlo Carena (Turin: Einaudi, 1992).

2. Siro Ferrone, *Attori Mercanti Corsari: La Commedia dell'Arte in Europa Tra Cinque e Seicento* (Turin: Einaudi, 1993).

Chapter 3

1. See Sergio Torresani, "I Comici Italiani nella Spagna del Cinquecento," in *Drammaturgia* (Brescia: Morcelliana, 1958), and the preface by Fernando González Ollé to *Lope de Rueda, Pasos* (Madrid: Ediciones Cátedra, 1981).

2. See Piero Camporesi, *La Terra e la Luna* (Milan: Garzanti, 1995) and also Arno Borst, *Computus* (Genoa: Il Melangolo, 1997).

3. See Piero Camporesi, *La Maschera di Bertoldo* (Milan: Garzanti, 1993).

4. See Vladimir Ja. Propp, *Morfologia della Fiaba* (Turin: Einaudi, 1984).

Chapter 4

1. See Flaminio Scala, *Il Teatro delle Favole Rappresentative* (Milan: Il Polifilo, 1976).

2. See Jean-Didier Vincent, *Biologie des Passions* (Paris: Editions Odile Jacob, 1986).

3. See Giovan Battista Della Porta, *Della Fisionomia dell'Uomo,* ed. Mario Cicognani (Parma: Ugo Guanda Editore, 1988).

4. In *Giulio Cesare Croce Dall'Emila all'Inghilterra,* eds. Roberto L. Bruni, Rosaria Campioni, and Diego Zancani (Florence: Olschki, 1991).

5. See Erasmus of Rotterdam, *The Praise of Folly,* trans. Clarence H. Miller (New Haven: Yale University Press, 1979); and Maurice Lever, *Le Sceptre Fe et la Marotte, Histoire des Fous de Cour* (Paris: Fayard, 1983).

Chapter 5

1. See Giovanni Testori, *L'Ambleto* (Milan: Rizzoli, 1972).

2. We cite from the *Dizionario della Lingua Italiana* (Novara: De Agostini, 1995).

Chapter 6

1. See pp. 43–44 of this book.

2. See Fabio Ceccarelli, *Sorriso e Riso, Saggio di Antropologia Biosociale* (Turin: Einaudi, 1988).

Glossary

Actio   A Latin term meaning "action"; the "scenic action" of an actor onstage.

Agelasta   He or she who opposes laughter; anyone who cannot, or must not, or does not want to laugh.

Agnizione   "Recognition"; situations of disguise and cross-dressing, extremely frequent in Commedia, are always resolved by *agnizione,* that is, by the person being recognized, by the revelation, whether intentional or forced, of the character's true identity.

Arte   The trade, the profession of the actor; also, all the practices, the trade secrets, and the sum of experience of and in the trade. In its most positive sense, Arte is the artistic-professional patrimony of the actor. In its negative sense, Arte is the routine, the chore, the degrading slog of theater work.

Bambocciata   A puppet play; a seventeenth-century pictorial genre depicting scenes of daily life among the common people; a pejorative term for mask theater.

Batòcio   A Zanni weapon, a sort of wooden dagger with a flat double blade that makes a lot of noise when it strikes (in English, a "slapstick"). Zanni and his *batòcio* are inseparable.

Bisguizzo   A verbal *lazzo,* a play on words, a funny line.

Bravura   A monologue of the Capitano, enumerating his acts of heroism, his formidable military achievements, and equally formidable erotic ones.

Canovaccio   The written outline of a scenic action, whether of a single action or an entire comedy.

Castigamatti   The club used in ancient times to control the insane in asylums. For us, in general, anyone who takes on the task of punishing, castigating whoever deserves punishment.

Coglione   Literally, "testicle." In common language, a stupid person, a blockhead, a dummy, a potential victim of schemers.

Commedia Boschereccia   A Commedia play with a sylvan setting, with Commedia characters mixing with satyrs, nymphs, and sometimes centaurs.

Commedia Improvvisa (or, all'Improvviso)   Another name for Commedia dell'Arte.

Commedia Marinaresca   Commedia with a seaside or marine setting, with Commedia characters mixing with sea gods and mermaids.

Commedia Mercenaria   Another name for Commedia dell'Arte, so-called because the actor is paid to perform.

Commedia Pastorale   A play in a bucolic setting (a "pastoral") with Commedia characters mixing with shepherds and shepherdesses.

Concertatore   In Commedia, the director.

Concertazione   In Commedia, the "direction" carried out by the director.

Contrasto   The conflict between two Lovers, always because of a misunderstanding, in the form of a duet.

Corago   In Commedia, another expression for the director.

Epicomico   Not a genre, but an attitude. A *lazzo*, monologue, or similar mechanism that makes use of epic themes and tones that are necessarily universal. For example, when Zanni laments his hunger, the theme implicitly becomes universalized as Hunger, in its widest metaphorical/historical/human connotations. An actor who practices this attitude can also be referred to as "epicomic."

Fantesca   The first version of the Servant Girl, played by actresses beginning in 1560. Previously the character was called the Zagna, a masked feminine grotesque played by men. Subsequently, the Servetta, pretty and intelligent, replaces the clumsy, stupid Fantesca.

Follia   A Lover's monologue. When the character goes mad—always and only for love—he or she develops the theme of folly by concentrating into the monologue a large number of new and specific *maschemi*.

Frizzo (plural: frizzi)   A Zanni gesture of joy or euphoria.

Generico   An individual piece of repertoire of an actor or couple of actors: the *lamento*, the *follia*, or the *contrasto* for the Lovers; the *sproposito* for the Zanni; the *rimprovero* or the *maledizione* for the Magnifico; the *sproloquio* for the Dottore; the *bravura* for the Capitano.

Grommelot   Unintelligible gibberish that substitutes for real language. A phonetic expression of pure sound, made comprehensible by accompanying physical behavior, tone of voice, and intention. In Commedia, *grommelot* is used under particular dramatic circumstances, for example, when the character cannot or must not or does not wish to speak normally. In Commedia, the use of *grommelot* is neither obligatory nor common; it is an optional expressive instrument available to the artist.

Grottesco   A figure that contains elements of different natures: human, animal, vegetable, and fantastic. For us, the hypertrophic performance style characteristic of Commedia and particularly of the mask-characters.

Infarinato   Term used to define the nonmasked male servant, generally dressed all in white. His face is all white, *infarinata* (covered by flour), made so with makeup.

Lamento   Monologue for a Lover, made desperate by love.

Lazzo (plural: lazzi)   Any comic action. A *lazzo* can be a quick gag or a brief scene with a purely comic function, complete unto itself.

Maledizione   Monologue for the Magnifico, who curses everybody, in terrible detail, furiously, because he has been the victim of a great wrong. For example, his money has been taken or he has been beaten or cruelly mocked.

Maschema (plural: maschemi)   Every permanent characteristic peculiar to a particular character, by which that character is recognized. The *maschemi* are present in the physical, verbal, and vocal behavior of a character, in the anatomy and the gesture, in the dress and the accessories. A certain hat, a certain voice, a habitual expression, a characteristic gesture: all are *maschemi*. The term is a neologism that I invented "in the field"; it comes from practice, born of the need to define precisely an expressive principle that is present everywhere in Commedia (and not only Commedia).

Mestierante   Anyone who practices the Arte in a routine way, with no quality.

Morosofo   The opposite of *agelasta*. The "philosopher of folly" who practices purposeful folly; the public fool; the professional fool; he or she who wants to, can, and must make others laugh. The comic actor.

Nudatio Mimarum   The striptease, present in comic theater in ancient Rome.

Opera Eroica   Epic, tragic fable, characterized by heroic characters and actions.

Opera Regia (also, Opera Reale)   In the repertory of Commedia companies, this term indicates a tragedy (as opposed to a comedy).

Pappolata   A huge lie, typical of the Capitano. His bravura is a great *pappolata*.

Rimprovero   A tirade by the Magnifico, aimed at teaching morals to his son or daughter.

Sbrofadei   Something like gnocchi, from the ancient cuisine of Bergamo.

Scenario   The detailed *canovaccio* of the entire comedy, described scene by scene, including practical and poetic instructions, but without the specific lines spoken by the actors, which are entrusted to the invention of the actors onstage.

Servetta   A female variant of the Servant in Commedia. She is pretty, smart, vivacious, and affianced to the Second Zanni (Arlecchino, Pulcinella, or another character of that series).

Sproloquio   A monologue for the Dottore. The term contracts *sproposito* (malapropism) with *soliloquio* (soliloquy, monologue). The *sproloquio* is always inconclusive but of great comic efficacy.

Sproposito   A monologue for Zanni. Always comic and always in *actio*.

Stronzo   Quintessential Italian insult, rather vulgar. Literally, it means "piece of shit" and is addressed to a person whose conduct is unbearably horrid or inappropriate.

Tormentone   The term given to a theme that recurs insistently, systematically, at regular intervals, to the degree that it finally seems it will never end. The English term "running gag" is close to the idea. The *tormentone* has the character, obviously in an ironic sense, of excruciating, relentless torment, of torture.

Zagna (plural: Zagne)   The feminine of the Zanni.

Zagnara   The world of the Zanni, in its physical sense as well. A realm frequented exclusively by Zanni. A hypothetical "land of the Zanni."

Zanni   The given name of the character of the servant in primitive Commedia. In general, written in lowercase (*zanni*) and used as a technical term (that is, not by characters during performance) for any servant in the Commedia dell'Arte.

Zannismo   Zanni-like behavior, whether on the part of a Zanni or other character. Any expression typical of a Zanni.

Zerbinotto   A full-time wooer of women, a cavalier offering devoted service to women. Mannered and rather effeminate. He exists historically only in the masculine variant. In Commedia, all the various male Lovers can be *zerbinotti,* as well as the Infarinato, as the situation demands.

Allegri, Luigi. *Teatro e Spettacolo nel Medioevo*. Bari: Laterza, 1988.

Apollonio, Mario. *Storia della Commedia dell'Arte*. Florence: Sansoni, 1982.

Barbieri, Nicolo. *La Supplica/Discorso Famigliare a Quelli Che Trattano de' Comici*. Edited by Ferdinando Taviani. Milan: Il Polifilo, 1971.

Barbina, Alfredo. *Giangurgolo e la Commedia dell'Arte—Il Calabrese in Commedia*. Soveria Mannelli: Rubbettino, 1989.

Bärtsch, Albert. *Holzmasken*. Aarau: AT Verlag, 1993.

Bragaglia, Anton Giulio. *Pulcinella*. Florence: Sansoni, 1982.

Bruni, Roberto L., Rosaria Campioni, and Diego Zancani. *Giulio Cesare Croce dall'Emilia all'Inghilterra*. Florence: Leo Olschki Editore, 1991.

Campanelli, Alessandro. *Il Dottor Balanzone*. Bologna: Pàtron, 1965.

Camporesi, Piero. *La Maschera di Bertoldo. Le Metamorfosi del Villano Mostruoso e Sapiente, Aspetti e Forme del Carnevale ai Tempi di Giulio Cesare Croce*. Milan: Garzanti, 1993.

Carandini, Silvia. *Teatro e Spettacolo nel Seicento*. Bari: Laterza, 1997.

Ceccarelli, Fabio. *Sorriso e Riso, Saggio di Antropologia Biosociale*. Turin: Einaudi, 1988.

Cosmacini, Giorgio. *Ciarlataneria e Medicina*. Milan: Raffaello Cortina Editore, 1998.

Croce, Giulio Cesare. *Storie di Vita Popolare nelle Canzoni di Piazza di G. C. Croce: Fama Fatica e Mascherate nel '500*. Introduction and notes by Monique Rouch. Bologna: Clueb, 1982.

———. *Il Tesoro/Sandrune Astuto*. Edited by Fabio Foresti and Maria Rosa Damiani. Bologna: Clueb, 1982.

Della Porta, Giovan Battista. *Della Fisionomia dell'Uomo*. Edited by Mario Cicognani. Parma: Guanda, 1988.

De Villaines, Beatrice, and Guillaume d'Andlau. *Les Fêtes Retrouvée: Fêtes et Traditions Populaires Belgique, France, Luxembourg, Suisse*. Tournai: Casterman, 1997.

Di Maio, Romeo. *Pulcinella—Il Filosofo Che Fu Chiamato Pazzo*. Florence: Sansoni, 1989.

Duchartre, Pierre-Louis. *La Commedia dell'Arte*. Paris: Librairie Théâtrale, 1955.

———. *The Italian Comedy*. New York: Dover, 1966.

Falavolti, Laura, ed. *Commedia dei Comici dell'Arte*. Turin: Utet, 1982.

Ferrone, Siro. *Attori Mercanti Corsari: La Commedia dell'Arte in Europa Tra Cinque e Seicento*. Turin: Einaudi, 1993.

Greco, Franco Carmelo. *Pulcinella Maschera del Mondo*. Naples: Electa, 1990.

Jacobelli, Maria Caterina. *Risus Paschalis e il Fondamento Teologico del Piacere Sessuale*. Brescia: Queriniana, 1990.

Lattanzi, Alessandro and Paologiovanni Maione, eds. *Commedia dell'Arte e Spettacolo in Musica Tra Sei e Settecento*. Atti del Convegno Internazionale di Studi (Naples, September 28–29, 2001), Naples: Editoriale Scientifica, 2003.

Le Théâtre du Geste. Paris: Bordas, 1987.

Lever, Maurice. *Le Sceptre et la Marotte*. Paris: Fayard, 1983.

Mariti, Luciano. *Commedia Ridicolosa*. Rome: Bulzoni, 1978.

Miklasevskij, Kostantin. *La Commedia dell'Arte*. Venice: Marsilio, 1981.

Molinari, Cesare. *La Commedia dell'Arte*. Milan: Arnoldo Mondadori, 1985.

Nicolini, Fausto. *The World of Harlequin, a Critical Study of the Commedia dell'Arte*. Cambridge: Cambridge University Press, 1958.

Nicoll, Allardyce. *Il Mondo di Arlecchino*. Milan: Bompiani, 1965.

Pandolfi, Vito, ed. *La Commedia dell'Arte*. 6 vols. Florence: Le Lettere, 1988.

Prota-Giurleo, Ulisse. *I Teatri di Napoli nel 600*. Naples: Fiorentino, 1962.

Reggiani, Giulio, Dino Chiarini, and Luciano Manini. *Narciso da Malalbergo: Storia di Una Maschera Bolognese*. Bologna: Patron, 1995.

Richards, Kenneth, and Laura Richards. *The Commedia dell'Arte*. Oxford: Shakespeare Head Press, 1990.

Rudlin, John. *Commedia dell'Arte*. London: Routledge, 1994.

Scafoglio, Domenico, and Luigi M. Lombardi Satriani. *Pulcinella /Il Mito e la Storia*. Milan: Leonardo, 1992.

Scala, Flaminio. *Il Teatro delle Favole Rappresentative*. Edited by Ferruccio Marotti. Milan: Il Polifilo, 1976.

Taviani, Ferdinando. *La Commedia dell'Arte e la Società Barocca: La Fascinazione del Teatro*. Rome: Bulzoni, 1991.

Taviani, Ferdinando, and Mirella Schino. *Il Segreto della Commedia dell'Arte*. Florence: La Casa Usher, 1986.

Tessari, Roberto. *Commedia dell'Arte: La Maschera e l'Ombra*. Milan: Mursia, 1989.

Tofano, Sergio. *Il Teatro all'Antica Italiana*. Milan: Rizzoli, 1965.

Torresani, Sergio. *Invito alla Lettura di Carlo Goldoni*. Milan: Mursia, 1990.

———. *Invito alla Lettura di Ruzante*. Milan: Mursia, 1994.

Toschi, Paolo. *Le Origini del Teatro Italiano*. Turin: Boringhieri, 1955.